The Natural Speaker

The Natural Speaker

Randy Fujishin
West Valley College

PEARSON

Boston ▪ Columbus ▪ Indianapolis ▪ New York
San Francisco ▪ Upper Saddle River ▪ Amsterdam ▪ Cape Town
Dubai ▪ London ▪ Madrid ▪ Milan ▪ Munich ▪ Paris ▪ Montréal ▪ Toronto
Delhi ▪ Mexico City ▪ São Paulo ▪ Sydney ▪ Hong Kong ▪ Seoul
Singapore ▪ Taipei ▪ Tokyo

Publisher, Communication: *Karon Bowers*
Program Manager: *Anne Ricigliano*
Editorial Assistant: *Jennifer Nolan*
Senior Marketing Manager: *Blair Zoe Tuckman*
Managing Editor: *Linda Mihatov Behrens*
Project Manager: *Crystal McCarthy*
Senior Operations Specialist: *Mary Fischer*
Manufacturing Buyer: *Mary Ann Gloriande*
Art Director, Cover: *Jayne Conte*
Cover Designer: *Bruce Kenselaar*
Cover Photo: *lunamarina/Fotolia*
Media Production Manager: *Diane Lombardo*
Media Project Manager: *Tina Rudowski*
Full-Service Project Management: *Jogender Taneja/Aptara®, Inc.*
Composition: *Aptara®, Inc.*
Printer/Binder: *Courier*
Cover Printer: *Courier Westford*

Library of Congress Cataloging-in-Publication Data

Fujishin, Randy.
 The natural speaker/Randy Fujishin, West Valley College.—Eighth Edition.
  pages cm
 Includes bibliographical references.
 ISBN-13: 978-0-205-94627-3 (Student Edition)
 ISBN-10: 0-205-94627-5 (Student Edition)
 1. Public speaking. I. Title.
 PN4129.15.F85 2014
 808.5'1—dc23

                                                    2013042151

10 9 8 7 6 5 4 3 2

ISBN 13: 978-0-205-94627-3
ISBN 10:   0-205-94627-5

For Vicky

My gift in this lifetime

Other Books by the Author

Natural Bridges: A Guide to Interpersonal Communication

Gifts from the Heart

Creating Communication

Creating Effective Groups

Your Ministry of Conversation

Discovering the Leader Within

CONTENTS

Our greatest fear is speaking in public. In countless surveys, public speaking outranks death, losing one's spouse, financial bankruptcy, illness, war, and snakes as the number one thing that terrifies us most. How is it possible to overcome this fear? We can overcome it by realizing that our fear and our physical and emotional reactions that are symptomatic of that fear are natural and can be changed.

For almost two decades, *The Natural Speaker* has helped students of all ages truly connect with others through the power of speech. It has given countless students the tools needed to research, prepare, and deliver poised and commanding speeches that build on each speaker's natural strengths and reflect each speaker's natural style. This edition is no exception and reflects the latest research and trends in the field.

New to the Eighth Edition

- How do You Feel about Public Speaking?
  This is an introductory discussion that accesses and explores the student's perceptions and feelings about speaking in front of an audience. This discussion will ease the student into the process of imagining speech preparation, practice, and delivery before actually presenting a speech.

- Success in a Hybrid Public Speaking Course
  Many colleges are now offering hybrid public speaking courses, where the lectures, class discussions, and student activities are conducted online, and the actual speeches are delivered in-person in a classroom. Specific suggestions for the hybrid public speaking student are outlined and discussed. The student is also encouraged to participate in ways that will make the hybrid learning experience successful and rewarding.

- Using Social Media to Increase Speaker Delivery Effectiveness
  Social media is rapidly becoming the preferred medium for college students to communicate with one another. Easy, creative, and impactful ways to use many forms of social media are suggested to increase the speaker's speech preparation, audience analysis, speech advertising, sharing of presentation materials and media, posting the speech for worldwide viewing, and follower feedback.

- Helping the Audience Understand your Evidence
  A simple yet effective method to present documented evidence that will not only establish the credibility and relevancy of the information but will also enable the speaker to make evidence memorable to the listener—in both informative and persuasive speech presentations—is outlined.

- Developing Speaker Ethos
  This section provides specific suggestions on ways that any speaker can increase his or her ethos or source credibility with the audience before, during, and

after a speech. By engaging in these very simple behaviors, the speaker can communicate his or her goodwill to the audience and demonstrate a depth of character that elicits trust.

• Question-and-Answer Sessions
The student is given a practical and easy-to-remember approach to responding to audience questions at the end of any presentation. Special consideration is given to making certain that all of the audience hears the questions, limiting the speaker's response, and dealing with difficult questions. By using this approach to answering audience questions, the speaker gains skill and confidence.

• New Chapter on "Speaking for a Lifetime"
This new chapter develops the idea that the student will continue to use public speaking skills long after the course has ended. Rather than groaning a sigh of relief after delivering the final required speech for the course, the student is encouraged to consider using and developing these public speaking skills for the rest of his or her life.

• Developing the Heart of a Speaker
In this section, the student's journey to become a speaker for a lifetime will be guided by the goal of developing the right kind of heart—the heart of a speaker. By developing a love for the audience, a love for the speech topic, and a love for himself or herself, the speaker will discover a greater awareness, understanding, and commitment to becoming a speaker for a lifetime.

About This Book

The most important skill you will ever develop in this life is your ability to connect deeply with another human being. A hundred years from now, it won't matter what level of education you achieved, the kind of a car you drove, or the amount of money you earned.

What will matter is that you connected with the hearts of others. That you welcomed others. That you served others. That you encouraged others. That you loved others. Without this ability to connect with other human beings, your life will be unhappy and empty. From the moment you are born, you are driven by an undeniable urge, a need to connect with others deeply and meaningfully.

One of the most powerful ways to connect with others is through speech. Your ability to effectively and passionately address a group of people not only enhances your educational, professional, and personal lives, but it also can also enlarge, empower, and help those who listen to you. Public speaking, the training you might be dreading most, could surprisingly become a communication skill that you really appreciate, use, and enjoy in the years to come.

This book is offered so that you can give a speech that will be a benefit and an encouragement to others. It is a simple guide to improve and enhance the natural speaking strengths you already possess, while providing a basic understanding of speech research, organization, and delivery. In the process of learning and developing these skills, you will be inviting the natural speaker within you to appear.

Chapters 1 and 2 explore the nature and principles of communication, your communication attitude, and six interpersonal communication skills that are vital to effective communication in your everyday life. You will also be encouraged to give yourself permission to grow in all of these areas. Chapter 3 will introduce you to the basic components of speech organization.

Chapters 4 and 5 explain topic selection and speech content materials. In these chapters, you are given a practical guide to constructing a speech from start to finish in an effective and comprehensive way.

In Chapter 6, the role of listening in public speaking is presented. The topics of the listening process, barriers to listening, bridges to listening, and benefits of listening will be explored. Throughout this chapter, you will see that the effort expended to improve your listening skills for public speaking will also bring about immediate improvement in your interpersonal and relational listening.

Chapter 7 highlights the physical components of speech delivery and practical methods for delivery improvement. The emphasis of this chapter is on developing those speaking strengths you already possess and adding new skills that will enhance your natural style.

Chapter 8 covers the principles of sharing information with your audience. Also presented are simple suggestions for effective informative speaking, language use, and dealing with audience questions. Chapter 9 examines the fundamentals of persuasive speaking. Aristotle's three persuasive appeals—ethos, logos, and pathos—are discussed, and ways to incorporate each appeal into your speech are explained.

And Chapter 10 invites you to become a speaker for your lifetime. Impromptu speaking, special occasion speaking, and developing the heart of a speaker are explained in a simple and encouraging way.

The purpose of this book is to give you the basic skills to present a speech that is effective, natural, and beneficial for you and the audience. Your decision to develop your natural speaking abilities is one that will reward you, both professionally and personally, for the rest of your life.

Acknowledgments

I want to thank my editor, Karon Bowers, for her wisdom, support, and friendship through the years. I would also like to especially thank Jennifer Nolan, the editorial assistant, who guided and encouraged me through this eighth edition process.

In addition, many thanks to the reviewers of the eighth edition for their time and expertise: Amanda Feller, Pacific Lutheran University; Cristy Stefnoski, Lord Fairfax Community College; Molly May, Monterey Peninsula College; Chris Kennedy, Western Wyoming Community College.

I gratefully acknowledge my mother, Helen Fujishin, for her constant love and blessings; my four sisters, Diane Sakauye, Melanie Cottengim, Nanette Vidales, and Teresa Gruber, for their love and support for as long as I can remember; my esteemed colleagues Meg Ferrell and Dr. John Hannigan; my good friend, Paul Sanders, for his brotherly love, chainsaw skills, and laughter; and my friend, Steve Richmond, for showing me how a Godly man is to live and ride a motorcycle across America.

Finally, I want to express my deepest love, admiration, and devotion to my wife, Vicky, my gift for this lifetime and to our sons, Tyler and Jared, both in ministry, who bless us beyond words.

Randy Fujishin

Instructor and Student Resources

Key instructor resources include an Instructor's Manual (ISBN 0-205-98218-2) and Test Bank (ISBN 0-205-99696-5), available at www.pearsonhighered.com/irc (instructor login required). Also available is Pearson's MySearchLab™, a valuable tool to help students conduct online research. Access to MySearchLab is available at no additional cost in an optional package with new copies of this text or for purchase at www.mysearchlab.com (access code required).

For a complete list of the instructor and student resources available with the text, please visit the Pearson Communication catalog at www.pearsonhighered.com/communication.

Chapter 1

COMMUNICATING WITH OTHERS
YOUR MOST IMPORTANT SKILL

LEARNING OBJECTIVES

After reading this chapter, you should be able to:

1.1 Define communication

1.2 Define the components of communication

1.3 Explain the principles of communication

1.4 Explain the concept that attitude is more important than aptitude

1.5 List the communication skills for your life

Never before had Paul sat for so long in total silence with another human being. Paul, a young psychologist, was in a therapy session with his client, a middle–aged woman with lifeless eyes, arms that hung limply at her sides, and a posture that displayed the shame and anger that often accompany victims of physical abuse.

It was during Paul's first year of clinical training as a marriage, family, and child therapist that he had worked with her. The woman came to therapy with a long history of depression and withdrawal. As a novice therapist, Paul encouraged her to open up and share her feelings. But during the first two sessions, all the woman did was sit in silence. He asked the usual questions therapists are trained to ask, and she responded only with silence. She simply stared out the window at the peaceful mountains in the distance as the two of them sat in the small, cramped office.

During the course of therapy, she did make some progress. After two months, she responded in short sentences to some of Paul's questions. She even smiled a time or two. Yet, within four months, she quit coming to her sessions. Paul left messages on her answering machine inviting her back to therapy, but she did not respond. Paul never saw the woman again.

To this day, Paul is haunted by something she said at the end of one of her final sessions. After he asked her why she spent the vast majority of her time in therapy in silence, she slowly admitted, "Most times it's less painful to be silent than to talk. I think it would be much easier to live my entire life not having to communicate with anyone."

Can you imagine a life without communication? Immediately your existence would change in dramatic ways, leaving you with an entirely different life—an empty, hollow life.

No longer could you talk with friends over coffee or laugh with your family at a picnic. No longer could you whisper sweet nothings to your spouse or discuss the latest movie with a neighbor. No longer could you debate an issue at a business meeting or negotiate the price of a used car. No longer could you apologize for a wrong or ask for forgiveness from a wounded friend. In short, no longer would you be fully human. We need communication as a bridge to others in this life.

> *Once a human being has arrived on this earth, communication is the largest single factor in determining what happens to him in the world.*
> —Virginia Satir

Hell was once described not as a burning pit of endless agony, but as a cold, lonely, isolated place where each person was sentenced to spend eternity alone on an island. No bridges between the islands. No way to span the gulf between people. Forever alone. A life without communication would be hell.

1.1 What Is Communication?

Although there are numerous definitions for communication, the following definition is very simple and has been around for a long time. *Communication* is the process of sending and receiving messages. The sender sends a message through a channel, within a specific environment, to a receiver. The receiver responds with feedback to the sender; noise can interfere with the fidelity or accuracy of the message. Communication can be both verbal and nonverbal. *Verbal* communication consists of all language that is spoken and written, whereas *nonverbal* communication is all communication that is not spoken or written.

1.2 The Components of Communication

The communication process is made up of seven components. They are the sender, message, environment, channel, receiver, feedback, and noise.

Sender

The *sender* is the originator of the message. In other models of communication, the sender can also be called the source of the message. The process of communication begins at this point with a speaker who wishes to communicate an idea or feeling. It's important to note that the sender doesn't simply send a message. She must first decide what she wants to communicate and then encode the message. *Encoding* is the process of converting the message into language and terms that will be understood by the receiver. Once the message is encoded, it is sent to the receiver.

Message

The idea or feeling the sender wants to communicate is called the *message*. The message can be any idea, thought, emotion, or feeling the sender wishes to communicate.

Whether it's a flirtatious wink across a crowded room or a college commencement address, the message is still the thought or feeling the sender wants to communicate.

Environment

The *environment* includes the time, place, and occasion of the communication event. The time at which communication occurs can influence the communication between people. Talking to someone early in the morning or late at night can affect how we interact. The physical surroundings also play an important role. Is the communication event inside or outside? How does the lighting, temperature, arrangement of the furniture or chairs, size of the room, and a host of other physical variables influence the manner in which we communicate with others? The specific occasion for the event also determines to a large extent how we communicate. What is the purpose of the occasion? Is the occasion formal or informal? How many people are involved? These environmental variables need to be considered when we communicate.

Channel

The *channel* is the means by which a message is transmitted. Messages can be transmitted through channels of hearing, sight, smell, taste, and touch. A sender can use a variety of channels to communicate her message. For instance, if she wants to communicate affection to someone special, she can choose to tell the person with words, hug the person, send cookies, write a letter, or offer perfume. In public speaking, the auditory and visual channels are used most often. But it's important to keep in mind that the more channels utilized by the sender, the more impact the message has on the receiver.

Receiver

The destination of the message is called the *receiver*. Without the receiver, communication does not occur. In public speaking, the receiver of the message is the audience. In the communication model, the receiver receives the message and then must decode the mes-

> *Speech is civilization itself.*
> —THOMAS MANN

sage. *Decoding* is the process of translating the message so that it has meaning for the receiver. A wink of the eye from the sender can be decoded or interpreted in many ways. It can be a nonverbal sign of flirting, a sign that there's dust in the eye, or even the first symptom of an epileptic seizure. The decoding process is vital in communication.

Feedback

The response of the receiver to the sender is called *feedback*. Although feedback is really a message from the receiver to the sender, the term helps us see the circular movement of this communication model. It should be stressed that the receiver can send the return message through all the same channel options as the sender when she encodes and sends the response.

Noise

Noise is any disturbance or interference in the communication process. *External noise* is any physical interference that diminishes or reduces the meaning of the message. Examples of external noise include background talking, a jackhammer banging outside the building, or even a distracting mannerism of the speaker. All of these and more can interfere with the communication process. Psychological or semantic interference, on the other hand, is called *internal noise*. Internal noise can cause us to misinterpret or decode the message in a way not intended. A word with multiple meanings is a common example of internal noise. For instance, an audience may interpret the speaker's statement, "In Japan, students respect their teachers," in a variety of ways depending on their individual interpretations of the word *respect*.

1.3 The Principles of Communication

Now that you have an idea of what communication is and the elements that make up the process, you are in a better position to examine some principles that govern communication.

You Cannot Not Communicate

Even when you don't think you're communicating, your nonverbal behavior is constantly giving off important messages. Your posture, your eye contact or lack of it, and the manner in which you walk or even sleep send messages loaded with meaning to the outside observer. Freud wisely observed, "He who has eyes to see and ears to hear may convince himself that no mortal can keep a secret. If his lips are silent, he chatters with his fingertips and betrayal oozes out of him at every pore." Your body, your movements, your use of time, the distance you stand from others, and even your clothes broadcast constant and powerful messages to observers. You are always communicating.

Communication Is Irreversible

Many times we wish we could retract a critical word or erase an angry response that we have made. Unfortunately, this is not possible. An apology for harsh words can be sincerely accepted, but the memory of the event can live on for the remainder of a person's life. Human memory is a funny thing. The least of gestures, the smallest of words can haunt us long after the event. It might be wise for us to remember the recommendation, "One seldom regrets unspoken words."

Communication Is a Process

Many years ago, Heraclitus observed, "You never step into the same river twice." The river has changed—the water clarity is different, the temperature is different, the current is different, the depth is different, and the width is different. The river may look the same, but it's a different river. In fact, you too have changed—the very cells of your body are different—since you last stepped into its waters.

This same principle holds true for communication. A smile might have worked while requesting something from a friend last week. But this week, the same smile elicits mild rejection. Why? Because you cannot repeat any event in exactly the same manner. Things have changed. Both participants have changed in countless subtle and not so subtle ways. It is impossible to replicate the hundreds of minute variables that influenced you just a week ago. Everything has changed to some degree during the week.

Have you ever seen the same movie twice? It's amazing how many new things you see the second time around that went unnoticed during your first viewing. Your emotional response to the film may also change because of the personal changes and emotional experiences you have had since you first saw the movie.

Communication is a process. Life is a process. The soldier who goes off to war returns a different person. The old woman dying in the city hospital bed is not the same person who ran along the country lane 70 years ago. That, however, is the beauty of life. As we get older, we can explore, experiment, change, and grow as we get older so that on our deathbed, we will have very few regrets.

Communication Is Learned

There are some nonverbal communication behaviors that seem to be universal, such as smiling and crying. But the majority of verbal and nonverbal communication is learned. The specific language that a child grows up with is learned early in childhood, as are the nonverbal communication behaviors that are appropriate for a specific culture. For instance, in U.S. culture, we value and encourage direct eye contact, especially in the public speaking arena. Yet a native of the Japanese culture would interpret the same direct eye contact as a sign of rudeness and lack of respect, especially when the speaker is addressing an individual of higher status.

Just as a fish is unaware of the water surrounding it, an individual might not be aware that communication is learned because he too is surrounded by the language and culture of his society. However, when a person learns a new language, visits a foreign country, or acquaints himself with a person from a different culture, he begins to realize that his way of talking and perceiving the world is but one of many. There are many realities out there, and perhaps one important indicator of maturity is the realization that "our way" isn't necessarily the only or best way.

The most important aspect of this principle is that ineffective ways of communicating can be replaced by learning new, more effective methods. People often think that because they can talk, they can communicate effectively, too. This is far from the truth. Ernest Hemingway once warned us "not to confuse motion for action." The same holds true for talking and communicating. Communicating effectively in our interpersonal and professional lives requires study and practice. Effective communication skills can be learned, and they must be learned if we are to experience a life that is meaningful and worth living.

Communication Needs to Be Cross-Culturally Appreciated

Perhaps the most significant lesson we can learn is that communication is often culture specific. Granted, the principles of communication mentioned thus far apply to all cultures. Individuals from all cultures learn to communicate. They cannot not communicate. Their communication and their lives are in process. And once they communicate a message, intentionally or unintentionally, the effect is irreversibly felt by others.

> *Every culture views beauty in different ways. You expand your world each time you see beauty through the eyes of others.*
> —BARBARA DOSKER

But we must not make the mistake of thinking that what we value in terms of communication competencies is desired by all people in every culture. This is not always the case. For example, in this book, you will be encouraged to maintain direct eye contact with your listeners, use expressive gestures, employ vocal variety, and share personal illustrations in your speaking. For the purposes of addressing most American audiences, these and other skills will serve a positive and desirable function. But if you were addressing a group of Japanese businesspeople in Tokyo, these same behaviors might be interpreted as overly forward, disrespectful, annoying, and even rude. The Japanese often view direct eye contact as an invasion of personal space. The use of exaggerated gestures and vocal variety does not fit their more restrained and formal style of communication. And personal disclosure would be inappropriate, if not suspect, in a large group of strangers.

"Well," you sigh, "I just won't ever give a speech to a group of Japanese businesspeople in Tokyo!" Maybe not, but the United States is a country that is home to hundreds of different cultures. That's the beauty of our nation! If you really analyzed any audience in America, you'd be surprised at the heterogeneous mix of the cultures and ethnic backgrounds of your listeners.

The purpose of this public speaking book is not to provide you with a list of the communication skills and behaviors valued by each of these different cultures. We'll leave that book to someone else. But you are encouraged to become aware of, sensitive to, and respectful of these differences. This is not to say you must shift your communication style with each audience you address. That would be an impossible task. But you are being challenged to examine the notion that "your way is the only way."

You need to become more aware of the subtle, and not so subtle, differences between cultures. Not only must you raise your level of awareness concerning these differences, but you also need to be more sensitive to them, not only in your speaking but also in your daily interactions with others. And finally, you must respect these differences in your speaking and listening with all people. The next section will help you meet this challenge.

1.4 Attitude Is More Important than Aptitude

Before proceeding to the next chapter, it is important to mention the attitude of the communicator, for the attitude of the speaker is the most important factor in effective communication.

A person's attitude is far more important than his aptitude in communicating with others. An individual can be highly trained and skilled in the communication arts but may possess an angry or critical attitude. It is this negative attitude that is sensed below the level of spoken language, and the receiver or audience ultimately will respond to it rather than to the words.

The attitudes that distinguish truly effective communicators from less effective ones are worth mentioning here. Effective communicators seem to possess an attitude of self-acceptance. They accept who they are without having to prove a great deal to others. They exhibit an attitude of other-centeredness, which enables them to empathize with, care for, and respond to others. Rather than constantly being consumed with the need or desire to control others or gain their approval, these self-accepting individuals can dance to the beat of a different drummer with greater ease and grace. They don't spend a lot of time looking over their shoulders or down their noses.

Flexibility is another attitude that characterizes these individuals, for they are more likely to experiment with new behaviors, take risks, and make mistakes. They appear gentle in their dealings with others. And finally, these individuals possess a sense of openness and authenticity that makes them comfortable to be around, demanding little energy. We walk away from these individuals feeling enlarged rather than diminished.

The most telling attitude of effective communicators is their sense of joy—not just a temporary happiness or a practiced, interpersonal warmth, but a joyfulness that seems to come from deep within. Usually these individuals have lived a while, they have managed to survive and accept some of life's tragedies, and still, they have chosen to embrace the beauty and mystery of life.

You know when you've been in their presence, for they usually make you feel calm, relaxed, and trusting. Just as certain animals can sense fear in some people and love in others, you can feel the attitude of joyfulness in these individuals. At such times, words really don't matter all that much.

Without these positive attitudes shaping and influencing the communication process, most communication skills training is wasted. Ultimately, the heart is more important than the head.

1.5 Communication Skills for Your Life

Before we actually begin learning about the concepts and skills of effective public speaking, let's spend a few moments examining your personal communication life, because how you communicate interpersonally lays the foundation for your attitude and skills in public speaking. Effective public speaking must be audience centered.

There have been individuals who were powerful, persuasive public speakers. They could command the attention of hundreds of people with their words alone. Their relationship with the audience was impressive, as the masses swayed in unison to their every word.

But their relationship with the audience wasn't necessarily indicative of their relationships with individuals in their personal lives. Some of these outstanding public speakers had miserable personal lives, wracked with pain, emptiness, and longing. Their great speaking skills could impress hundreds in the audience but could do very little to bridge the gulf between themselves and those who should have mattered— family and friends.

In this book, you will learn skills and concepts that will help you speak effectively to an audience. But before you run out and book speaking engagements, we need to begin with a brief discussion on a topic that is enormously important to your life—your interpersonal communication impact on others.

Every time you talk with someone, you either enlarge or diminish that person by your interaction. Suppose that you and another person are engaged in casual conversation for a few minutes and then you say good-bye. As you walk away from that individual, how are you feeling? What kind of emotional impact did he have on you? Maybe he had a diminishing impact, and you say to yourself, "Yuk! I'm glad to be away from that negative, depressing guy. I was feeling all right before I talked with him." Perhaps he didn't have any noticeable effect on you, and you're saying, "I wonder where I parked that darn car of mine." Or just maybe, his impact on you was enlarging, and you're exclaiming, "I felt pretty down before I talked with him, and now I feel better. The world doesn't look as depressing as it did just a few minutes ago."

Do others enlarge or diminish you? Don't count the neutral impact as a third category, because neutral impact is similar to a negative impact. So clump those two together into the "diminish" category. If you still want three categories, that's okay. The discussion will work either way.

Remember that communication is a process, and your past history, your state of mind, your physical condition, and a host of other factors come into play here. And yet ultimately, you have an impact on others every time you interact. You either enlarge or diminish another person by your interactions. With every word, sound, gesture, expression, glance, movement, pause, and touch you share with another person, he or she is changed in ways that are both subtle and striking.

There are six specific ways you can enlarge others by your interpersonal communication with them: not taking communication so personally, listening without verbal interruption, listening reflectively, complimenting others, reframing, and touching.

Not Taking Communication So Personally

Most of us listen to what others say in terms of how it affects us personally. We ask questions such as: "Is that right or wrong (from *my* point of view)?" "How does that affect *me*?" "What does the speaker think or feel about *me*?" "How do *I* feel about what was shared?" "How do *I* respond?" With all of these questions, did you notice where the focus of attention was? It was on our response, our evaluation, our point of view—in short, we take center stage; everything revolves around us. We take it all so personally.

> *We can alter our lives simply by altering our attitudes of mind.*
> —WILLIAM JAMES

That's not necessarily a bad thing. We need to evaluate the merits of a sales presentation, we need to form an opinion of our new manager, and we need to check our emotional response in a conflict situation. But to overemphasize a self-centered approach to all communication is not healthy. We need to develop the ability to suspend judgment when listening to another person. We need to develop the art of psychological and emotional disengagement—to take our ego out of gear once in a while. When we always take what is said personally, we get hooked into many unnecessary arguments, conflicts, and struggles.

An effective technique that can help you to disengage your ego, and not take everything that is said so personally, is to ask these questions when you're listening to someone else:

"What is this person's point of view?"
"What does this say about this person?"
"How is this person feeling?"
"Where is this person coming from?"
"How does this person see the situation?"
"Who is this person?"

Did you notice the different focus of attention? No longer do we take center stage. The speaker is the focus of attention—her point of view, her feelings, her frame of reference, her character and personality. We're not taking in all that is said in terms of how it affects us. We are broadening our perspective to include the one who is talking. We have concentrated on the speaker, and, consequently, we have also distanced ourselves from her. We are not taking her communication so personally.

The ability to not take communication personally is the first step in communication—to be able to hear what the other person is saying without a screen of self-centered questions filtering and clouding what is being said. Without this ability, communication with others will be superficial and often defensive. Without this ability, we will be hearing only the echoes of our own mind, instead of the thoughts and feelings of the other person.

Listening without Verbal Interruption

Now that we can accept what is being said from an other-centered point of view, we can begin to listen without verbal interruption—the ability to be silent for a period of time when someone else is speaking.

Did you know that when we are talking with another person, we verbally interrupt the other person every 12 seconds? Every 12 seconds! "That's wonderful!" "That's terrible!" "I'm sure!" "I'm all . . ." "That reminds me of a time when I . . ." "If I were you, I would . . ." "No, that's not true, because . . ." "Well, it was even worse for me, because I . . ." And the interruptions go on and on. Every 12 seconds. Back and forth. On and on we interrupt.

And we wonder why we don't feel like we've been really listened to, really taken seriously, really understood at a deep level. Because of the constant interruptions and judgments, advice and direction, we realize there is no safe harbor to simply say what's on our minds and in our hearts without being interrupted from all sides every 12 seconds. Maybe that explains why we pay certain people $100 to $150 an hour to just sit quietly and listen to us in therapy.

One of the most enlarging behaviors we can share with another person is to listen without verbal evaluation—without interrupting every 12 seconds! What an oasis that would be. Perhaps the most loving thing we can do for another human being is to listen quietly, deeply, without interruption.

The next time your spouse, your child, or a neighbor begins talking with you, ask yourself the question, "Should I give this person 12 seconds before I interrupt, or should I allow 120 seconds?" If you wear a watch with a sweep second hand, time yourself if you can do it without being too obvious. See what happens if you remain silent for two entire minutes! Many times the other person won't even notice your silence and will continue talking. Other times, he or she might ask, "Is something wrong?" "Are you all right?" Such questions could be indicators that the other person is accustomed to your interruptions. Don't feel bad. Just respond by saying, "Everything is fine. I just think what you're saying is important, and I didn't want to interrupt you."

Listening Reflectively

In addition to not taking communication too personally and listening without verbal interruption, another enlarging communication behavior is to listen reflectively.

> *It is better to ask some of the questions than to know all the answers.*
> —JAMES THURBER

To listen *reflectively* means to mirror back to the speaker what he is saying.

When you are listening to someone, think in terms of, "What is this person trying to communicate to me?" "What is this person saying?" "What is this person feeling?" As you begin to get a sense of exactly what this person is attempting to communicate to you, check it out—reflect or mirror back to the speaker. The simplest way to accomplish this is to begin your questions with

"Are you saying . . . ?"
"I hear you saying . . . ?"
"You think ... ?"
"You believe . . . ?"
"Are you feeling . . . ?"
"Your point is . . . ?"
"Do you mean . . . ?"

These are simple beginnings to your questions, but they will change the entire focus of your communication. Once again, where is the attention directed? You? Or the other person? Right, the other person!

There may be a change in the relationship with this person if you use reflective listening with any frequency. With practice, this reflective way of listening will begin to feel natural, and you will notice that your communication patterns shift from a self-centered posture to a more other-centered focus.

There are numerous advantages of this reflective listening technique. First, it shifts the focus from you to the speaker, and it encourages you to not take communication too personally. Ideally, it will also force you to listen without verbal judgment. Second, reflective listening will prove to the speaker that you care about what he is saying. This, in and of itself, is enlarging. Third, it improves the accuracy of communication. If your reflected statement is inaccurate, the speaker can clarify, explain, or illustrate in detail. Fourth, this type of listening takes the burden off you. No longer do you have to judge, give advice, or solve problems. You are simply acting as a mirror, reflecting the other person's image back to him. Fifth, you provide the speaker with a safe harbor where he can talk and be heard. It beats paying $100 to $150 an hour just to be heard accurately. In Chapter 7, we will examine specific ways you can listen to a speaker more effectively.

Complimenting Others

Mark Twain once admitted, "I can live two months on one compliment." A sincere compliment not only feels good, but it also can give new life to the person receiving it. We all know the feeling of satisfaction, joy, and even inspiration when a sincere compliment comes our way. We love to receive them, yet we are usually guilty of not giving them as often as we could.

The fourth communication skill for your life is that of complimenting others—sharing sincere praise. The first step in developing this skill is to decide to be a source of compliments. Begin to look for the best in others. Sure, all individuals have their weaknesses, faults, and areas for improvement. But shift your focus of attention and instead see their strengths of character, achievement, and effort.

Compliment Character.   The first type of compliment is to acknowledge the internal attractiveness of the person rather than look at his or her physical appearance. Complimenting character traits is better than complimenting physical traits because character traits do not diminish with age. Such things as kindness, generosity, optimism, gentleness, humor, trustworthiness, empathy, loyalty, and candor are just a few of the hundreds of character or personality traits you can appreciate and praise. Here are a few character compliments:

> "I really appreciate your thoughtfulness."
> "Your trustworthiness makes me feel secure."
> "I like your sense of humor."

Compliment Achievement.   A second form of complimenting is to compliment achievement. To do this, you simply acknowledge something that a person has accomplished or realized. The achievement can be as modest as remembering a telephone number or as monumental as overcoming some physical disability. Here are some examples of complimenting achievement:

> "Your speech was inspirational."
> "Congratulations on finishing your decorating project!"
> "I'm happy you were elected to the city board."
> "Great job!"

Compliment Effort.   You can compliment a person on his or her effort to achieve some task or goal, even if the person was unsuccessful in attaining it. In U.S. culture, we tend to compliment only the winners—those people who finish first and win the trophies. But you can compliment people for the effort they invest in a task or project. What's important is that they tried. It's not the destination but the journey that matters. Here are some examples of complimenting effort:

> "I'm really impressed with the effort you put into this project."
> "I love your determination!"
> "You ran a clean and honest race during this election."

Compliment the Invisible.   The final form of complimenting is a bit unusual. It involves complimenting people on the things they don't do—complimenting the invisible. There are countless things people don't do that are worthy of appreciation, yet we rarely think about those things. Maybe the person doesn't swear, chain-smoke, or interrupt constantly, so tell him or her that you appreciate it.

Once you begin to compliment the invisible, it can be fun and even entertaining. Here are some examples of complimenting the invisible:

> "I appreciate the fact that you don't swear."
> "I'm thankful you don't mention the mistakes of the past."
> "You could have criticized me, but you didn't. Thanks!"
> "I'm happy you don't watch television all night long."

Your willingness to see the best in others and verbally compliment their positive traits, efforts, and achievements is a life skill that will be a blessing not only to others but also a blessing to you.

Reframing What Is Said

A fifth way you can enlarge a person is to reframe his negative perception of a situation, circumstance, or person. The *reframing* technique involves seeing something from a different perspective or point of view. The French Renaissance writer Montaigne once cautioned, "We are hurt not so much by what happens, as by our opinion of what happens." In other words, our perceptions of an event are more important than the event itself.

How we choose to see something is instrumental in determining how we will respond to, deal with, and resolve problems that confront us. For instance, a man is fired from his job. Nothing can change the fact that he has been fired. But he can view the event from a variety of perspectives. The obvious viewpoint is that the firing is a terrible thing. He is out of a job, and he will need to begin looking for another one. It's a depressing situation. Many people in the man's shoes would stop here, go no further in their attempt to see this event from a different point of view, and would simply become hurt, angry, or depressed. Many people do not realize that there can be other ways of perceiving this same event.

It can be seen as a new beginning. He can finally pursue employment that might be more to his liking. It can be seen as a learning experience. What went wrong? How can he improve? What skills does he need to develop for future jobs? It can be viewed as a chance to take a break from the rat race. If he can afford it, he can use the next few weeks or months to rest and possibly take a vacation from the responsibilities of earning a living. It can be seen as a time to travel. He can sell everything he owns and hit the road. It can be viewed as an opportunity to be creative and start his own little company or business. This one event can be seen in a hundred different ways—no one way more valid than another.

Despite the many points of view from which we can choose to see a situation, we tend to hold onto the first interpretation that pops into our heads. We cement that perspective into our field of vision and limit our emotional responses to that point of view. In short, we get stuck. One experienced marriage and family therapist stated,

"As a counselor, I don't change my clients' situation; I simply help them see other ways of viewing the same situation." This seems to have a freeing effect on clients. It releases them from the bondage of seeing something from only one point of view. Depression can also be viewed as an invitation to grow. Anger can also be seen as a way of dealing with repressed sadness. The death of a loved one can also be a reminder to love those around

> *One question, one gentle word can change the course of a conversation and a life.*
> —ALFRED ADLER

us with greater appreciation. There are many ways of seeing. We need to be flexible in our perceptions and interpretations of those events that make up the fabric of our lives.

As a friend, you can enlarge others by opening their eyes to other ways of viewing a situation. If they share something "terrible" that has just happened to them, you can listen without verbal interruption, reflect what they are saying and feeling, and, if you can, reframe their situation. You can do this by simply stating:

"John, another way of looking at this is . . . "
"Mary, could this also mean . . . "
"Dad, another interpretation of this is . . . "

Your reframing doesn't have to be accepted by others as the truth, as insightful, or even as a solution to a problem. It's simply a way of allowing them to not get stuck with their own frame of reference. The purpose is to get them unstuck, to help them see with a different set of glasses, to assist them in looking at the same situation from a different perspective. You can be instrumental in freeing them from the prison of their own perceptions.

Touching Others

The final way to enlarge others is to touch them. This sounds like an obvious suggestion, but it is often overlooked as a means of making others feel acknowledged, cared for, and loved. There are times when words ring hollow and we need the comfort and reassurance that only physical contact can provide.

A little boy was frightened by a summer thunderstorm and ran to his father for comfort. The father attempted to reassure the boy by saying that the lightning and thunder were actually far away. "Anyway," added the dad, "God will always be with you for protection even though you can't see him." The boy listened to his father but continued to crawl up onto his lap. "I know that," the boy said, "but can I hug you anyway? I need something with skin on it."

At the end of the nineteenth century in Europe, orphaned children under the age of six months were dying for some unknown reason. The mortality rate for these infants in the orphanages of Europe was 100 percent. Experts tried to help by giving the infants more food, better lighting, special medicines, and even soothing music. But nothing seemed to work. The babies kept dying. This was so prevalent in Europe that it was referred to as the "Marasmus Syndrome." *Marasmus* in Latin means "to waste away." And that's what the babies continued to do—waste away. Apparently, these infants did not possess the will to begin life. Then the orphanages discovered that if these young infants were touched on a regular basis by "hired mothers"—women who were paid to handle, cuddle, and fondle the babies—they would live. The death rate dropped to the point at which an infant's death was the exception.

Could it be that we suffer from an adult form of the Marasmus Syndrome? Perhaps in our culture, we are wasting away from lack of touch. How many hugs do you receive a day? When was the last time you really hugged another human being for more than one or two seconds? One of the most powerful ways to enlarge another person is to touch them. Touching changes relationships. It changes lives.

There are entire books devoted to the importance of touching behavior, but for our purposes, remember that there are times when words don't bridge the gap between you and another person. When to touch? How long to touch? How to touch? These are questions only you can answer depending on the individual, the situation, and your intent. But keep in mind that touching others is one of the most powerful ways that we enlarge others, and ourselves.

COMMUNICATION ACTIVITIES

PERSONAL ACTIVITIES

1. **Enlarging communication behaviors**

   On a sheet of paper, identify three individuals whose communication behaviors have had an enlarging impact on your life. List specific behaviors that each person has demonstrated. If possible, thank each of the three individuals for their positive contributions to your life.

2. **Communicating in other cultures**

   Ask an individual from a different cultural background about his or her communication behaviors and attitudes. How do his or her behaviors and attitudes differ from your own? How are they similar? How did you feel about communicating with a person from a different cultural background?

3. **Seeing your communication improvements**

   On a sheet of paper, list three specific ways you have improved your communication behavior in the past five years. Maybe you're a better listener, less judgmental, more assertive, more forgiving, less timid, and so on. How do you feel about each positive change? How has each improvement changed your life?

CLASS ACTIVITIES

1. **Analyzing a communication event**

   Consider a recent communication event from your life—asking a friend for a favor, trying to persuade your employer that you were deserving of a raise, or resolving a relationship conflict. Identify the seven communication components of sender, message, environment, channel, receiver, feedback, and noise, and explain how they contributed to the success or failure of the communication event. Be prepared to discuss your thoughts and feelings about this assignment in class.

2. **Listening to others**

   Use reflective listening when you are talking with a friend. After your friend has completed a statement, try reflecting it back to him or her ("Are you saying . . . ?" or "Do you mean to tell me that . . . ?"). How did it feel? How did your friend respond to your mirroring? Be prepared to discuss your reactions to this assignment in class.

3. **Reframing others**

   Pair up with another student in class and share a recent disappointment or upsetting event. Listen to your partner describe his disappointment or upsetting event for 30–60 seconds; then offer one or two *positive* reframes of that situation. "Well, Jill, another way of looking at this is . . . " or "Fred, a positive way of seeing this is . . . " Discuss your responses to the activity; then reverse roles and repeat the exercise.

====== *Chapter 2* ======

GIVING YOURSELF PERMISSION
WELCOMING A NEW YOU

LEARNING OBJECTIVES

After reading this chapter, you should be able to:

2.1 Explain how you feel about public speaking

2.2 Explain the speaker apprehension self-appraisal scale

2.3 Discuss your speaker apprehension self-appraisal ranking

2.4 Apply the concept of giving yourself permission to make mistakes

2.5 Describe your response to the permission list for speakers

2.6 Explain the concept of giving yourself permission to overcome your fear of speaking

2.7 Explain the concept of why are you so nervous?

2.8 Summarize three reasons why public speaking is different from conversation

2.9 List five encouraging words about stage fright

2.10 Explain the question "will I ever get rid of these butterflies?"

2.11 Discuss the concept of adventure and growth, not safety

2.12 Identify seven ways to be successful in a hybrid public speaking class

Kuan knocked on his professor's door and heard her say, "Come on in, the water's fine!" Even though the purpose of his visit was to drop her Public Speaking class, he still smiled at her sense of humor.

"Well, what brings you to me, Kuan?" his professor said cheerfully.

"I just wanted to tell you that I've enjoyed your class these past two weeks, but I need to drop the course."

"Why?" she asked.

"I have a 4.0 grade point average in college, and I know I won't get an A in your class," he said reluctantly. "So I'm thinking about transferring to a college that doesn't require Public Speaking for graduation."

"All that effort just to keep a 4.0?"

"Well, I've always been a straight A student, and the public speaking class is a real problem if I can't get an A."

"Maybe your real problem is not public speaking," she offered. "Maybe your *real* problem is your desire to be perfect."

"I don't want to be perfect," he said. "I just want to get straight As."

"A wise man once said that 'He who is attached to much, will suffer much.' You might consider being less attached to your desire to be perfect. You might think about letting go of perfection and consider being an 'excellent student' or maybe even just a 'good student.' In fact, you might need to be gentler on yourself in other areas of your life as well."

"I've never thought of it that way," Kuan whispered almost to himself.

"This Public Speaking class could provide you with your greatest learning, Kuan—to give yourself permission to make mistakes, because it's through our mistakes that we learn and grow."

After a long silence, Kuan announced, "I'll stay in your class."

"Hey, that's great! And when you give your first speech, make a mistake or two so I feel needed as a teacher."

"Now that's a promise," Kuan chuckled as he rose and shook his professor's hand.

2.1 How do You Feel about Public Speaking?

Before we begin discussing the idea of giving yourself permission to make mistakes, let's take a moment and imagine what the process of giving a speech might be like. It might be helpful to take an imaginary glimpse into the future before we actually begin—somewhat like looking at a map before setting out on the actual journey itself. Let's take a few moments and glance at a map of the places you will be exploring as you learn to speak to an audience.

We will begin our exploration by responding to the Speaker Apprehension Self-Appraisal Scale.

2.2 Speaker Apprehension Self-Appraisal Scale

Read each of the following 10 speaking situations and circle your response on the 5-point scale. Upon completion of your 10 responses, add up your total points circled and refer to the Speaker Apprehension Scale provided.

1. Having a friendly conversation with a close friend, I would feel

1	2	3	4	5
Confident	Relaxed	Neutral	Anxious	Terrified

2. Having a conversation with a stranger, I would feel

1	2	3	4	5
Confident	Relaxed	Neutral	Anxious	Terrified

3. Research and outlining a formal speech, I would feel

1	2	3	4	5
Confident	Relaxed	Neutral	Anxious	Terrified

4. Practicing a formal speech, I would feel

1	2	3	4	5
Confident	Relaxed	Neutral	Anxious	Terrified

5. Sitting alone in the speaking room 30 minutes before I speak, I would feel

1	2	3	4	5
Confident	Relaxed	Neutral	Anxious	Terrified

6. Sitting in front of the audience one minute before I speak, I would feel

1	2	3	4	5
Confident	Relaxed	Neutral	Anxious	Terrified

7. Speaking to an audience of 30 strangers, I would feel

1	2	3	4	5
Confident	Relaxed	Neutral	Anxious	Terrified

8. Speaking to an audience of 30 friends, I would feel

1	2	3	4	5
Confident	Relaxed	Neutral	Anxious	Terrified

9. Speaking to an audience of 30 communication instructors, I would feel

1	2	3	4	5
Confident	Relaxed	Neutral	Anxious	Terrified

10. Speaking to an audience of 30 infants in their cribs, I would feel

1	2	3	4	5
Confident	Relaxed	Neutral	Anxious	Terrified

2.3 Speaker Apprehension Self-Appraisal Ranking

Although this scale is simply a rating of how you *might* respond to different speaking situations, it can provide you with some things to ponder as we begin looking at public speaking and your attitude toward your audience and toward yourself.

There are no right answers, and your responses would most likely fluctuate depending on a host of variables, including your psychological frame of mind, your emotional state, the specific people in the audience, your speech topic, what you had for breakfast, and so forth. But these 10 situations give you a more specific idea as to your level of apprehension.

Add up your total scores and let's see how you did.

Score of 10–20. Comfort with Speaking.

Your level of confidence and comfort in speaking would provide you with a healthy emotional foundation to address an audience without anxiety.

Score of 20–40. Acceptable Tolerance to Speaking.

Your level of speaker anxiety is normal and would provide you with a satisfactory foundation to address an audience with proper preparation and practice.

Score of 40–50. It's Good You're Reading This Chapter.

Your level of anxiety is high, but there's good news. Your level of self-satisfaction after reading this chapter could be much greater than the level of self-satisfaction of those who didn't respond with as much anxiety. In fact, some of the most satisfied speakers, after completing a public speaking course, are those individuals who initially reported the greatest anxiety before receiving instruction and practicing their speaking skills.

Regardless of your score on the Speaker Apprehension Scale, you'll be pleased to realize that you can decrease your level of speaking anxiety by changing the thoughts you have about speaking in front of others. Let's begin by taking a look at some interesting aspects of the situations you just responded to.

How did you feel about your level of apprehension when you envisioned having a conversation with a stranger or a friend? Normally, your anxiety is much lower when talking one-on-one with another person, regardless of the degree of familiarity, when compared to addressing an audience. How did you feel?

How were your feelings when you imagined you were researching or practicing your speech by yourself? Once again, your level of anxiety is relatively low when compared to actually standing in front of your audience and speaking.

It's not surprising that speakers usually report increased feelings of apprehension when they envision themselves in the speaking room 30 minutes before their talk and especially when they're getting ready to be introduced to the audience. How did you feel?

And finally, how did you feel when you imagined yourself delivering your speech? Did the kind of audience make a difference? Audience membership can make a big difference. Speaking to friends probably didn't make you feel as apprehensive as speaking to a group of strangers and especially not as anxious when addressing a group of communication instructors.

However, the final speaking situation is interesting. How did you feel about speaking to an audience of 30 infants in their cribs? Probably not apprehensive at all. Why? Although you were in the presence of 30 human beings while you spoke, most likely you didn't feel anxious at all. You might have even felt comfortable or even confident. Why?

The answer is that the infants weren't going to evaluate or judge you. They're just babies facing you with those innocent eyes and wonderful smiles. The other audience groups were knowledgeable and experienced enough to evaluate your speaking effectiveness, especially the communication instructors. But not the babies in their cribs. Interesting. Think about that for a moment. Your fear of speaking is primarily based upon your fear of evaluation, and ultimately rejection. All performance anxiety is founded upon the fear that we will be judged to be inadequate, undesirable, and, in the end, unlovable.

But that doesn't have to be your frame of reference when it comes to public speaking. You can change your ideas and expectations about what it means to share your thoughts and feelings in front of others. It all begins with giving yourself permission to not be perfect.

2.4 Giving Yourself Permission to Make Mistakes

Someone once said, "If you're not failing every once in a while, you're living life too cautiously." One of the primary stumbling blocks to our personal growth is our fear of making a mistake: making the wrong decision, choosing the wrong profession, marrying the wrong person, looking foolish in the eyes of others. We are often paralyzed into not acting at all and not taking any step because we fear it might be the wrong one.

But aren't mistakes an important part of the learning process? Isn't that how we truly learn? Not from reading it in a book or listening to someone else, but by experiencing it ourselves. The first time we tried to walk as infants was probably awkward, if not humorous. And our initial attempt at riding a bicycle without mom or dad holding on to the seat must have been a sight. Remember, we learn from our mistakes. That's the beauty of this journey.

R. H. Macy, founder of Macy's Department Stores, tried seven times to get his department stores started but failed each time. Can you imagine his sense of failure even after the first or second attempt? But on the eighth venture out, he succeeded. Just think of all the Macy's stores you've visited over the years. Would you have had the courage, as Mr. Macy did, to risk even a second attempt, let alone an eighth? The saddest thing is not that we didn't succeed, but rather that we didn't even try. We learn from our mistakes.

As you read this book, you will be asked to try new behaviors and new ways of seeing yourself. Don't take yourself too seriously on this journey. Give yourself permission to make mistakes along the way. Give yourself permission to be gentle on yourself.

2.5   A Permission List for Speakers

Before we begin talking about the mechanics of speaking in front of others, we need to take a few moments to examine your attitudes toward public speaking. People will often train as public speakers without ever once asking themselves if this is a skill they would like to improve. They struggle through all of the preparation and practice required for effective public speaking, and yet they neglect to explore some very fundamental issues involved in this highly charged communication event. They never give themselves permission to improve their speaking skills.

> *Be gentle on yourself.*
> —Joy Browne

This may sound strange to you—giving yourself permission to improve your speaking skills. Usually, public speaking training is imposed on you by someone else. For example, it may be required by your college or university for graduation, or your manager at work may think you would benefit from such a course. Rarely do you, after an afternoon of introspection, decide suddenly that your speaking skills are lacking and your life would be dramatically improved if you learned to speak more effectively on your feet.

So let's take a few moments to explore this whole area of giving yourself permission to speak. Read the following statements and circle the response that most accurately describes your feelings.

1. I give myself permission to express myself.   yes/no/unsure
2. I give myself permission to stand up in front of others.   yes/no/unsure
3. I give myself permission to ask others to listen to me.   yes/no/unsure
4. I give myself permission to experience something new.   yes/no/unsure
5. I give myself permission to feel uncomfortable.   yes/no/unsure
6. I give myself permission to speak in front of others.   yes/no/unsure
7. I give myself permission to not be perfect.   yes/no/unsure
8. I give myself permission to make mistakes.   yes/no/unsure

  9. I give myself permission to try new speaking skills.   yes/no/unsure
10. I give myself permission to improve my speaking.   yes/no/unsure
11. I give myself permission to not know all the answers.   yes/no/unsure
12. I give myself permission to teach others.   yes/no/unsure
13. I give myself permission to persuade others.   yes/no/unsure
14. I give myself permission to let others have their opinions.   yes/no/unsure
15. I give myself permission not to seek the approval of others.   yes/no/unsure
16. I give myself permission to enjoy my time speaking in public.   yes/no/unsure
17. I give myself permission to like my voice and my body.   yes/no/unsure
18. I give myself permission to be gentle on myself.   yes/no/unsure
19. I give myself permission to be myself.   yes/no/unsure
20. I give myself permission to love myself.   yes/no/unsure

Did it feel unusual or unnatural "giving yourself permission" to do or feel these things? Usually, permission to think, feel, or do something comes from someone or something outside of yourself. It comes from the government, the boss, the teacher, the church, the school, your parents, your friends, or your spouse.

However, in the 20 permission statements you just considered, the permission was coming from *you*, not someone else. It didn't matter whether you responded with "yes," "no," or "unsure" because it was you who was doing the deciding. No one else. You were the one who was giving permission or not giving permission. You were even the person deciding if you were "unsure" about each statement. No matter how you responded, each of the 20 times, you were in the control tower deciding how each decision landed.

This concept of where permission resides is often called the *locus of power*. Do you decide things for yourself, or do others decide for you? It's the subtle difference between "I have to ..." and "I choose to... ." Try this: in a normal speaking voice, say, "I *have* to give a speech." Say it again. How did that feel? Now try saying, "I *choose* to give a speech." Again. How did that feel? Did you notice a difference between the two statements?

With the "I have to" statement, you may have noticed less commitment in your voice, perhaps even less energy. When you said, "I choose to give a speech," you may have felt more definite, more determined. If not, try the "choose" statement again. Feel anything different? If you think that feels awkward or strange, try saying "I choose not to give a speech" a couple of times and explore how that statement feels to you.

You might be thinking they're just words—"I have to ... ," "I choose to ... ," and "I choose not to... ." But words are powerful, and these particular words—"have to" and "choose to"—bring you to an interesting place in your personal decision making. Who makes your decisions? Are they made for you most of the time (I have to ...)? Or do you choose and decide for yourself (I choose to ... ; I choose not to ...)?

Much of your sense of independence, personal strength, and internal resilience depend directly on your decision to think and decide for yourself during your lifetime.

As you marked your responses to the 20 permission list items above, you may have been surprised by the number of statements you have never consciously considered before this moment. These are not questions we often ask ourselves. And it would not be unusual if you responded more frequently with "no" and "unsure" than "yes" because most individuals often feel they have nothing really important to share that would warrant the attention of a group of human beings. Many people, after completing this questionnaire, report that they rarely feel anyone would want to listen to them speak.

If your answer to these items was "yes" the majority of the time, you are the exception to the rule, and your training in public speaking should be easy, if not downright enjoyable. If, however, you were unsure, responding with lots of nos, or you thought this was a dumb set of questions, don't be discouraged. Your training in public speaking might just change your perception of who you think you are.

> *No one can make you feel inferior without your consent.*
> —ELEANOR ROOSEVELT

Before you begin your training in public speaking, we need to spend a few moments examining one of our most common fears—the fear of giving a speech in front of a group of people. The 20 statements on the permission list asked if you gave yourself permission to overcome your fear of speaking. No matter how you responded to these questions, you will benefit from a brief discussion of overcoming stage fright.

2.6 Giving Yourself Permission to Overcome Your Fear of Speaking

The thought of speaking before an audience can often arouse a great amount of anxiety. It outranks death, losing one's spouse, financial bankruptcy, illness, war, and snakes as the number one thing that terrifies us most.

Most people would probably agree with this survey. Very few people actively seek speaking opportunities, sneak into speech tournament competitions, or grab the microphone from the speaker at a PTA meeting and deliver an impromptu talk. Very few.

Many of us would prefer avoiding anything even resembling a public speaking event. Whenever someone is needed to introduce the bride and groom, deliver a brief sales presentation, speak at a luncheon, preside at the annual awards dinner, or even say a prayer at the family reunion, most folks disappear into the woodwork or run for the hills. The stress of speaking before an audience is great for many of us.

Three Ways We Stress Out When Speaking

There are three primary categories of stress responses that people report when they experience stage fright. *Physical sensations* make up the first category of stress responses that can occur when we are preparing to speak. The physical sensations can begin long before the actual day of the speech and may appear in the form of sleepless nights, an upset stomach, dizziness, and tingling in the hands and legs. During the speech itself, the physical sensations can include trembling knees, sweaty palms, lightheadedness, dry mouth, and nervous coughing. The exact physical sensations vary from person to person, of course, but almost everyone experiences some degree of physical discomfort or uneasiness when speaking in front of others.

The second category of stress responses includes *emotional responses* that can be experienced before, during, and after the speaking performance. They can include feelings of being overwhelmed, fear, loss of control, depression, panic, anxiety, help-lessness, inadequacy, abandonment, shame, and anger.

The final category is the *psychological responses* that can be experienced when delivering the speech. This includes loss of memory, negative self-talk, jumbled thought patterns, nervous repetition of words or phrases, and the use of verbal pauses such as "ah," "um," and "you know."

To complicate matters, these three categories of stress responses can and often do interact with one another, increasing your level of stage fright. For instance, the physical sensations of trembling knees can give rise to feelings of being out of control and feeling helpless or terrified. These feelings in turn can cause a psychological block so that the words of your talk are lost.

Sound like fun? Well, before you throw this book in the garbage and swear that you would rather hide away in some cave in Tibet than risk these terrible ills, hold on. It's not all that bad.

Even skilled speakers experience some of these responses when addressing an audience. But the difference between you and them is that they understand the speaking process. They understand that such responses are natural. It's all part of being human. They realize that these responses can be changed. These speakers have pre-pared and practiced their speeches, and when they do experience any of these sensa-tions of stage fright, they know how to bring themselves back under control. They know the skills and techniques to get themselves to breathe gently, center their focus of attention, and return to their talk. This chapter is designed to enable you to do the same. But first, let's look at why you are so nervous.

2.7 Why Are You So Nervous?

Before you can overcome a problem, you must admit that there is a problem and then understand the reasons for its existence. Most people, when confronted with a fear or anxiety, either deny its existence or fail to adequately investigate the reasons for it.

As to the first issue of denial, very few novice speakers are grandiose enough to boast that they have no fears regarding public speaking. Without exception, most beginning speakers are very conscious and aware of their fears, but they don't seem to know why they are afraid.

One mystified speaker angrily lamented, "Why am I so frightened? I know how to talk."

"My friends all tell me I am witty," another complained, "but when I get up to speak in front of a group, I just go blank."

And one executive grumbled, "I've had this speech written out for nearly a month, but as soon as I stand up before my audience, my eyes get blurry and my brain turns to mush. I just don't understand why."

Why, they ask.

Why is it so difficult to just speak in front of a small group of 10 or 12 people, many of whom you may know? Why is it so hard to deliver a talk when you've been talking all your life? Why is it so demanding to speak, even when you're prepared ahead of time? Why should you be so nervous?

Only One of Me and Lots of Them

Let's look at the same public speaking scene, without the sound. There is a group of people seated in a room, all facing one direction. Then, one of them stands, walks to the front of the room, turns, and faces the other people, who are still seated. As she stands above the seated audience, the speaker's mouth begins to move, and her hands gesture occasionally. All eyes are on her. She looks at the group. Her mouth is moving. Their mouths are shut. She gestures. They do not. Her mouth stops moving. The seated individuals clap their hands. She turns and walks down from the podium, finds her chair, and sits down. Now, everyone in the group is seated again.

What just happened? Well, if you simply watched the event and did not analyze the content of the speech, you would discover a very striking thing. The speaker becomes separate from the people she is talking to. She is no longer just one of them. Instead, she is in front of them. She is standing above them, while they are seated below. She is talking, while they are silent. She is moving and animated, while they sit motionless. She is glancing at individual members, while every eye in the audience is on her. In fact, she now controls the event, while they have little or no control. She determines the ebb and flow of the experience, while they watch for her cues. When she finishes, they applaud. She walks back down to find her chair, while they are seated and are still clapping. In short, the speaker becomes the leader of the group, and the people in the audience become her followers.

> *If you're never scared or embarrassed or hurt, it means you never take any chances.*
> —JULIA SOREL

Now, if you are the president of the United States or the conductor of the New York Philharmonic, such an experience in front of all those people would not be frightening (maybe). Having all of those eyes riveted on you, watching your every move, listening to your every word—you, the center of attention—might not be too frightening, if you're trained for such experiences.

2.8 Public Speaking Is Different from Conversation

The fact that you've carried on conversations all your life doesn't help now. The fact that you are witty doesn't help now. The fact that you've written the speech beforehand doesn't help now. All of these things don't help now because you're not involved in conversational skills.

You are involved in presentational skills. You are, in short, presenting yourself, both body and mind, to a group of people who are watching your presentation. You are no longer one of them. You are separate from them. You are presenting; they are observing. That's why it's so frightening to speak in front of an audience. No one has ever told you what to do in this situation. Sure, you've spent your entire lifetime learning how to carry on a conversation, how to informally talk to others in small group settings or at intimate gatherings at quaint restaurants. But it is unlikely that you've ever been trained to present yourself to a group of people. So remember to give yourself permission to be gentle on yourself as you learn to be different from "the rest of them"—your audience.

Public speaking is an activity that involves mental and physical presentation skills that are different from social conversational skills. Being an effective public speaker requires physical coordination, mental concentration, content organization, skills practice, and a great deal of experience. Just as it would be foolish to thrust a beginning surfer into large waves her first time out, it would be equally foolish to expect the beginning speaker to be cool, calm, and collected the first time before an audience. Formal presentation skills require as much, if not more, practice and skills improvement as surfing, or any physical sport for that matter.

There are many books and teachers who sincerely believe that if a novice speaker could just relax, she would decrease her stage fright and would thus become a better public speaker. Positive thinking, self pep talks, creative visualization, and self-hypnosis are often encouraged as means of improving your speaking skills. There is some research to support such claims, but there are no shortcuts to learning these formal presentational skills.

Without the practical experience, there can be little behavioral change. You can visualize, think, and dream all you want that you can ride a surfboard. But it's the practical, hands-on experience that enables you to paddle out, stroke just enough to match the speed of the wave, stand up, and maintain a trim position as you ride the swell to the beach.

That's what we'll be doing. Learning not only the whys but, equally important, the hows. We'll learn step by step how to do everything from walking up to the podium to returning to and sitting back in your chair.

2.9   Some Encouraging Words about Stage Fright

Now that you know some differences between public speaking and conversation, let's consider some encouraging words about stage fright.

It's Natural to Be Anxious

The human body reacts to any perceived threat with certain physical, psychological, and emotional responses. To not do so would be cause for serious concern. It's natural to feel some anxiety and fear as you face an audience.

You Are Not Alone

Everyone experiences some degree of stage fright before, during, and even after a speech. There is not one person in your audience who would not feel some degree of stage fright if she or he were in your place. So take heart: you're not alone. We're all in this together.

You Appear Much More Relaxed Than You Feel

When speakers view a video playback of a speech, they are all, with very few exceptions, surprised at how relaxed they appear on the monitor. Feedback from audience members immediately after the talk confirms this interesting phenomenon. The speaker experiences a great deal more internal anxiety than she exhibits externally to others. You may feel really nervous on the inside, but chances are you don't appear nervous to your audience.

Have Something Important to Say

Abraham Lincoln once stated, "I shall never be old enough to speak without embarrassment when I have nothing to say." Those words still ring true today. If you feel strongly about what you are going to share with your audience, you are less likely to be fearful of them. Speak only when you have something important to say. That is an essential rule of thumb for public speaking, as well as in your daily life.

> *To grow, we must travel in the direction of our fears.*
> —JOHN BERRYMAN

Concentrate on What Is Said

Be more concerned with the main idea you are going to share with your audience than the exact wording of your message. Don't get fixated on the details of your talk. Instead, focus on the main idea of the speech. Keep looking at the big picture, not the minutiae.

Practice Your Speech

There are very few speakers who can give well-developed speeches in an impromptu fashion, with no prior practice. Practice is one of the most important factors in confident speaking for speakers at all experience levels. There is no substitute for actually practicing your speech in a standing position. Remember, public speaking is a physical skill as well as an intellectual, psychological skill.

Visualize Success

After you have practiced your speech two or three times, find a quiet place to relax and visualize yourself successfully delivering your presentation. Sit in a comfortable chair, relax your entire body, close your eyes, take a deep breath or two, and visualize the speaking situation. See the room, the audience looking at you, the podium, and yourself all dressed up, ready to communicate your message enthusiastically to your listeners. Visualize yourself beginning the introduction, effortlessly moving from point to point in the body of your speech and then concluding the talk with conviction. Imagine the audience smiling, nodding, and leaning forward in their chairs to hear every word you say. Finally, imagine the audience smiling and applauding warmly as you end your speech. Let the applause linger for a while in your ears, and then take a deep breath, open your eyes, and let your body remember the scenes from your visualization. Try this exercise once each night before you give your speech. It will make a difference.

Release Your Tension before You Speak

Some speakers jog in the morning before giving a speech. Others talk nervously about their anxiety to a friend the night before. There is a television news anchor in New York who goes through five minutes of light stretching exercises in her dressing room before she goes on camera. Systematic relaxation exercises work for some, while other speakers prefer to simply pace backstage before they deliver their speech. One of the most effective relaxation exercises is simply to breathe deeply from your stomach. Keep your eyes open, but don't fix your gaze at any one thing. Just breathe deeply and evenly. You'll discover that all your bodily rhythms will become more calm and centered. Experiment to discover what works best for you. It's your life.

Experience Reduces Anxiety

The more speaking experience you have, the less likely you are to be frightened by your next speech. It's like that with most things. The more you do it, the less frightening it is. There once was a man named Clay in the central California farmlands who flew a crop duster, an airplane used to spray insecticides on the strawberry fields. Day after day, Clay would make that old red plane loop, spin, twirl, and zip over those strawberry fields. When asked if flying like that ever frightened him, he responded, "At first it did, but after 27 years of flying a duster, I've sorta gotten used to it." The same holds true for speaking.

The Audience Is on Your Side

Think of your own reactions when you've been an audience member. Did you want the speaker to fail? To look like a fool? Probably not. The vast majority of us want the speaker to succeed. We want the speaker to be interesting, informative, stimulating, and entertaining. The last thing we want is for the speaker to fail in her attempts to communicate. Audiences really are empathic, encouraging, and supportive, if given half a chance. One of the most uplifting thoughts you can have as you face an audience is the belief that they wish you well and want you to succeed. They really are on your side.

> *There is only one of you in all time.*
> —MARTHA GRAHAM

2.10   Will I Ever Get Rid of These Butterflies?

We've talked about giving yourself permission to make mistakes and to overcome your fears, and still you're probably wondering, "Will I ever get rid of the butterflies once and for all?" Well, there's a well-known story about a 60-year-old woman who was enrolled in a public speaking class at a local college. On the night she was scheduled to deliver her first speech, she was overcome with terror at the prospect of talking in front of all those people. She couldn't bring herself to walk up to the front of the class when her name was called, so the instructor walked over to her and asked her how she felt.

The woman replied, "I'm scared. My stomach is filled with butterflies, and they're flying around chaotically." With some gentle encouragement from the teacher and students, the woman slowly walked to the front of the class and spoke to the group.

The following summer, that same woman was at a family gathering. During dinner, the woman's granddaughter asked, "Grandma, Daddy said you took a speech class and learned how to talk. He said you had butterflies in your stomach. Did you finally get rid of them?"

"No, I didn't get rid of those butterflies," the woman replied proudly, "but at least now they fly in formation."

Carl Jung wisely observed, "We rarely solve life's biggest problems. We merely outgrow them." In your life's journey, you will outgrow many of the fears and problems you are struggling with today. Your butterflies will most likely always accompany you when you speak in public, but with time and practice, they will be flying in formation.

2.11   Adventure and Growth, Not Safety

Many people run from new opportunities, especially if those opportunities involve thinking differently, behaving differently, and feeling differently. Most of us suffer needlessly because we fear the unknown. Rather than venture into the unknown, we would rather resign ourselves to a situation that is painful because it is also familiar, predictable, and in some ways safe. But perhaps we were intended to explore the unknown in our life's voyage.

> *A ship in a harbor is safe,*
> *But that's not what*
> *ships were built for.*
> —ZEN SAYING

For most of us, learning how to speak in front of others involves venturing out into the unknown. We are like ships in a harbor, not really comfortable with the prospects of setting sail into open sea because every voyage requires some element of risk, and maybe change. But that's what learning is all about—changing, improving, and being freer than you were before.

Just keep in mind that the purpose of life is not to be perfect. It's to try new things as we grow older. To learn more about this world, our friends, and ourselves. We should learn to discover and communicate what we think, how we feel, and who we are as we journey during our lifetime.

Now it's time to leave the harbor.

2.12   Success in a Hybrid Public Speaking Class

With online courses becoming more popular due to geographical demands, institutional budgetary constraints, and student convenience, public speaking courses are often being offered as hybrid classes. A hybrid public speaking course will require that much or all of the content material, assignments, quizzes, and exams be accessed on the Internet. Online chat rooms or discussion boards will facilitate student/instructor discussion, interaction, and feedback, while students will meet in person with other students at an onsite location to deliver their speeches on specified dates. This hybrid approach to public speaking requires additional student responsibilities and commitment that a regular course might not. Here are seven suggestions that will help you achieve greater success in a hybrid public speaking class.

Determine Your Level of Hybrid Readiness

Hybrid courses are different from onsite, face-to-face courses, and your hybrid public speaking course may present some challenges that you need to consider if you are to be successful in this approach to learning. Here are five questions you need to honestly reflect upon before you commit to a hybrid course.

1. Do you like to work independently?
2. Are you good at meeting deadlines?
3. Are you willing to ask for clarification and/or assistance?
4. Do you feel confident working with computers and the Internet?
5. Do you manage your daily and monthly schedules effectively?

If you answered "yes" to four or five of these questions, you will most likely be successful in meeting the requirements of your hybrid public speaking course. If, however, you answered "no" to two or more of the questions, you might reconsider using a hybrid approach to your public speaking course, especially if you have difficulty with the time management issues raised in questions two and five.

Make A Personal Commitment for Hybrid Success

A hybrid public speaking class does not offer the daily, face-to-face interaction with the instructor and students that a regular course does. All of the nonverbal communication cues that are so readily available in an onsite class are now largely replaced with PDF readings, links to related websites, online forums or chat rooms, and e-mail communications with your instructor and fellow students. This approach to learning offers less face-to-face interaction, stimulation, and encouragement and demands more self-motivation and discipline on your part.

You will need to make a personal commitment to the additional responsibilities and requirements your hybrid class will demand of you. That means that for the next semester, you will have to devote yourself to structuring your life to meet the assignment, exam, and speech deadlines without the in-person reminders and reinforcement that an onsite class offers. Make a personal commitment for success and stick to it every day of the semester.

Manage Your Time Effectively

The most essential element for success in your hybrid public speaking course is time management. Simply put, if you manage your time effectively, you can succeed in completing your hybrid public speaking course. If you don't manage your time effectively, you will be less likely to succeed. Here are four helpful suggestions for effective time management.

First, construct a semester-length calendar generated from the course syllabus assignment deadlines for your class. Note *every* reading, homework assignment, online forum/discussion, quiz/exam, and speech deadline for the entire semester on your calendar. Use color coding of due dates to help you indicate the type of assignment or work. You might even place reminders of assignment due dates three days ahead. In other words, three days before a big assignment or speech is due, give yourself a heads-up reminder.

Second, conduct a daily and weekly check of assignments that are due. Your beautiful semester calendar won't do you any good if you don't check it once in awhile. I suggest that you check it daily and keep on top of all of your class responsibilities.

You can even schedule in weekly "homework time" periods in a specific color so you can "see" when you should be working on each assignment, day by day. It's best to assign your "homework time" periods in one or two hour blocks so you have adequate time to complete assignments, without burning out.

Third, elicit the help of a friend to hold you accountable to your semester calendar—someone to ask you each week if you've been following your homework calendar for the course. It's amazing how powerful knowing that someone will be asking you every Sunday night for the entire semester if you're current on all of your assignment preparations and submissions can be. That's what friends are for.

And fourth, submit *ALL* of your assignments, exams, and speech material on time. This is the secret to online success. More than anything else, submit all work on their due dates. Better yet, submit all work one or two days early, if possible. This not only indicates to the instructor that you are responsible, committed, and a little neurotic (in a good way), it also will give you a feeling of accomplishment and pride (in an even better way). Remember, if you manage your time effectively, the hybrid public speaking course can be a wonderful experience. If not, you'd better change your time management practices right now. I mean, right now.

Establish a Relationship with Your Instructor Early On

You might be reluctant to visit your instructors during office hours, but you need to make changes when it comes to a hybrid course. If your instructor holds office hours, visit him or her during the second week of the semester. By that time, most of the initial confusion of the first week of classes has settled, and both you and your instructor are in a place where you can meet one another in a more relaxed atmosphere. It will be beneficial for you to shake hands with your professor, get a feel for his or her personality, and establish the beginning of a relationship. Since your face-to-face interactions with your professor will be limited in a hybrid course, meeting him or her in person during the second week will take the mystery out of the relationship, and you'll be more apt to communicate online or in person if the need should arise.

You might even visit your professor a couple of times more during the semester, just to touch base, clarify any questions you might have, and glean any pearls of wisdom his or her knowledge and experience can afford you. Communicate with your instructor, in person. It will make a big difference.

Participate in Class: Online and In-Person

In addition to submitting all of your work on time, one of the things you can do to really benefit from a hybrid public speaking course is to participate in all of your online forums, discussion groups, and e-mail communications. Since there is little face-to-face interaction with the instructor and students, your participation in all online assignments is vital to your contribution and success in the class. Keep current on all online assignments, feedback discussions, and forums. Contribute your responses, feedback, and opinions in a manner that is clear, meaningful, and respectful. Refrain from arguing online. Keep your remarks positive and your attitude uplifting. Since the instructor and students cannot see your face, your words will have to communicate your genuine and positive attitude. One final suggestion, think before you click the "Send" button on any online correspondence, especially if the discussion gets heated or intense. Once a message is sent, it can never be erased. So pause before you hit the "Send" button.

On the days you meet face-to-face with the instructor and other students, don't be intimidated or reluctant to contribute. Arrive to the classroom 5 or 10 minutes early and greet the instructor and other students. Sit toward the front of the room. Look for ways you might be helpful in getting the room arranged or the class organized. Ask the instructor if he needs any help. Contribution to the class begins even before the instructor welcomes the students.

Most likely, your face-to-face meetings will involve the presentation of various speeches. Be positive in all of your nonverbal communication. Pay attention to each speaker. Smile at the speaker. Nod your head in affirmation. Ask a question after each presentation if there is a Question and Answer session. Look for two or three things to compliment as each student speaks. And volunteer often to verbally compliment speakers after their speeches. Do all you can do to make the face-to-face onsite experience enlarging, friendly, and supportive. Your fellow students and instructor will be glad you did, and so will you. Make a positive difference in all that you do.

Establish Face-to-Face Support

In some hybrid public speaking classes, the instructor will assign you to a class group or "family" that you are required to meet with, in person, a number of times during the semester, in addition to the scheduled onsite speaking days. These face-to-face meetings with your class group add a personal dimension to the course experience for discussion, speech practice, and support.

If your instructor does not provide the opportunity for non-speaking-day, face-to-face group meetings, you might want to establish your own face-to-face support with two or three other students enrolled in your course.

During the first day or two of onsite speaking presentations, be on the lookout for two or three students who appear friendly, deliver good speeches, and participate in the discussions. Approach two or three of those students after class and ask them if they'd be interested in forming a small group to meet occasionally to discuss the class, practice speeches, and be encouraging of one another. You'd be surprised how delighted and willing students will be to join such a group.

Your meetings don't have to be formal, long, or numerous. Volunteer to have the first meeting at your house, dorm, or apartment. Provide some chips and soft drinks. And just see how the first meeting goes. It's best to meet every two or three weeks for one hour to discuss assignments, study for tests, or just touch base. Your group can be especially helpful if you practice your upcoming speeches in front of one another and provide some feedback on the practice speeches. Whatever your group does, remember that the purpose is to support and encourage one another in this journey of public speaking. And you might just make a friend in the process.

Finding Out-of-Class Speaking Opportunities

Your instructor might require that one or more of your speech presentations be delivered and recorded to an out-of-class audience. This type of speaking assignment requires some planning and additional effort on your part. Here are four suggestions that will make any out-of-class speaking assignment a successful one.

First, review the requirements for your out-of-class speaking assignment. What are the requirements in terms of speech purpose, type of audience, minimum size of audience, time limits, recording requirements, and due date? The answers to many of these questions will determine your approach to planning for the out-of-class speech.

Second, you will need to locate an audience for your speech. In some instances, instructors will permit you to deliver your speech to a group of students from your hybrid class or to a group of your friends. But the majority of instructors will have you locate an existing group to serve as your audience. Here's where many students in hybrid public speaking courses want to throw up their hands in disgust and drop the course because they can't think of any audiences. But slow down, take a deep breath, and be creative in your approach to this requirement.

There are many audiences within a few miles of where you're sitting right now that would be happy to have you deliver an interesting informative or persuasive speech. Consider contacting community service groups such as the Rotary Club, Lions Club, Kiwanis International, Soroptimist International, Knights of Columbus, Junior League, and the League of Women Voters. You can contact local political groups such as the Young Democrats, Young Republicans, and Young Libertarians. Consider reaching out to interest groups such as the Sierra Club, the National Rifle Association, Greenpeace, and the 4H Club. If you want to have a fun time scanning hundreds of interest groups, just Google "local interest groups," and you have enough to fill a Friday evening. Local churches often host weekly lunches where guest speakers are encouraged to present brief presentations on a topic of interest.

You can often give a presentation to a church youth group or college group, and the topic of your speech doesn't have to be religious in nature so long as it's relevant to the audience. You might even consider contacting a local company or corporation that hosts "brown bag" luncheons with a local guest speaker and sharing an interesting or relevant topic. And finally, you might even ask one of your former or current college instructors if you can serve as a quest speaker in one of his or her classes if your topic is related to their course content. There are hundreds of potential audiences within 25 miles of your home if you just invest a little research and effort.

Third, you will need to record your speech. Once you've located an audience of appropriate size to listen to your speech, you will need to record the speech so that your instructor can view your presentation for evaluation. Make sure you understand and can accommodate the recording requirements. Whether you are required to submit your speech on a flash drive, e-mail it to your instructor, or download it to YouTube or some other online site, make certain that you know how to accomplish this very important task. If you don't or are uncertain, contact your instructor to clarify or receive further instructions. This is the time to learn the process—not on the day of your off-site speech.

Fourth, have a friend or fellow student record your speech. Whether you use a camcorder, tablet, or smart phone to record your speech, it's easier to have an assistant who understands the requirements of the assignment rather than try to get one of the audience members to volunteer to record your speech a minute before you deliver your presentation. Have your assistant record the entire audience before you are introduced to serve as evidence for the audience size and frame your entire body during your presentation so your instructor can see as much of your delivery as possible. Also have your assistant record the applause and any questions and answers that follow your speech. Remember to treat your assistant to lunch or dinner after the event. You can never be too grateful.

An out-of-class speaking assignment could be viewed as one extra headache in your attempts to complete the course. Another way of looking at it is that it can be an opportunity to learn some real-world skills, to provide relevant and helpful information to an appreciative audience, and to achieve a level of personal accomplishment that is not always discovered in a college classroom. Who knows: someone in your audience might even offer you another opportunity to speak. This could open up a whole new career for you. Be positive. Be open to what life has in store for you.

COMMUNICATION ACTIVITIES

PERSONAL ACTIVITIES

1. **Giving yourself permission**
   Review your responses to the 20 statements in the permission list. Select one item that you did not agree with. Read the statement aloud five times in a definite, confident voice. Close your eyes and imagine you are actually experiencing the situation described in the statement. For example, "I give myself permission to not know all the answers." Imagine being asked a question by a teacher and simply responding, "I don't know." Imagine feeling comfortable with your response. Imagine the teacher smiling and saying, "That's okay. I don't know the answer either." Imagine that you and the teacher both begin to laugh. How did that feel to you? Try another permission statement if you had more than one "no" response.

2. **A different cultural perspective**
   Ask an individual from a different cultural background about his or her attitudes and feelings about the permission list presented in this chapter. How does his or her culture perceive the ideas raised by the statements in the permission list? How do you feel about his or her responses?

3. **Imagining the worst**
   Imagine you are delivering a five-minute speech about programming a VCR to a group of 25 high school seniors. Halfway through your speech, you draw a blank—you can't remember what you were going to say. What is the worst thing (or things) that could happen? Be specific. List all of the horrors that could happen. Look at your list. How would you respond to each of the items on your list? Be strong. Be assertive. Tell those high school seniors a thing or two. Did any of the audience members come to your rescue? How do you feel? Was it all that bad?

CLASS ACTIVITIES

1. **Receiving permission**
   Pair up with another student in class and take turns granting one another permission for the statements from the permission list. If you responded "no" to

any statement on your list, have your partner grant you permission to do that behavior. For instance, have your partner tell you in a firm and definite tone of voice, "I, (name), give you permission to make mistakes!" Ask her to say the statement three or four times. How did it feel? What did you think? After your partner has repeated this process with three or four other statements you disagreed with, switch roles and give your partner permission statements. Be prepared to share your reactions to this assignment in class.

2. **Group sharing: letting others know what you fear**

   The class is to be divided into groups of five students each. Each student is to share three or four things he or she fears. As each individual shares a specific fear, other students in the group can raise their hands to indicate that they too share that same fear. You'll be surprised at how many others share not only your fear of public speaking but other physical, psychological, and emotional fears as well. You are not alone. The group members can also discuss how they cope or deal with these fears.

3. **You appear more relaxed than you feel**

   This exercise will be videotaped in your class. Give an informal 30-second talk about your public speaking fears. You can share anything you'd like during this brief talk. After the entire class has spoken, view the presentations *without* sound. What did you look like? Did you look as anxious or frightened as you felt? How did the other students appear while they were speaking? Discuss your responses to this activity in class.

4. **Worst nightmare speech**

   Make a list of the five most terrible things an audience could do to you while you're speaking—throw paper, walk out of the room, shout criticism, sleep, "boo" and "hiss," or laugh. This will be like your worst nightmare. But, you'll discover, it's not that bad. Assign members of the class to role-play your "terrible" behaviors while you are speaking. Give an informal 30-second talk about a happy childhood memory and let the students act out their roles (the horrible behaviors). How was it? Was the experience as bad as you thought it would be? Did you laugh? Did the audience laugh? What feelings do you have? How did the exercise change your attitude toward speaking? Be prepared to discuss your reactions to this assignment in class.

Chapter 3

ORGANIZING YOUR SPEECH
KEEPING IT SIMPLE

LEARNING OBJECTIVES

After reading this chapter, you should be able to:

3.1 Explain the concept "keep it simple"

3.2 Define public speaking

3.3 List the three principles of public speaking

3.4 Define the four speaking methods

3.5 Explain speech organization

3.6 Discuss the body of the speech

3.7 Discuss the introduction of the speech

3.8 Discuss the conclusion of the speech

3.9 Construct a speech outline

3.10 Construct speaking notes for a speech

Have you ever experienced a time in your life when everything seemed to hit all at once? A hundred things to do. Appointments to keep. Projects to complete. Unfinished business pressing in from all sides.

Sam's first year of teaching college was like that. He was 23 years old, teaching three classes as a part-time instructor at a local community college, attending graduate school, volunteering a couple hours a day as a teacher's aide at a local child-care center, and washing dishes at the Garrett Restaurant in the evenings. In addition, Sam was conducting communication workshops for college students every other Sunday at a local church.

Somehow, Sam managed to juggle all of those responsibilities for the first three months of the year, until gradually he noticed changes in his behavior. He was getting angry over little things. And he wasn't sleeping as well as he once had. Getting up in the morning was becoming more difficult, and Sam found himself just lying in bed staring at the ceiling after the alarm went off.

Sam has since learned that these are some of the telltale symptoms of depression. But at that time, all he knew was that getting up in the morning was becoming more and more difficult. Knowing that something was wrong, Sam wanted to talk to

35

someone about his situation, but he didn't have the money to see a therapist. He was too embarrassed to share his problem with his family and too proud to discuss it with his friends. So he was stuck.

One Saturday morning, as Sam was sitting on the back porch of his second-story apartment, Annie shouted up to him with an invitation for coffee. Annie Loveless was a friendly 76-year-old woman who lived by herself in the apartment directly under Sam's. Annie was a gentle soul, and very wise. After her second husband died nine years earlier in Hollywood, she moved to northern California. The years had been good to her, and she seemed to glide through life with ease and grace.

After pouring a second cup of coffee, she asked Sam if he had been feeling well. He lied and said he was fine. A long silence followed his response, and Annie whispered, "I once heard that God invented time so everything wouldn't happen all at once." Sam smiled weakly and remained silent as he held his cup.

"You have a long life ahead of you," she continued. "Don't complicate and confuse your life with too many things, too many responsibilities. You need to ease your burden by cutting some things out. I think you need to simplify your life a little."

Annie was a good friend, and she had come to know Sam well during the year and a half he had lived at the apartment complex. Her words hit him with great force. During the next two weeks, Sam quit his dishwashing job at the restaurant, said good-bye to all those kids at the child-care center, and arranged to teach the college Sunday School class once a month instead of twice.

> *The ability to simplify means to eliminate the unnecessary so that the necessary may speak.*
> —HANS HOFFMAN

With only his teaching and graduate school to occupy the majority of his time, Sam felt as though the weight of the world had been lifted from his shoulders. His anger gradually subsided. His sleep began to return to normal. And soon, Sam discovered it was even easy to get out of bed in the morning when the alarm went off.

Not all responsibilities can be cast aside. Not all lives can be simple and uncomplicated in the web of relationships, ties, and duties we accumulate over the years. But we do have the freedom to make choices. We don't have to say yes to every request that is placed before us. Sometimes we need to choose simplicity over complexity. One or two good friends, instead of ten or fifteen. One or two organizational memberships, instead of seven or eight. A desk empty of clutter, rather than one piled high with old papers, books, unanswered mail, and yesterday's lunch wrappings. One single painting adorning a wall, instead of five. There is beauty and freedom in simplicity.

3.1 Keep It Simple

A young pastor, intent on impressing the congregation with his theological education, developed a lengthy, complicated, and verbose sermon style. The congregation would stir restlessly, eyeing the clock on the wall as this young pastor droned on and on, bringing up point after point after point.

This continued for some time, until one Sunday morning, the pastor's wife, also frustrated with his long sermons, slipped him a note before he went up to speak. At the top of the note was written "KISS." He smiled as he glanced over at his wife. Then he noticed at the bottom of the note, "Keep It Simple, Stupid."

Hopefully, you will never receive such a note. But the recommendation to "keep it simple" is one of the wisest bits of advice you will ever receive.

Your speech must be structured so that is easy to follow if you are to accomplish your goal of having the audience listen to your words and remember your points and recommendations.

Far too many novice speakers talk in a style that is difficult to follow. The listener gets lost in a maze of unrelated thoughts and ideas, with no clear theme connecting the endless parade of words. We often lose interest, and perhaps become annoyed with a speaker who cannot present his or her thoughts in a readily understood fashion. Before we examine the basics parts of any speech, let's look at the fundamentals of public speaking.

3.2 Public Speaking

Public speaking is defined as speaking before an audience. There are three primary purposes for giving speeches: to inform, to persuade, and to entertain. College lectures, a winery tour, and a demonstration of flower arranging are speeches that primarily inform. Examples of persuasive speaking include a fund-raising talk for the Asian Club on campus, a speech advocating blood donation, and a sales presentation for the latest computer software. After-dinner speaking and comedy club acts are examples of speeches that entertain. Usually, speeches are technically a combination of all three, but the primary goal of a given speech is to inform, to persuade, or to entertain.

3.3 Three Principles for Public Speaking

Before we begin discussing the various ways you can speak to an audience, three principles for public speaking will set you on the right path for giving effective speeches. For effective speaking, you should put the audience first, speak deep from the heart, and leave your audience wanting more.

Put the Audience First

The most important secret to successful public speaking is to put your audience first. It's a matter of having the right attitude. Many beginning speakers spend far too much time focused on themselves. They worry about how they'll sound, how they'll come across, and what the audience will think of them. Their focus is on self. Too often in relationships, dating, and marriage, we hold a similar "me-first" attitude, and the results can be damaging.

To be more effective, and less anxious, we need to shift the spotlight off of us as speakers and focus it instead on our audience. Our attention should be on the people who will listen to our speech. So when you begin thinking about a speech you will be giving, think in terms of your audience first. Who are they? What are they interested in? How do they feel? What do they think? How might I instruct them? How can I help them? How might I encourage them? This shift in focus not only helps your public speaking, but it also can improve your relationships as well.

Deep Speaks to Deep

The second secret to successful speaking is that "deep speaks to deep." Whenever you have an opportunity to address an audience, whether it's a one-minute impromptu speech at a wedding reception or a formal presentation at a dinner banquet, don't waste your audience's time on trivial matters. Our lives are already saturated enough with the insignificant details of celebrities' lives, frivolous e-mail, *Saturday Night Live* characters, and the tedium of never-ending electronic gismos and doodads.

Instead of adding to the trivia, invite your audience to consider topics of importance. Talk about subjects that really matter to you, deep in your heart. Select stories from your life and from your research that move the heart and challenge the mind. Share thoughts and feelings that are significant, are meaningful, and, in the end, matter. Every person in your audience, no matter how he or she appears on the outside, is on the same journey as you, from birth to death, consciously or unconsciously trying to find meaning in this life and attempting to make sense of it all. Appeal to that part of your listener. If you do, your audience will respond, because whether they realize it or not, they are moving through deep waters in this lifetime. Share important topics, for deep speaks to deep.

> *Deep speaks to deep.*
> —PSALM 42:7

Leave Your Audience Wanting More

There's an old saying that "the more you say the less you say, and the less you say the more you say." A speaker who goes on and on, and on and on, with little or no regard to the bored and restless responses of the audience can actually cancel out any positive contribution or effect he or she has had on the audience.

Even a dynamic speaker, with significant material, can eventually cause a once appreciative audience to become restless, frustrated, and even angry if the speech doesn't end within a reasonable length of time. What's a reasonable length of time? That depends on the occasion, the speaking environment, the speaker, and the audience. But here's when our first principle of public speaking comes in handy—put the audience first. Consider your audience. Observe them as you speak. Do they look bored? Tired? Restless? Or even frustrated? If they do, bring your speech to an end. No use talking your audience to death. Know when to stop.

When preparing your speech, put the audience first. Know what you want to say, and say nothing more. Don't use all the material you researched, although it might feel good to show off your efforts. Instead, select only the best material. Then, stay focused. Keep to your point. And conclude your speech. Bigger is not necessarily better. Longer is not necessarily more helpful or instructive. Observe the time limit of your speech, and don't go over it. In fact, end before the allotted time. Instead of giving a 20-minute speech, end at 17 minutes. Instead of giving a 10-minute speech, conclude at 8 minutes. Your audience will never rush the podium in a rage if you end a little sooner than expected. But they might do so if you drone on and on.

Avoid having your audience grumble, "When's she going to quit?" or "Isn't he finished yet?" Instead, earn their ultimate compliments—"I wish she'd spoken longer" or "I hope he'll speak again." Always leave your audience wanting more of you, not less.

3.4 Four Speaking Methods

Now that we've examined the three principles of public speaking, let's look at the different styles or methods of delivering a speech. The four basic methods or approaches are manuscript, memorized, impromptu, and extemporaneous.

Manuscript Delivery Method

The manuscript delivery method consists of reading a speech from a text or manuscript. The speech is written word for word, and the speaker does not stray from the prepared text as he or she reads to the audience.

One advantage of this delivery method is that the content of the speech is guaranteed so long as the speaker sticks to the text. This could be important if the exact wording of a speech is vital, as in scientific presentations or political addresses.

There are many disadvantages to this style of speaking. The obvious disadvantage to manuscript delivery is the lack of natural, spontaneous delivery on the part of the speaker. Eye contact is decreased because most speakers using this method read the entire speech, word for word, instead of establishing eye contact with their audience. Animated gestures, facial expressions, and body movement are limited by this style of speaking. Spontaneous speaker response to audience feedback is not easily attained with this delivery method, as the text is already determined. We've all known professors who relied on this style of lecturing, semester after semester, year after year.

> *The real art of speaking rests in exhausting your subject before you exhaust your audience.*
> —Adlai Stevenson

Memorized Delivery Method

The second method of delivery is memorized. In this style, the speaker memorizes the text of a speech, word for word, and then recites the speech without the use of a manuscript.

One advantage of the memorized delivery method is that the speaker is able to look at the audience more often because he no longer needs to rely on reading the manuscript that is in front of him. The speaker is also more spontaneous in gestures and body movement. This method is used by actors and Disneyland tour guides, to name a few.

The disadvantages of this method are many. Unless you are gifted at memorization, it's difficult to commit to memory even the briefest of talks. Memorization requires a great deal of time and effort, even for the best of speakers. To make matters worse, once you've memorized the speech, you face the possibility of forgetting a part of the speech when you're speaking.

Once the speaker forgets just one word, everything that followed that particular word is out the window. Swooosh . . . into the universe, never to be seen again. The speaker usually goes blank. And that's one of the most pitiful looks you can ever see on a human being—just *blank*. Don't let this happen to you.

Impromptu Delivery Method

Impromptu speaking consists of speaking to an audience on the spur of the moment, without prior preparation or practice. Most public speaking nightmares involve sadistic variations on this style of speaking, with hundreds of shrieking demons dancing around you, as you stand on the stage, naked, struggling to find words, any words, to begin your talk.

Doesn't sound like there's anything good or of redeeming value about impromptu speaking. But nothing could be further from the truth. Once mastered, impromptu speaking can change the way you see yourself and how you communicate with others. The confidence you receive from being skilled in impromptu speaking can change your self-concept.

Extemporaneous Delivery Method

Of the four methods of speaking, the extemporaneous method is perhaps the best style for most public presentations because it utilizes the best aspects of the other three, while balancing their respective weaknesses. Extemporaneous speaking is speaking that is prepared and practiced ahead of time, but for which the exact wording isn't determined until the speaker delivers the speech.

The speech is researched and outlined ahead of time. Normally, the outline contains only 25–30 percent of the total words that will be delivered in the speech. Usually, full-sentence outline structure is used, with an introduction, a body, and a conclusion. This outline is the skeleton of the speech and the meat of the talk; the other 70–75 percent of the wording isn't exactly determined until the speaker delivers the speech.

Practice is another requirement for extemporaneous speaking. Once the speech is researched and outlined, the speaker practices the speech—first with the outline and then with only note cards. Many extemporaneous speakers deliver their entire speeches from only one or two 4 × 6-inch note cards containing a brief key-word outline of points.

The speech should be practiced at least five to seven times in its entirety. Too little practice doesn't provide the command of the main points of the talk and the general flow of the speech. Too much practice increases the probability that the speech will begin to sound memorized. You need to balance the two extremes as far as practice is concerned. There should be balance in speech practice, as in life.

Once the speech has been prepared and practiced, the speaker is ready to deliver it. The primary advantage of the extemporaneous style of speaking is that the speaker is organized and knows what points need to be covered, much like the manuscript and memorized speaking methods—but without the loss of natural delivery and the threat of forgetting the words and content. Furthermore, the speaker has the spontaneity of impromptu speaking, without the added burden of having to create the speech while standing in front of the audience. The extemporaneous delivery method is the style you will most likely use in your public speaking class.

3.5 Speech Organization

Now that we have reviewed the fundamentals of public speaking, let's look at how to organize a basic speech that is easy for your listeners to follow.

More than 2,000 years ago, the Greek philosopher Plato said that every speech should have only three parts: an introduction, a body, and a conclusion—just like our existence: birth, life, and death. This simple formula for speech organization still holds true today. Whether you're giving a 2-minute impromptu talk at a wedding reception or a 20-minute sales presentation to a group of prospective buyers, the organization of your speech should be the same.

> *True eloquence consists of saying all that should be said, and that only.*
> —FRANÇOIS DE LA ROCHEFOUCAULD

Before launching into a more detailed examination of each of these three components, let's preview the basic functions of the introduction, body, and conclusion.

The *introduction* should capture the attention of the audience, clearly state what your speech is about, and preview the main points of your talk. Your introduction should comprise only 10–15 percent of your total speaking time. The *body* of the speech contains the two or three main points of your talk, along with the supporting material necessary to develop each point contained in the body, and with clearly stated transitions between each point. The body of the speech should make up 75–85 percent of your total speaking time. The *conclusion* of the speech presents a summary of your main points and a final thought to leave with your audience. The conclusion should be brief and should comprise only 5–10 percent of your total speaking time.

3.6 The Body

We'll examine the body of the speech before we discuss the introduction. This may seem a little odd, but we need to realize that we can't work on our introductory attention getter and preview of main points until we know what the main points will be and how they will be organized. Let's begin with the main-point selection and organization.

> *If you have an important point to make, don't try to be subtle or clever. Use a pile-driver. Hit the point. Then come back and hit it again. Then hit it a third time.*
> —WINSTON CHURCHILL

Main-Point Selection

The specific purpose of the presentation, often referred to as the *thesis statement*, states the purpose of the speech and divides the speech into its key parts or main points. The remainder of the body of the speech develops, clarifies, explains, or proves those main points. Let's examine one specific purpose.

Specific Purpose: To inform the audience about three uses of public speaking training.

As you see, the specific purpose establishes the goal in speaking (to inform the audience) and what you want to share (three uses of public speaking training). What are those three uses? They constitute the three main points of the speech. In complete sentence form, those three points are

Main Points
    I. Public speaking improves your presentational skills.
    II. Public speaking helps you become more effective in business.
    III. Public speaking improves your self-image.

Selecting main points is not difficult, so long as you remember that each of the implied areas of the specific purpose will be one of the main points of your speech.

Let's have you try your hand at providing three main points for a specific purpose statement. Suppose you had to share with your audience three things that make you happy—any three things that bring you joy, make you feel good, give you a rush. The specific purpose statement would be

Specific Purpose: To share with the audience three things that make me happy.

Now, complete the main points with three things that make you happy. Use short, complete sentences for each point.

    I. _____
   II. _____
 III. _____

That wasn't too difficult, was it? You've just completed outlining your first main-point structure for the body of an informative speech. Not bad!

Main-Point Organizational Patterns

For your purpose as a beginning speaker, the following five main-point orders will most likely suit your needs: topical order, chronological order, spatial order, advantage-disadvantage order, and problem-solution order. Each of these five main-point organizational patterns is designed to present your main points in a way that is easy for the audience to understand and remember and satisfies the requirements of your specific purpose.

Topical Order. With topical order, the order of the main points is left to the discretion of the speaker. The main points can go, for example, from specific to general or from least important to most important. Often, the topic suggests its own arrangement of main points. Look at how the following example makes use of this organizational pattern.

Specific Purpose: To describe three characteristics of a good marriage.

    I. The partners share in open communication.
   II. The partners support the personal growth of each other.
 III. The partners resolve conflict in a nonthreatening manner.

Now that you've gotten the hang of topical order, let's have you complete the following:

Specific Purpose: To discuss three things I appreciate about my college education.

    I. _____
   II. _____
 III. _____

Chronological Order. Chronological order is the kind of organizational pattern in which the main points follow a time order or sequence. It shows your audience there is a definite order in which the main points develop. The order of main points is not left to the discretion of the speaker but rather is determined by the process itself.

This type of organizational pattern works well with speeches that describe how something is made, how something happened, or how something works. Notice the chronological order in the following example:

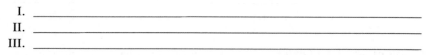

Out of intense complexities emerge intense simplicities.
—Albert Einstein

Specific Purpose: To explain how to bake cookies.

    I. The first step is to gather your materials.
   II. The second step is to prepare the ingredients.
 III. The third step is to bake the cookies.

Now, try your hand at providing the main points for the following specific purpose, utilizing time order:

Specific Purpose: To explain how I wake up in the morning.

    I. _____
   II. _____
 III. _____

Spatial Order. The third organizational pattern we examine in this chapter is spatial order. In spatial order, the main points are arranged in physical or geographical sequence. This pattern could be employed in a speech that described the floor plan of your house, the digestive tract of the human body, or the structure of a guitar. See if you can visualize the spatial structure in the following example:

Specific Purpose: To describe the arrangement of the Town Hall.

    I. The first floor contains the receptionist area and clerks' offices.
   II. The second floor houses the city officials' offices.
 III. The third floor is where the city records are stored.

How would you list the main points for the following specific purpose statement?

Specific Purpose: To describe the three parts of a whole egg (not a scrambled egg).

    I. _____
   II. _____
 III. _____

Advantage-Disadvantage Order. The fourth main-point order is advantage-disadvantage. There might be a time when you want to present both sides of a case or proposal. The purpose of your speech would be to fairly and equally communicate the pros and cons of an issue or case. Here's an example of advantage-disadvantage main-point order.

Specific Purpose: To inform the audience about the advantages and disadvantages of enrolling in a summer school class.

    I. There are advantages to enrolling in a summer school class.
       A. A summer school class enables you to focus your attention on one subject.
       B. A summer school class is completed in only four to six weeks.

II. There are disadvantages to enrolling in a summer school class.
   A. A summer school class requires longer daily class meetings.
   B. A summer school class requires three times the daily homework.

See if you can think of the subpoints for this advantage-disadvantage speech.

Specific Purpose: To inform the audience about the advantages and disadvantages of working full-time while attending college.

I. There are advantages to working full-time while attending college.
   A. _____
   B. _____

II. There are disadvantages to working full-time while attending college.
   A. _____
   B. _____

Problem-Solution Order.   The fifth main-point order is problem–solution. Many times you will want to propose a specific solution to an existing problem. This is a persuasive speech structure that is discussed in a later chapter, but for now, we will briefly outline the format known as problem–solution order.

Proposition: You should support a federal law fining violators $1,000 fine for running a red light at a traffic intersection.

I. This federal fine will generate revenue.
II. This federal fine will lower insurance rates.
III. This federal fine will saves lives.

See if you can construct three points to this problem–solution proposition.

Proposition: You should support an 8 percent federal income tax.

I. _____
II. _____
III. _____

Now that you've chosen your main points and the organizational pattern you will use, you need to turn your attention to selecting the developmental material. How your audience will receive, understand, and appreciate what you have to say will depend largely on how you develop the main points of the body.

Many a speaker exhausts his audience before he exhausts his subject. Limit your material.
—MARK TWAIN

In the next chapter, you will learn how to research a speech topic using the 4 × 6-inch note card method—storing each piece of research evidence on a note card. Let's assume you've already completed researching a speech topic and that you now have three times the amount of material required for your talk. Now we must begin the task of selecting the appropriate supporting material for your main points.

Selecting Your Developmental Material

The easiest method for selecting supporting material for your speech is called the "pile method." To use the pile method, simply place the various 4 × 6-inch research cards in one of three piles (if you have three main points), according to content. At the end of this process, each pile or stack will contain various definitions, statistics, expert testimony, examples, stories, comparisons, explanations, or visual aids that support a particular main point.

Now the fun part begins—the selection of the actual pieces of supporting material you will use for each main point. Here are some suggestions that will guide you in your selection as you stare at the various piles of research cards scattered in front of you.

Have at least one piece of evidence for each point. Provide at least one piece of evidence to support each of your main points. This will provide a solid base of support for your speech.

Provide a variety of supporting material. Don't just cite statistics in each point or tell anecdotes throughout your speech. Provide a variety of supporting material for your listeners to consider. If you researched your topic sufficiently, you should have little difficulty giving your audience a variety of supporting material.

Distribute your supporting material evenly. Develop each main point of your speech equally. Don't invest three pieces of evidence on one main point and not support the other two points. Provide the listener with an equal balance of supporting material for each point.

Adapt your material to the particular audience. This suggestion is vitally important if your message is to be received by your audience. Audiences respond favorably to information that relates to their interests, their knowledge, their demographics, and their attitudes. Adapt your research information in ways that your particular audience can understand, relate to, and appreciate. For instance, if you're talking about the advantages of public speaking to a group of Asian immigrants, who may be reluctant to speak, you could adapt your information and show how effective presentational skills can be desirable in job interviews, work performance, and academic success.

Transitions within the Body of the Speech

Now that you have your main points selected and developed with supporting material, you will need to move your listeners smoothly from one point to the next. Although there are numerous transitions available to serve this function, numbered transitions are the simplest and most informative type to use.

The *numbered transition* is a sentence stating which main point you will be presenting and its content. For instance, "The first characteristic of a good marriage is open communication" or "The third and final step in negotiation is the closing phase."

The numbered transition is useful because it tells the audience not only what you will be speaking about next but also where you are in the speech. This type of "signposting" encourages the audience to pay closer attention to what is being said and helps them retain the information.

A second technique that helps the audience move from one point to another is a moment of *silence* before you state your numbered transition. A two- or three-second pause between the last word of your preceding main point and your numbered transition serves as a welcome rest for your audience to digest what has been said.

After you end your introduction or one of your main points in the body of the speech, simply stop with a *two-* or *three-second pause* (one thousand one, one thousand two, one thousand three) and then proceed to your numbered transition. The use of pauses is a dramatic and visible sign of speaker confidence. Using the two- or three-second pause gives you time to breathe, focus, and relax. We should pause more in our daily lives, too.

3.7   The Introduction

Once the body of the speech is completed, you can begin working on the introduction. The introduction serves two primary functions. First, it captures the attention of the audience with an attention getter. Second, it previews the main points you will be presenting in the body of the speech. The introduction should take no more than 10–15 percent of the total speaking time.

The Attention Getter

The first objective of the introduction is to *capture the attention of the audience*. This can be accomplished by any number of attention getters, such as an audience question, an amusing anecdote, a startling statement, a startling statistic, a hypothetical situation, a quotation, or a joke. No matter which attention getter you choose, it should relate directly to the topic you will be presenting, and it should appropriately match the overall tone of your speech. You wouldn't want to begin a serious speech with a joke, nor would you start a humorous speech with a sad anecdote. Let's take a look at an example of types of attention getters.

> *As long as you can start, you'll be all right. The juice will come.*
> —ERNEST HEMINGWAY

Audience question. "How many of you have ever danced with a brown bear, ridden sidesaddle on a horse, or jumped through a burning hoop? Well, I have. And today, I'd like to speak about my career in the circus."

Amusing anecdote. "Two monks were walking toward a stream when they were approached by a beautiful woman. She asked if they could help her cross the swiftly moving water. The older monk agreed to help. He then carried the woman across the stream in his arms and let her go on the other side.

"As the two monks continued their journey for some time, the younger monk turned and asked the older monk, 'Why did you carry that woman across the stream? You know our vows don't permit us to touch women.'

"'I carried the woman across the river, that is true,' replied the older monk. 'But I let her go when we got to the other side. It seems that you are still carrying her.' Today, I am going to talk about letting go of past hurts."

Startling statement. "More individuals are murdered by people they know than by complete strangers. Although this may seem unbelievable, this statement is nonetheless true. Today, I am going to talk about murder in the United States."

Startling statistic. "In 1998, teachers in Japan ranked in the top 15 percent of all wage earners in that island nation. Today, I'd like to talk about the salaries of teachers in the United States."

Hypothetical situation. "Imagine yourself sitting on a warm, sandy beach in Hawaii. You can see the deep blue sea stretching out to the horizon. You can hear the waves in the distance, and the smell of the late afternoon ocean breeze surrounds you. A relaxed, wonderful feeling engulfs you. Stay there for a moment. Today, I'd like to share with you some highlights of my last trip to Hawaii."

Quotation. "Psychotherapist Heinz Kohut once said, 'The ability to soothe your own soul in the face of adversity is the most powerful skill you can develop in your lifetime.' Today, I'd like to speak about the benefits of positive self-talk."

Joke. "One of my problems is that I internalize everything. I can't express my anger, so I grow a tumor instead. Well, maybe I'm stretching the truth a bit, but I do have difficulty expressing anger. Today, I want to talk about the hazards of not expressing your anger."

There are many other attention getters you might consider as you construct your introduction. Other methods include referring to the occasion, referring to the previous speaker, building up suspense, using a visual aid, establishing common ground with the audience, pointing to a historical event, complimenting the audience, and stressing the importance of the speech topic. Remember that whatever attention getter you decide on, it should relate directly to the topic, and it should appropriately match the overall tone of the speech. Keep your attention getters relatively short because the entire introduction should comprise only 10–15 percent of your total speaking time.

Preview of Main Points

After you have given your attention getter, you should pause for one or two seconds and then present your preview of main points. The purpose of the preview of main points is to give your audience a foreshadowing of what's to follow. It prepares their minds to receive the points you will be speaking about. The preview of points should be only one sentence in length. A common mistake is to say too much in the preview, almost giving a mini-speech for each point previewed. Keep it brief and to the point— only one sentence. Here are some examples of acceptable previews of main points:

"The three steps to making cookies are gathering your materials, preparing your ingredients, and, finally, baking the cookies."

"The three parts of the guitar are the head, neck, and body."

"Running can improve your physical stamina, reduce psychological stress, and increase your spiritual awareness."

"The three components of a healthy relationship are caring, communication, and companionship."

After you've given the preview of main points, pause for one or two seconds before you state your first numbered transition. This pause will give your audience time to digest the preview of points.

3.8 The Conclusion

After you have finished your final point in the body of the speech, it is important to have a two- or three-second pause *before* you begin your conclusion. Actually say to yourself silently "one thousand one, one thousand two, one thousand three" before you start your conclusion. This brief pause will let your audience know that you will be ending shortly.

The first words out of your mouth during the conclusion will be your summary of main points. Please do not say, "In conclusion . . . ," or "I guess it's time for me to quit," or "Well, I'd better end now." Those transitions into the conclusion are unnecessary and awkward.

Your conclusion should summarize your main points in one sentence and leave your audience with a final thought. The conclusion should require only 5–10 percent of your total speaking time. In a five-minute speech, that's approximately 15–30 seconds. That might not sound like a great deal of time, but it will be sufficient to recap your points and provide the audience with a closing thought.

Summary of Main Points

The summary of main points should be a *one-sentence* review of the three or four points you made in your speech. One simple sentence will do. Nothing more. Here are some examples of main-point summaries:

> "Today, I've shared the three steps to making cookies: gathering your materials, preparing your ingredients, and, finally, baking the cookies."
> "In my talk this morning, I described the head, the neck, and the body of the guitar."
> "So remember, running can improve physical stamina, reduce psychological stress, and increase spiritual awareness."
> "Today I spoke about the three components of a healthy relationship, which are caring, communication, and companionship."

Final Thought or Appeal

After you have summarized your points, it's best to leave your audience with one final thought. This thought can be a return to your attention getter, an appeal, a quotation, a vision for the future, or a call to action. The final thought shouldn't be very long. Present a concise and focused thought for your audience to remember. This is not the time to begin another main point. Here are some examples of the various methods:

> **Return to attention getter.** "Like the young man in my opening story who wanted to know the secret of living a long life, I hope you will examine your life and attempt to reduce the stresses in it."
>
> **Appeal.** "As we have seen, drug use among our teenagers is at a record high, and many of us adults have been denying its existence. Our denial will not rid us of the drugs. Our denial will not put the drug dealers in prison. Our denial will not save our children's lives. It's time that we opened our eyes and began thinking about the horrors of teenage drug use."

Quotation. "John Steinbeck once observed, 'A marriage is like a journey. The certain way to be wrong is to think you control it.' I hope that you will relax a little more in your marriage or in your relationships in the future and follow the guidelines I've outlined this morning on how to give your spouse more personal space."

> *The secrets to successful speaking are to be organized, be brief, and then be seated.*
> —Norman Thomas

Vision for the future. "I see a future for our club with 1,000 members, not just 28. I see a future in which our club will donate thousands of dollars to local charities, not just $200. Our club will be a place for all women of Oakland to meet, build lasting friendships, and, most important, give something back to the community that provided us with our beginning. Do you see this vision also?"

Call to action. "The election is two weeks away. If you share my beliefs for a strong America, if you share my desire for a prosperous America, if you share my dream for a free America, I ask you to invest in the future of our great land. I ask you to contribute just $100 to my campaign fund this very morning. My assistants will be distributing the contribution forms to you in a few moments."

Don't feel limited to these final-thought devices. You can use a combination of two of them, or make up your own final statement format. Remember to keep the final thought short and to the point, however. Don't ramble. Your final thought for a 5-minute speech shouldn't be longer than 30 seconds.

Once you have completed your final thought, smile and pause for two or three seconds and then walk back to your seat. If you are permitted a question-and-answer period, remain at the podium and wait for the applause to end. Once the applause has ceased, pause a second or two and then request questions from your audience. In either case, the pauses are very important. It shows your audience that you are in control.

3.9 Constructing Your Speech Outline

Now that we have introduced the various components of the introduction, body, and conclusion, we need to spend a few moments reviewing some guidelines for writing a speech outline. Although some professional speakers do not use any outline in the preparation of their talks, they are few in number. The majority of speakers, both beginning and professional, use some form of outlining to help them plan and test their speech ahead of time. The outline is your most important tool in constructing a well-developed and easy-to-follow speech.

> *The wisdom of life consists in the elimination of nonessentials.*
> —Lin Yutang

The *speech outline* is a short, complete-sentence model of your speech. From this outline, you can test the organization, logic, and development of your entire speech. The total number of words in your outline shouldn't exceed 30 percent of the actual number of spoken words in your speech.

Here are some guidelines that will assist you in your construction of a speech outline:

Use a standard set of symbols. As you organize the body of your speech, use a standard set of symbols. The main points of the speech will be divided by roman numerals (I, II, III), subpoints will be designated by capital letters (A, B, C), and minor headings will be designated by arabic numerals (1, 2, 3).

Use complete-sentence structure for major headings. Complete-sentence structure for your major headings will help test the logic and development of your speech structure. Although you can use a key-word outline note card when you deliver your speech, a full-sentence outline will permit an analysis of your main- and subpoint structure.

Each main point should reinforce or clarify your specific purpose statement. This is one of the most important tests of your speech outline. Does each main point actually develop your specific purpose statement by reinforcing or clarifying it? If a main point does not, it should not be included in your speech.

Each main point and subpoint should contain only one idea. If a main point or subpoint contains more than a single thought or idea, it will confuse you and your audience. The logic of your speech structure is weakened when you present multiple ideas in a main point or subpoint. If you see an "and" in one of your main-point or subpoint headings, you will need to decide on one of the two ideas to present, or you can split them into two headings if it's appropriate. For example:

   I. The second advantage that jogging offers is that it increases your physical endurance *and* your psychological well-being. (*Incorrect*—Notice the "and" in the sentence? Let's change it.)

  II. The second advantage that jogging offers is that it increases your physical endurance.

 III. The third advantage that jogging offers is that it increases your sense of psychological well-being.

Subpoints should support main points. Check to make sure that not only do your main points support your specific purpose statement, but your subpoints support your main points as well. This is called *subordination of points.* Each subpoint should be directly related to the main point it falls under. If not, it needs to go. For example:

   I. The second floor of City Hall houses the city officials.
   A. The mayor is located in the west wing of the second floor.
   B. The city manager is located next to the mayor.
   C. *The city records are located on the third floor.*
      (Point C does not relate directly to the main point. It needs to be placed under another main-point heading that deals with the third floor.)

Limit your main points to a maximum of four. Don't overburden your audience with too many main points. The average listener cannot remember more than three or four main points, regardless of the length of the speech. Three main points are usually best for any speech.

Write the introduction and conclusion word for word. Because the introduction is so important in capturing the attention of the audience and the conclusion needs to bring your speech to a concise ending, there is little room for ad-libbing or impromptu speaking. Therefore, your introduction and conclusion should be written out verbatim in the outline.

Limit the outline to 30 percent of the total speech wording. The entire number of words in your outline, introduction, and conclusion should not exceed 30 percent of your total speaking words. More than 30 percent will make your outline resemble a manuscript speech, and your final presentation will run the risk of having a manuscript or memorized delivery style.

Later in this chapter you will find a sample outline of a tribute speech. Notice the various components of the speech—the specific purpose, introduction, body, conclusion, and reference list.

3.10 Speaking Notes

When you're delivering your speech, you might feel more confident having a few notes up at the podium. If you do, here are some guidelines when constructing and using your speaking notes.

Use Note Cards

Use either 3 × 5- or 4 × 6-inch index cards when constructing your speaking notes. Don't use regular-size paper, because the size is more obvious and papers tend to make noise when handled. Index cards are easier to manage and won't fly off the podium if a breeze comes up. Number your note cards on the upper right-hand corner so you can quickly place them in the correct order if they get mixed up.

Use Key Words and Phrases

Your speaking note cards should contain only key words and phrases. Unlike your formal outline, you don't need complete sentences in your speaking notes. Instead of writing your entire introductory attention getter word for word, you can simply write, "Story about monks." Your preview of points can be a list of three words, rather than the entire sentence. Instead of writing out each main-point transition in the body of the speech, you can simply write, "I. Workshops" or "II. Career." In the same way, each of your subpoints can also be represented by one or two key words. The review of points in the conclusion can be listed once again as three or four words, and your final thought might be shortened to a couple of words or a phrase.

The purpose of the key-word approach is simply to jar your memory so you can quickly recall the main points of your presentation without all the details of your formal outline. You can also use your note cards to list the essential information of any evidence you'll be presenting. For instance, you need only list the documentation and the actual statistic or expert testimony you will present. Your note card can also indicate when you will be presenting any visual aids in your speech.

Use Delivery Reminders

In addition to displaying key words and phrases, your note cards can also remind you to pause, speak louder or softer, look at the audience, and a variety of other delivery guidelines. You can make "//" notations to pause before important points or simply write "PAUSE" in red ink. You might want to use "<" to remind yourself to speak louder or ">" to speak softer at certain points in your speech. Or you can write out the words "LOUDER" and "SOFTER" on your note card. It's usually a good idea to remind yourself to "LOOK AT YOUR AUDIENCE" or "REMEMBER EYE CONTACT" every once in awhile on your speaking note cards. Some speakers simply draw two eyes in red ink occasionally on their cards to remind them to look at their audience.

Use Note Cards Sparingly

Remember, this is not a manuscript speech or a formal outline you're trying to get on these speaking note cards—this is just key words and phrases. One to three words for every 15 seconds of speaking time is a good rule of thumb. So for a five-minute speech, 20 to 60 key words at most ought to do it.

SAMPLE TRIBUTE SPEECH OUTLINE
A TRIBUTE TO GEORGE MCCLENDON

Specific Purpose: To pay tribute to George McClendon.

Introduction

Have you ever spent a weekend with a Trappist monk who runs marathons? Well, I have! Today, I'd like to tell you about a man who influenced my life in a significant way. His name is George McClendon. George is a practicing Gestalt therapist in Watsonville, and I met him two summers ago when I was enrolled in one of his U.C. Extension courses. I'd like to tell you about his wonderful relationship workshops, his 20-year career as a Trappist monk, and his marathon running.

Body

    I. The first thing I want to share with you is that George McClendon teaches excellent relationship workshops.
        A. His weekend relationship workshops for counselors emphasize a Gestalt approach to systems theory.
        B. George conducts his workshops with wisdom and empathy.
    II. The second thing I want to share is George's 20-year career as a Trappist monk.
        A. George spent 20 years in an Oklahoma Trappist monastery.
        B. He helped build the monastery from the foundation to the roof.
    III. The final thing I want to tell you about is George's newfound interest in marathon running.
        A. At age 53, he began jogging as a part-time hobby.
        B. Six months later, he completed the Big Sur Marathon.
        C. Randy Fujishin, in *Gifts from the Heart*, reminds us that, "We need to encourage our loved ones to grow—to follow their dreams."

Conclusion

Today, I've talked about George McClendon's relationship workshops, his life as a monk, and his marathon running. He is truly an inspiring individual who has taught me to appreciate life and dream big dreams. I hope you get a chance to meet him.

References

Fujishin, R. 2003. *Gifts from the Heart*. Lanham, MD: Rowman & Littlefield.

Use Note Cards Openly

When referring to your note cards, don't try to hide them or glance away from your audience when referring to them. Be open about your use of the cards. Just don't rely on them too much. Simply place your cards on the podium in chronological order from left to right and glance down at them when you need to. That's all. They're in place if you need them, but they shouldn't prevent good eye contact and directness with your audience.

SAMPLE CORRESPONDING KEY-WORD OUTLINE

Introduction

Weekend with monk? George.

Workshops, career, running

Body

    I. *Workshops*
       Gestalt approach
       Wisdom, empathy

   II. *Career*
       Trappist monk
       Built monastery

  III. *Running*
       Marathons at 53
       Big Sur Marathon
       (Fujishin reference)

Conclusion

Workshops, career, running

Hope meet George

COMMUNICATION ACTIVITIES

PERSONAL ACTIVITIES

  1. **Simplifying your life**
     Make a list of all the duties, responsibilities, and chores you have to complete in the next week. Write down everything—from going to that job interview

to feeding the cats. Your list should be substantial. Now, circle the three tasks that are the most important—if you couldn't do any of the others, these are the top three you would need to complete. Now, underline the next three most important tasks. Don't cheat, only three of them! Cross out the remaining tasks. That's right, you have only six tasks you can do. The rest will go uncompleted, at least for the week. How would your life change if you could do only these six things? How do you feel? What would your week be like? On the day you die, you will leave 100 things undone.

2. **Soothing the many sides of you**

   Get a piece of typing paper (or any 8½ × 11-inch paper) and fold it into thirds. Label the first column "BODY," the middle column "MIND," and the third column "SPIRIT." For each column, take a few minutes to brainstorm a list of activities that you enjoy or find rewarding. For example, for "BODY" you might include bathing, eating, playing in the sand, flossing, stretching, and skipping pebbles on water. Do this for each column. Look at your lists. How does each feel? Have you done any of these activities lately? If not, which ones could you do today?

3. **Organizing thoughts in other cultures**

   Ask an individual from a different culture how important the concept of clear, logical thought patterns is to him or her. Does she or he value critical thinking? How does this person feel about our emphasis on clear organizational patterns in speech construction? What forms of oral discourse or presentation are emphasized in his or her culture, if any?

4. **Organizing your life's priorities**

   One of the most valuable life skills you can develop is your ability to distinguish between what is important to you and what is not. On a piece of paper, list 20 things you would like to accomplish this year. Then rate each item using the following scale: 1 = Vital, do immediately; 2 = Essential, do in the next week; 3 = Important, do in the next month; 4 = Nonessential, do in the next year; and 5 = Disregard, eliminate from the list. Limit your ratings to four of each of the five rankings. In other words, only four 1s, four 2s, and so on. This will force you to decide what is important and what is not. How did this exercise go for you? What did you learn about organizing your life by using priority rankings?

CLASS ACTIVITIES

5. **Group discussion: five words or less**

   Divide the class into groups of five or six. Each group is to discuss for 10 minutes some aspect of communication suggested by the instructor. Students are free to express their thoughts and feelings, except no one is permitted to use more than five words during any given opportunity to address the group. No more than five words at a time. It's helpful in this exercise to count each of your five words on your fingers. This will give you a good feel for each word that comes out of your mouth. How does this way of talking feel to you? How do the other group members feel? Did you notice any communication interaction changes because of this limit? This may be the first time you have ever valued the currency of your language. Remember, the more you say, the less you say. And the less you say, the more you say. Be prepared to discuss your reactions to this activity with the rest of the class.

6. **Three highlights of your life speech**

   Construct a formal outline detailing the speech topic (specific purpose), "To inform the audience of the three highlights of my life." Remember to include supporting material in the subpoints of the speech. Prepare, practice, and present a three- to five-minute informative speech. Your speech should contain an introduction, body, and conclusion.

7. **The three sides of "me" speech**

   Prepare, practice, and present a three- to five-minute speech about interesting aspects of your physical, intellectual, and spiritual self. Review Personal Activity 2 in this chapter to get some ideas on how to develop your points. Your speech should contain an introduction, body, and conclusion.

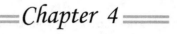
SELECTING YOUR TOPIC
CHOOSING YOUR PATH

LEARNING OBJECTIVES

After reading this chapter, you should be able to:

4.1 Explain the concept that it's your choice

4.2 Explain brainstorming topics

4.3 Discuss determining your speaking purpose

4.4 Identify the two elements of your specific purpose

4.5 Explain selecting your main points

4.6 Summarize the four areas of analyzing your audience

4.7 List ways to gather information about your audience

4.8 Complete a speech preparation questionnaire

Tyler waited for the last student to leave the classroom before he approached his teacher. "How can I help you, Tyler?" smiled the professor.

"Well, I can't think of a topic for my speech. I mean, there're so many possible topics, and yet I can't seem to think of a good one."

"A little overwhelmed?" asked the teacher.

"I guess so."

"Give me one topic you've been considering."

"I could talk about *Hamlet* since I wrote a paper on that play last semester," Tyler stated happily. "Then I wouldn't have to do any research."

"You could," nodded the teacher, "but convenience doesn't always provide you with the best selection."

"What do you mean?"

"There are times in life when you need to choose with your heart—to go beyond what is convenient, easy, or even logical," suggested the professor. "What moves your heart, Tyler? What makes you mad, glad, or even sad?"

"People who run red lights make me mad. And dads who leave their families and don't try to stay in touch with their kids makes me sad."

"I see," said the teacher. "How about glad? What makes you joyous?"

"Well, I love going out for coffee with friends. I really enjoy my advertising and marketing class. And I love playing my guitar." After a long pause, Tyler added, "I guess I'm most happy when I'm helping Pastor Steve with the Junior High Youth Group."

"Congratulations, now you've got some topics worth speaking about—topics that move your heart," said the teacher. "And when you deliver a speech with heart, it makes all the difference in the world."

"A speech with heart," smiled Tyler as he left the classroom.

The professor thought back to his first speech in college as he put papers into his briefcase and whispered, "And a speech with heart can even lead to a profession with heart."

4.1 It's Your Choice

Whether your speech is for a public speaking class, a sales presentation, an awards dinner, or a retirement roast, you will rarely be assigned a specific speech topic. It is more likely that you will be given a great deal of freedom and latitude in your selection of a topic.

On the surface, this may sound desirable. But it often presents the beginning speaker with one of the most challenging tasks in the public speaking process—the sole responsibility to choose, from the hundreds of thousands of possible subjects, one topic to speak on.

Sound easy? Maybe not. Many experienced speakers report this is the most difficult part of speech making—simply choosing something to talk about. Individuals experiencing difficulty at this point complain there are either too many topics or not enough. But no matter which of these two predicaments they find themselves in, they do not choose a topic.

That is where the trouble begins.

We're not going to examine the many possible psychological and emotional reasons individuals have difficulty deciding on speech topics, or anything else for that matter. It is apparent that indecision, and the immobility that follows, hampers many of us in our daily lives. Should I marry or not? Should I date this person or not? Should I leave the job or not? Should I stay in school or not? And the list goes on and on.

Indecision is something we must contend with in our daily lives, as well as in the speech-making process. But remember that indecision is a decision in and of itself—the decision not to decide. And that's okay. Many people spend a great deal of their lives not deciding.

But that will not work for your public speaking life. You must decide on a specific topic before you can begin preparing for your talk, so select a topic that you feel strongly about—a topic with heart. In this chapter, we examine the five steps involved in selecting your topic and choosing the main points for your speech. The five steps are (1) brainstorming possible topics, (2) determining your speaking purpose, (3) determining your specific purpose, (4) selecting your main points, and (5) analyzing your audience.

> *Give the world the best you have and the best will come back to you.*
> —MADELINE BRIDGES

4.2 Brainstorming Possible Topics

The first step is to *brainstorm* possible topics. The primary purpose of brainstorming is to generate a large number of ideas without evaluation. In other words, the goal is to not judge your ideas as you write them down for consideration, but simply to come up with as many ideas as possible. This technique may feel strange initially because much of our daily energy is spent evaluating and judging the rightness and wrongness, the goodness and badness, the effectiveness and ineffectiveness of just about everything we experience.

The first task in brainstorming is to *get away to a quiet place* that is free from distractions and interruptions. You don't want friends talking, the telephone ringing, or the dog barking as you generate your list of ideas for the speech topic. Once you've found a quiet, private place to work—such as your office, kitchen, or dining room—get a pad of paper, a pen or pencil, and a kitchen cooking timer.

Set the timer for 10 minutes. The reason you need a timer is to focus your efforts for a specific period of time. Remember: "work expands to fill the time allotted," so if you're given three weeks to decide on a speech topic, you'll generally take the entire three weeks. Once the clock is set for 10 minutes, get comfortable with your pencil and pad and perhaps a cup of coffee or tea, and you're set.

The second task in brainstorming is to *get crazy* and write down anything that comes to your mind as a possible speech topic. Most people can think of one or two topics when faced with a blank sheet of paper, but get really crazy and write down *any* idea that comes to mind.

> *Imagination is more important than knowledge.*
> —ALBERT EINSTEIN

The most important requirement of this technique is to *free yourself from self-evaluation or criticism.* What will restrict and hinder you the most in selecting a speech topic is your negative response to your own suggestions and ideas. You need to give yourself permission to get a little loose and generate ideas, any ideas, no matter how wild or crazy. Let your handwriting get crazy too. Throw out all the restrictions you normally impose on yourself. As you get crazy during this second step of the brainstorming process, keep in mind the following four suggestions:

1. Don't evaluate or judge any of your ideas.
2. Quantity of ideas is desired, not quality.
3. The wilder the ideas are, the better.
4. Combine ideas to create new ones.

To give you a picture of what this process might produce, let's pretend that Yari has to speak on the topic of "public speaking." Let's see how many brainstorming topics he can generate in 10 minutes. Yari grabs a pencil, takes a sip of coffee, and she's off and running.

Fear
Notes
Being a president
Immigrants to America

Advantages of public speaking
Uses of public speaking training
Podiums
Training for public speaking
Talk show host
African Americans in television
Making money speaking
Being a teacher

Learning to think logically
Being persuasive
Ways public speaking can help me grow personally
Being a tour guide
Hip-hop music
Speech contests

Speaking as a lawyer
Public speaking professions
Being a speech coach for the movies
Being on radio
Tiger Woods
Being confident

Having people think I'm smart
Stage fright
Telling stories to others
Being funny
Getting a job as a sports announcer

Going into advertising
Giving speeches for the church
Teaching people to not be afraid of audiences
Middle East conflicts
Being a speech tutor
Sharing my feelings with others

Selling cars
Ways public speaking can improve my interaction with others

Buzz! The 10-minute alarm just went off. Pencil down, Yari. Good job! Now finish off that cup of coffee while we count your brainstorming topics. There are 37. A pretty productive brainstorming session. And who says there's nothing to talk about with the topic "public speaking"?

Now, you might have cheered for some of the items on his list and sneered at others, but that's your evaluating mind in action. And the first rule of brainstorming is for you *not* to evaluate any of the ideas or suggestions during this brainstorming process. Once you get the hang of not judging, the process really takes off.

After you've generated a long list of possible topics, you're set for the selection stage. Your task is to *select one topic from the list of topics*. You might want to take some time, a few hours to a couple of days, between your brainstorming session and the selection step. Your brain may need a rest after that 10-minute brainstorming session, and it's good to leave the list for a while, just to give your unconscious time to mull it over.

After you feel rested, it's time to examine your list of possible topics and select the one that you'd like to speak about. As you look over your list, cross out the topics that you're not interested in or that might not be of interest to your particular audience. If possible, select topics you have previous experience with or knowledge of. Also, select topics you would enjoy researching.

Now Yari is set to begin this part of his task—eliminating the weak, flimsy, or unsound topics from her list. As she looks over the list, she eliminates the vast majority of brainstorming possibilities because she isn't interested in them or she doesn't possess a great deal of previous experience or knowledge of them. Yari finally selects three topics he finds interesting and is willing to spend time researching. The topics are "Being a speech coach for the movies," "Ways public speaking can help me grow personally," and "Uses of public speaking training."

After a day or two, she finally decides on the topic "Uses of public speaking training" as her speech topic. That's a topic of interest to her and of possible interest to her audience (college students in the beginning speech class).

We finally have a topic for the speech. We are now in a position to determine our speaking purpose, the second step in the process.

4.3 Determining Your Speaking Purpose

Once you've determined the topic of your speech, you must decide what effect you want to have on the audience. It's important that you decide on that effect because it will determine how you phrase your specific purpose statement and the selection of your main points.

As you will recall, the three purposes of speaking are to inform, persuade, and entertain. Although a speech may contain a little of each category, you will need to decide which *primary effect* your talk will have on the listeners. Will it be to inform? Persuade? Or entertain?

For the topic we've chosen, "Uses of public speaking training," we could choose any one of the three primary purposes for speaking. We could inform the audience about the uses of public speaking training. We could attempt to persuade our audience that public speaking does have many practical uses. Or we could entertain the audience by sharing humorous uses of public speaking training.

> *Nothing is particularly hard if you divide it into small jobs.*
> —HENRY FORD

Yari chooses to inform her audience about the uses of public speaking training. She doesn't want to persuade her audience or entertain them. Her speaking purpose is to inform. Now she's ready to go to step 3.

4.4 Determining Your Specific Purpose

Now that you've decided on your speaking purpose, you must determine your specific purpose. The *specific purpose* states exactly (1) what you want to do with your audience and (2) what you want to tell them. For instance, the specific purpose "To persuade my audience to get annual physical examinations" specifies both goals. First, it states what you want to do with the audience—"to persuade." And second, it states what you want to tell them—"to get annual physical examinations." Notice that the specific purpose is stated in the infinitive form of a verb (to . . .), so it clearly stipulates which of the three speaking purposes it is setting out to accomplish.

Here are some examples of specific purpose statements under their respective headings of speaking purposes.

Speaking Purpose	*To inform.*
Specific Purpose	To demonstrate how to change a flat tire.
	To report the results of a recent survey.
	To explain the art of flower arranging.
Speaking Purpose	*To persuade.*
Specific Purpose	To motivate my audience to jog a mile a day.
	To convince my audience to buy life insurance.
	To increase my audience's willingness to vote.
Speaking Purpose	*To entertain.*
Specific Purpose	To amuse my audience by explaining how to pig out.
	To amaze my audience with a demonstration of magic.

Let's return to Yari's speech topic—"Uses of public speaking training"—and put it into a specific purpose statement. Because she wants to inform her audience, Yari needs to state her specific purpose using the infinitive. The specific purpose becomes

"To inform the audience about the uses of public speaking training."

In the first part of the specific purpose, she specifies what it is she wants to do with the audience—"*To inform the audience.*" In the second part of the specific purpose, she specifies what she wants them to know—"*about the uses of public speaking training.*" After we have selected the main points of a speech, we will reword this second section of the specific purpose to reflect the actual main points we will use in the speech.

4.5 Selecting Your Main Points

Now that you have your specific purpose, you need to begin brainstorming possible main points for the body of the speech. The main points are those two or three supporting thoughts or ideas you wish to present in the body of the talk. These main points make up the skeleton or structure of the speech body and provide the direction the speech will take.

A common mistake beginning speakers make at this point of the process is settling for the first two or three main points that come to mind. And they don't think of any other main points. They stop the process right there and call it quits.

This is a mistake. Your first thoughts are not always your best, and this method of selecting main points runs the risk of missing better main-point possibilities that would surface only *after* you've researched the speech topic sufficiently. It is only after you have spent considerable time and effort researching your subject that the main points of your speech begin to appear. From this collection of researched information you will begin to brainstorm the main points of your speech. The process of researching your speech topic will be covered fully in the next chapter.

Brainstorming Main Points

After researching your topic, the brainstorming technique you just learned can be extremely helpful. Instead of brainstorming possible speech topics, use the same technique to generate possible main-point ideas for your topic. Yari can begin the brainstorming process by using the specific purpose she has selected: "To inform the audience about the uses of public speaking training."

With a second cup of coffee in hand, Yari has set the alarm for 10 minutes, and, once again, she begins the brainstorming process. But this time, she's generating main points from the material she's gathered in her research efforts.

Improves your speaking
Get to listen to speeches
Get to meet people in class
Satisfy the oral requirement for State College
My friend is in the class

Learn to speak up in my other classes
Become more skilled in my interpersonal interactions
Appear more attractive to the opposite sex
My parents will be proud of my speech
Improves self-image

Learn to relax when under pressure
Improves presentational skills
Improves my oral interpretation skills
Makes me a better salesperson
Makes me more persuasive

Maybe I'll get a date
Learn about speaker credibility
Improves effectiveness in business
My friends will want to have me teach them skills
Be more effective in beating traffic tickets

Get a summer job
Income will go up in the years to come
People will like me
My grades will improve
My boss will like me

Makes me more pleasant
Learn to think more quickly

Buzz!! That's 10 minutes. Yari puts the pencil down and takes a sip of coffee. She generated 27 items or possible uses for learning public speaking. Each item could serve as a main point that could support her topic—"The uses of public speaking training." Once again, some ideas are better than others, but the goal in brainstorming is quantity, not quality.

The next step, as in the brainstorming process for topic selection, is to examine the list and eliminate the weaker items on the basis of speaker interest, previous knowledge and experience, and possible audience interest in the main points.

After completing the elimination process, Yari finally decides on "Improves presentational skills," "Improves effectiveness in business," and "Improves self-image." She finally arrives at the following tentative outline for his speech:

> *Specific Purpose: To inform the audience about three uses of public speaking training.*
>
> *Main Points:*
>   **I.** Public speaking improves your presentational skills.
>   **II.** Public speaking helps you become more effective in business.
>   **III.** Public speaking improves your self-image.

The speech topic and main-point structure do not mysteriously appear. Their creation takes some time and effort by you, the speaker. It involves the commitment to sit down by yourself and brainstorm possible topics and main points. It requires making decisions about the topic and main points you are going to be working with as you research, outline, and practice before you present your speech. Some people are not prepared or willing to make this commitment, like the young man in the professor's office at the beginning of this chapter. The choice is always yours.

4.6 Analyzing Your Audience

There was a young man who desired to win the heart of a certain woman in his neighborhood. He wanted to make a good first impression, so he purchased a few gifts to make his introduction all the more impressive. He went to the store and bought a case of onion-flavored chips, his favorite food. He bought every CD ever recorded by Alan Jackson, his favorite singer. And finally, he went to the animal shelter and purchased two young hound dogs, his favorite kind of dog.

The young man was now ready to present these gifts to the woman and ask her for a date. So he grabbed the case of onion-flavored chips, carefully stacked the Alan Jackson CDs on the top of the case, and clutched the leashes of the two barking dogs and wobbled down the street to her house.

> *Often the most creative people are also the most prepared.*
> —LEE IACOCCA

As he knocked on the young woman's front door, the dogs began jumping on his chest, spilling the CDs off the case. As he reached for the CDs, the case of chips fell to the ground, and the dogs began biting the case and tearing into the bags of chips. When the young woman came to the door holding her cat, the dogs began snarling at the cat, and the woman screamed, "Get those horrible monsters off my steps! I hate dogs! And what's that horrible onion stench? I'm allergic to onions!"

As the young man tugged on the leashes trying to get the barking dogs off the porch, the woman yelled, "And take these wretched Alan Jackson CDs with you—that man's got no talent!"

"Does this mean you don't want to go out with me?" shouted the young man. The woman slammed the door as hard as she could, while her cat hissed a final warning behind the window.

Now, you're probably asking yourself what does this story have to do with public speaking? Or with anything for that matter. Actually, plenty. Like the young man in the story, we often view the world and others through a self-centered perspective—what we think, what we feel, what we like, what we want—rather than putting ourselves in the shoes of others. In our lives, we will connect more effectively and more meaningfully when we take the time to learn about and understand others.

This journey from self to others is a lifelong journey; it is a journey toward maturity. Without this ability and willingness to see the world through the others' eyes, we will be hampered in our attempts to understand others, to connect with others, to establish lasting relationships, to get a date, and even to give a speech.

Audience analysis is the process of trying to understand your audience so that you can improve your communication with them. In other words, you need to learn as much about your audience as you can so you can adapt your speech in ways they will receive, understand, and appreciate. No barking dogs, spilled CDs, crushed chips, or hissing cats for you!

It's important to remember that without the audience, there is no speech, and there is no speaker. The audience is the reason for the speech. Too often, the beginning speaker isn't even conscious of this fundamental truth. He spends an inordinate amount of time and energy worrying about how he will be perceived by the audience, without even once stopping to consider exactly who he will be talking to.

Analyzing your audience is essential to your entire speech process. Without it, your chances of selecting, researching, and presenting an interesting and captivating speech are severely limited. The process of audience analysis should guide your inquiry and decisions regarding your topic selection, the points you pick, the material you gather, and the manner in which you present your content.

> *Talk about what interests your listeners and you'll discover an interested audience.*
> —DALE CARNEGIE

Therefore, the analysis should begin immediately as you select your speech topic and main points. There are four areas of audience analysis that you should examine as you select your topic and main points. They are audience interest, knowledge, attitude, and demographics.

Audience Interest

Will the audience be interested in this topic? Ideally, you, as the speaker, will be interested in the topic you are considering. But will your audience be interested? It was once stated that "there are no uninteresting topics, only uninterested listeners." The topic of flower arrangements might be an extremely boring topic to the folks at a BMW Motorcycle convention, but of great interest to a convention of florists. On the other hand, the topic of motorcycle valve adjustment techniques would most likely have every member of the motorcycle convention hanging on the edge of his or her motorcycle seat, whereas the florists would have long walked out of the auditorium.

It's vital that you consciously shift your attention to your audience and their interests and not stay stuck on what only interests you. One definition of a bore is someone who can talk about things that interest only him. So begin thinking in terms of the other person—the listener in your audience. This emphasis on being sensitive to what others are interested in is helpful in your personal life as well.

Audience Knowledge

The second area you need to examine as you analyze your audience is their knowledge of the topic. After you've determined that your audience will be interested in the specific topic you would like to speak about, you have to determine the audience's knowledge of that topic.

You don't want to speak below their knowledge level of the topic. That could bore and perhaps even insult your audience. If you spoke on the topic of "basic oil painting stokes" to a group of experienced oil painters, you might not only bore them, but you also run the risk of insulting them. On the other hand, you don't want to speak above their knowledge level either. To speak on the topic of "the joys of advanced calculus" to a group of students enrolled in beginning algebra would likely only confuse and frustrate them, since they have no knowledge and experience in calculus.

Audience Attitude

Analyzing the attitude of the audience is the third area of examination. What is the attitude of the audience regarding your topic? Are they in favor? Are they opposed? Or are they neutral in attitude? If they are neutral, how might you present your material to arouse their interests? Or if they are hostile to your topic, how might you neutralize or lessen their hostility? You may even decide to eliminate the topic altogether if their attitude toward it is hostile or nonreceptive.

Audience Demographics

The final area of analysis is audience demographics. Will the audience be male, female, or a mixture of both? What is the average age of the audience? What is the age range? What are the occupational backgrounds of the audience members? What is the educational background? Is their income high, low, or average? Is there a group affiliation? Are the members associated with a particular political, professional, or interest group?

One of the most important demographic factors you need to consider is the cultural backgrounds of your audience. No longer are the audiences of the United States strictly Anglo-European, but are now a mixture of many cultural heritages. African American, Asian American, Mexican American, Native American, and numerous other cultural backgrounds populate the audiences you will be addressing now and in the years to come.

Adopting and developing a spirit of cultural awareness and sensitivity is necessary and desirable if you are to be an effective speaker. It is not the intent of this book to describe the cultural differences of these various groups, but rather to invite you to begin or continue exposing yourself to cultures different from your own.

Here are four ways you can begin your intercultural journey. First, you can interact with students in class who are culturally different from you. Initiate interaction during class activities and in group assignments. You can even invite them for lunch or dessert after class. Making friends is a wonderful way to learn about different cultures. Second, you can enroll in an intercultural communication course. Such a class will provide you with a basic understanding of and appreciation for communication between cultures. You can also take any course that offers a cultural emphasis, such as Asian American literature, African American history, or Native American art. Third, you might even attend special speaking functions or social gatherings hosted by one of the many cultural clubs on campus. And finally, you can read both fiction and nonfiction books on a particular cultural heritage.

By exposing yourself to the literature, experiences, and personalities of people from different cultures, you will increase your awareness and sensitivity to their way of seeing the world and themselves. Ideally, this increased awareness and sensitivity will be reflected in the speech topics you select and the manner in which you develop them.

4.7 Gathering Information about Your Audience

Now that we've discussed the four areas of audience analysis, let's examine four different ways you can gather information about a particular audience. You can learn more about your audience by direct observation and from surveys, interviews, and the contact person.

Direct Observation

The first way you can gather information about your audience is by direct observation—by looking at and listening to them. If you have access to the audience you will be speaking to, you can attend one of their meetings and simply look around and observe. How many people are there? What is their gender makeup? Mostly men? Mostly women? How about the age of the audience? Young? Older? Mixed? And how about the ethnic makeup of the group? One particular ethnic group? Or a mixture of many? Remember to take notes as you observe the group so you can refer to them later as you prepare for your speech. If you're giving the speech to your college class, you enjoy a tremendous advantage because you've had plenty of opportunity to observe the other students in past class meetings. Take advantage of that.

In addition to visual observation, you might keep your ears open, too. By simply listening to what's going on during your visit, you can learn a great deal. What are the discussion topics of their meeting? What are the audience members' responses to the discussion topics? What are the topics of their conversations before and after the meeting? What are the things they talk about and like? What are the things they don't like? What is the attitude of the group? Did you happen to hear anything that would indicate their level of knowledge concerning your particular topic or their attitude about your topic? You can learn all of these things just by listening. Remember to take notes on any important thoughts and feelings that might be helpful as you prepare your speech.

Surveys

The second way you can gather information about your audience is to survey them. A survey is a collection of questions that the audience can respond to that provides you with valuable information. Keep the survey brief, maybe three to five questions, so the people will be more willing to fill it out. Who wants to answer 30 or 40 questions?

There are three primary types of survey questions. *Closed questions* require brief one- or two-word answers. Questions such as, "Do you know what a hound dog is?" or "Do you like hound dogs?" are closed questions since they can be answered by a simple "yes" or "no" response. *Open questions* such as, "What things do you know about hound dogs?" or "What are the characteristics of a good pet?" require a more developed response. You can see how the responses to open questions can involve much more than just yes or no answers. The third type of survey question is the *categorical question*, which measures responses by degrees. Here are two examples of categorical questions:

"What best describes your knowledge about hound dogs?"

_____ None _____ Little _____ Some _____ Considerable _____ Expert

"What is your attitude toward hound dogs?"

_____ Hate _____ Dislike _____ Indifferent _____ Like _____ Love

Did you notice how the information gathered from categorical questions can be helpful not only in determining if an individual possesses knowledge about your topic or his attitude toward your topic but also in providing the degree of knowledge or attitude. This information can be extremely beneficial in determining speech content, structure of main points, and even whether or not your topic should even be presented.

The secret is to limit your survey questions to five. More than that will discourage respondents from completing your survey. And make certain that you include questions that measure the level of knowledge and the attitude toward your speech topic. These two items are crucial to your research and preparation of any speech. Your audience's level of knowledge will help determine your speech content, and their attitude about your topic will assist you in choosing the most appropriate speech structure for your topic.

Your survey questions should be on one single sheet of paper, and it's best if they complete the surveys anonymously, assuring more honest responses. You need not survey the entire audience, although that would be ideal. Even 25 percent of the audience would provide valuable information. It's best if the surveys are distributed, completed, and collected as soon as possible to enable you to begin your research once you gather and interpret the data.

Interviews

The third method for gathering information is the interview. If it's possible, arrange to interview a few members of your audience before you begin researching your presentation. Conduct five-minute interviews with two or three of the audience members, using both open and closed questions to collect information about their interest, knowledge, and attitudes toward your topic. Keep the interviews brief since you're trying to get a general idea of the audience you'll be addressing. Open questions are most useful, especially when you ask for the interviewee's perceptions of the group's interest, knowledge, and attitude levels. Keep in mind that the individuals you interview will provide only a sampling of opinions and positions, but they usually will provide a general outlook or direction that can be helpful in your speech construction.

The Contact Person

The final source of audience information is the contact person for the speaking event. Your contact person usually possesses an intimate knowledge of the audience you have been asked to address and can also provide you with a wealth of information about their demographics, interests, knowledge, and attitudes. In addition to answering your questions, the contact person can provide specific information regarding the speaking event itself, such as the speaking occasion, your placement on the agenda, time limits, available equipment, size of audience, your seating location, and a host of other essential bits of information.

Audience analysis is essential to constructing and delivering an effective speech. Without learning about your audience and tailoring your message so that it will be received by them in the most productive fashion, your speaking efforts just might be as successful as the young man with the onion-flavored chips, Alan Jackson CDs, and the two barking hound dogs. Don't let that be your fate. Get to know your audience: what they like, what they know, and how they feel. It will not only make your speaking more successful, but it also might even enhance your relationships with others.

4.8 Speech Preparation Questionnaire

Before you research your speech, you need to research your audience and the speaking occasion to ensure the success of your speech. The first step is to locate a contact person, someone who is in charge of the speaking event, and interview that individual over the phone or in person. if possible, it would also be wise to visit the auditorium or room where you will be speaking to get a feel for the place. The following preparation questionnaire provides some questions you might want to ask the contact person.

SAMPLE SPEECH PREPARATION QUESTIONNAIRE

Speaking Date _____ Time _____

Contact Person _____ Phone _____

Address _____

Speech Occasion _____

Topic requested _____

Speaking purpose _____ entertain _____ inform _____ persuade

Speech time limit _____

Facility Location _____

Directions _____

_____

Size of auditorium/room _____

Podium _____ Microphone _____ Lighting _____

Audience

Name of group _____

Age range of group members _____

Cultural/ethnic considerations _____

_____

Interest in topic _____

_____

Knowledge of topic _____

_____

Opinion of topic _____

_____

Special considerations _____

_____

COMMUNICATION ACTIVITIES

PERSONAL ACTIVITIES

1. **Brainstorming about yourself**

   Make a list of the positive things about yourself following the brainstorming rules, giving yourself 10 minutes for the activity. Remember not to evaluate—quantity is the goal. How did it feel to brainstorm all of these wonderful things about yourself? A little different and strange? We need to do things like this more often. It's good for our self-image.

2. **Interviewing for intercultural speech topics**

   Conduct an informal 10-minute interview with a student in class or an individual at work who is from a different cultural background than yours. Ask him or her to brainstorm a list of topics that make them mad, glad, or sad. Once the individual has completed the list, invite him to explain any of the items in terms of cultural relevance or interest. Don't judge or evaluate his comments. Simply listen and learn.

3. **Personal appreciation list**

One of the real challenges for any public speaking student is to come up with speech topics. Even though you know the brainstorming steps, it can be a frustrating process, which can result in you throwing up your hands and admitting that you can't think of even one idea. If this is your experience, try completing this appreciation list. It might help you discover some interesting things about yourself and point to some possible speech topics.

1. Your favorite class is (was) _____.
2. Your favorite book is _____.
3. Your greatest personal achievement is _____.
4. The historical figure you'd most like to share dinner with is _____.
5. Your favorite hobby is _____.
6. The most fascinating or enjoyable place you ever visited is _____.
7. An organization or group you volunteered or worked for is _____.
8. The person, idea, or belief you would die for is _____.
9. The most interesting or fascinating fact you know is _____.
10. If you had six months to live, you would _____.

CLASS ACTIVITIES

1. **Increasing your cultural awareness through reading**

Select one magazine, periodical, or newspaper that represents a specific cultural group. Your college library will have a number of such publications. Thumb through one magazine or newspaper and read two articles of interest. What is the perspective or point of view of the articles? Is it different from yours? How is the perspective similar? How did you feel about the articles? Be prepared to share your responses in class.

2. **Group discussion: brainstorming speech topics**

Divide the class into groups of five or six students. Have each group brainstorm possible speech topics of interest for 10 minutes. All group members are to record the suggestions so that everyone will have a list of possible topics. Remember the rules of brainstorming—no evaluation, quantity not quality, the wilder the better, and combine ideas. Have fun with this activity. Be creative in your thinking!

3. **Group discussion: audience analysis**

Divide the class into groups of five or six students. The task is to brainstorm five reasons an audience would purchase a new vacuum cleaner from the group. Each group is to brainstorm five different reasons for each of the following four audiences: a fraternity, a group of elementary schoolteachers, a motorcycle club, and a retirement home. Be prepared to discuss your lists with the class.

Chapter 5

GATHERING YOUR MATERIAL
WHAT YOU SOW IS WHAT YOU REAP

LEARNING OBJECTIVES

After reading this chapter, you should be able to:

5.1 Identify seven things to look for when gathering your speech material

5.2 Explain where to look for speech information

5.3 Explain how to record your speech information

5.4 Discuss how to help the audience understand your evidence

The icy wind blasted against the thin walls of the tent as sheets of snow fell from the black sky above. Huddled in their warm tent, three Sherpa guides calmly sipped their tea in silence as they listened to the groans of nature outside. In their silence, they contemplated the ascent from the base camp to the first rim of Mt. Everest the next morning. During the hours that followed, not one word would be exchanged among the three men. Each would sit comfortably in the silence. At ease with one another and within themselves, they had nothing to say, and only the sounds of the storm filled the tent as they sat.

The three Americans in the tent beside theirs were busily discussing the departure from the base camp. They talked about the weather conditions, hoping the storm would subside by early morning. They reminisced about past expeditions. They noisily exaggerated their earlier achievements as they argued over which of them was the most skilled climber. The tent was filled with the heated words of their good-natured arguments as the storm raged outside.

When asked by one of the Americans many weeks after the expedition why he didn't always feel the need to talk, one of the Sherpa guides replied, "There is no need to talk if there is nothing to say. I am comfortable with my silence." The American who posed the question couldn't really grasp the import of the Sherpa's answer.

Many years ago, Dionysius warned, "Let your speech be better than silence, or be silent." Much of our American public speaking, in the classroom as well as in the public forum, often resembles the mindless chatter of our televisions. Superficial topics and unimportant issues characterize a great deal of what we bring to our podiums. This tabloid mentality of the mass media permeates our daily conversation.

We need to occasionally be silent in this noisy culture of ours. We need to quit talking and listen—really listen to others without constantly interrupting. We need to listen with our whole being and not just with our ears. We need to turn off the television. We need to turn off the car stereo and simply hear the hum of the car engine as we drive. We need to turn off the iPod and listen to the rustling of the leaves and the wind in the trees.

We need to experience silence and see what it has to teach us about others and ourselves. All of nature and life is singing to us outside our tents, and we need to take the time to simply listen. Maybe then our speech will reflect a deeper understanding of life and all it has to offer.

> *The secret of success is to know something that everyone else doesn't.*
> —HENRY FORD

Giving a speech involves much more than confidence, delivery practice, and direct eye contact. It requires that what we share with our audience is indeed important, interesting, and ultimately, life enhancing. This chapter will help you in this area of speaking. We will examine the process of gathering the content material for your speech—what to look for, where to look, and how to record the information.

5.1 What to Look For

As you begin researching your speech topic, you must know what types of supporting material to look for. Although there are a variety of systems that classify supporting material, most speech experts agree on the following seven classifications: definitions, examples, explanations, comparisons, statistics, expert testimony, and visual aids.

Definitions

One of the most helpful and readily accessible forms of supporting material is the simple *definition*. The novice speaker often overlooks the dictionary on her desk as she begins the process of gathering material for her presentation. Yet a definition is not only a powerful tool in clarifying terms for the audience's understanding; it also helps focus the speaker in her research and preparation for the speech itself. A practical use of a definition might be seen in a husband's attempt to convince his wife they should take a one-week vacation to Hawaii: "You know, Janet, *Webster's Dictionary* says a vacation should be 'a period of suspension of regular work or study.' I would define a vacation as eight days and seven nights in Hawaii. How would you like to vacate for a while?"

You should always define the most important term or two for any speech. For example, if you were to give a talk on "honesty in relationships," you would want to define the term *honesty* and include that definition in the introduction or the first main point of the speech. You could simply say, "And what do I mean by *honesty*? Well, *Webster's Dictionary* defines honesty as 'the quality or fact of being truthful, sincere, or frank.'" It's always worthwhile to define your terms early in the speech to clarify and limit the scope of your presentation.

One thing you might keep in mind is that a definition should not confuse the audience. Try to avoid technical terms that themselves need defining or definitions that are too lengthy. Select definitions that are brief and easily understood. You don't want to lose your audience before you even get started.

Examples

We use examples every day to support our assertions and positions. If we tell a friend he's usually late for lunch dates, one of the first things he'll most likely say is, "Oh, yeah? When have I ever been late?" In other words, he's asking us to give an example to support our assertion.

One of the most widely used supporting devices is the example. The *example* is a specific instance of a generalization or assertion. *The Random House Dictionary* (we're using a definition already) defines *example* as "One of a number of things, or a part of something, taken to show the character of the whole." Remember the husband attempting to convince his wife to visit Hawaii a few paragraphs ago? Well, he could use an example such as: "Honey, you're going to love Hawaii. It's such a beautiful place to relax. I was there once when I graduated from high school, and I was impressed with the lushness of the vegetation and the warmth and clarity of the water. I was never more relaxed in all my life."

A good rule of thumb is to have at least one example in each of your main points in the speech. The example is a powerful tool the speaker can use to paint a specific picture in the minds of the audience.

Examples can be brief or detailed, factual or hypothetical. If an example is factual and familiar to your audience, you need only refer to it briefly, as your audience is acquainted with the incident. If you're speaking about famous sports achievements, you could briefly refer to the example of "U.S. swimmer Michael Phelps' eight Olympic medals at the 2004 summer games." If the audience is not familiar with an example you are using, you will need to develop it in more detail, with names, dates, and facts. A more detailed example is often called an *illustration*. These illustrations can take the form of anecdotes, personal experiences, stories, or parables.

A *factual example* is an incident that actually took place. Suppose you are speaking about the advantages of buying flood insurance. Your example could be drawn from a family whose flood-damaged home was replaced after Hurricane Katrina in 2009, where the bill was paid by the insurance company.

A *hypothetical example*, on the other hand, can also be impressive. You might put the audience in the shoes of an imaginary homeowner whose home was destroyed by a flood but was not covered by flood insurance: "Suppose you own a home and choose not to purchase flood insurance. And suppose your home is destroyed by a flood. How do you pay for the thousands of dollars in damage? How will you cope with the stress of the added financial burden?" A hypothetical example is also called a *hypothetical situation*. It can be extremely effective in getting your audience to consider a situation from a different point of view.

Explanations

An *explanation* is used to make an idea clear and easily seen in the mind's eye of the audience. Once again, the husband could use an explanation when convincing his wife to visit Hawaii: "I'm convinced you'll love Hawaii because you enjoy beautiful scenery, you like to swim in warm water, and whether you admit it or not, you do like to get away from the kids." How could she turn this down? But she's still holding firm to her refusal to go to Hawaii.

Well, let's leave those two for a while and examine the three types of explanations you can use: analysis, exposition, and description.

Analysis is the process of explaining or studying something by examining its parts. You might want to explain to your audience how to bake a cake by breaking the process into three parts: gathering the materials, mixing the ingredients, and, finally, baking the cake.

> It is harder to conceal ignorance than to acquire knowledge.
> —JOHN DEWEY

The purpose of *exposition* is to give your audience information that will increase their knowledge of a topic. Much of any speech is devoted to expounding or explaining so that the audience understands more about the topic. A speech on how to make money selling real estate, grow a garden, or improve communication within a marriage may use exposition.

Description uses the five senses of taste, touch, sight, smell, and hearing to let the audience know what is being presented. Often, the use of description is the most powerful method of painting a picture for your audience. Suppose you are trying to describe a beach scene to your audience. Instead of simply saying, "It was a beautiful beach," you might describe the scene by saying, "Imagine yourself sitting in the warm sand (touch), and the sound of the waves lapping on the shore (hearing) relaxes you. You smell the salt air (smell), and the blue ocean stretches out as far as you can see (sight)." Which one describes the scene in more detail? The use of description can have a powerful effect on the minds of your audience.

Comparisons

A *comparison* presents qualities or features that are similar. One of the most effective ways to present a new idea is to compare it to something the audience is familiar with. Often, comparisons attempt to show the connection between what the audience knows and what they do not know. The husband in our continuing vacation saga could use a comparison such as: "Hawaii's water is like Florida's, only clearer. The climate of Hawaii is like Southern California's. And the people of Hawaii are as friendly as our own family."

A comparison can be either figurative or literal. *Figurative comparisons* describe similarities between things that are otherwise different. "He's as slow as molasses" and "The heart is like a pump" are examples of figurative comparisons.

A *literal comparison* is an actual comparison. This type of comparison gives your listeners a clear mental picture of what you're talking about. You can tell your audience that the airplane weighed as much as seven pickup trucks or that the tomato was the size of a softball.

Contrast is a way of noting differences between two things. Here, the emphasis is on differences rather than similarities. An example of contrast can be seen when a mother tells her daughter that when she was 20 years old, annual college tuition was $3,000. But now, an annual tuition bill of $30,000 is not unusual. Things sure have changed.

Statistics

Many of your listeners will be interested in and impressed by statistics. *Statistics* are numerical facts, such as: one of four Americans will experience some form of cancer in his or her lifetime; 50 percent of all marriages will end in divorce; and Z-Company stock has doubled in the past five years. Once again, in his attempts to persuade his wife to go to Hawaii, the husband might use a statistic: "One of every three Americans prefers vacationing in Hawaii to any other place in the world."

Wisely used, statistics can have a powerful impact on your audience. Unwisely used, they can bore, confuse, and even deceive the audience. When using statistics, try to keep them simple and easily understood by the average audience member.

There are some important rules to keep in mind when you use statistical information in your speech:

1. **Ensure the accuracy of the statistics you are using.** You should take statistics from reliable sources. Is the magazine, book, journal, newspaper, or website a trusted and proven source? Is the author or the researcher of the statistics credible Verify these things before using the information.
2. **Your statistics should be recent.** What may have been true just five or ten years ago could be outdated now. Try to have your statistics reflect research that is no more than five years old. The more recent, the better.
3. **Limit your use of statistics.** Once you have researched a topic thoroughly and have collected reams of statistical information about your subject, there is a tendency to want to use all of the data in your speech. If you did, you would run the serious risk of overwhelming your audience. You must realize that your listeners can accept and remember only a few statistics during the course of a speech. It is better to have a few well-placed statistics in your speech than to overload your listeners with an avalanche of numbers. Choose those statistics wisely.
4. **Use your statistics for comparative purposes.** For instance, when discussing the number of lawyers in America, you might tell your audience that in 2008, 1 of every 308 Americans was a lawyer. But the picture changes when you compare that statistic to 1967, when only 1 of every 1,210 Americans was a lawyer. The comparison gets even more interesting if you compare our statistics with those of Japan, where in 2008, only 1 of every 5,330 Japanese citizens was a lawyer.
5. **Round off your statistics.** Present your statistics in a way that will make them easy for your audience to understand. Instead of saying that the average annual wage of a field worker in Chile is $388.73, round off your statistic so that it will be more easily heard and remembered by the audience. Thus, the average wage of the field worker in Chile becomes $390 annually. Much easier to hear and remember.

   > *The harder you work the luckier you get.*
   > —GARY PLAYER

6. **Use visual aids to present your statistics.** For many people, it is difficult to visualize even the simplest statistic as it is being rattled off by the speaker. If the speaker mentions too many statistics and numbers, the audience often will simply tune out. If you have a lot of statistics to present, you might try presenting them in the form of a visual aid—a chart, graph, table, or diagram. We examine this in more detail later in the chapter.

Expert Testimony

The testimony of an expert or authority on a particular subject adds credibility to your speech. The most important benefit of *expert testimony* is to show your audience that you are not alone in your thinking—that your ideas and convictions are also held by experts in the field.

You're probably wondering if that wife has decided to visit Hawaii yet. She hasn't. What will it take to convince her? Maybe the husband could present some expert testimony: "Sylvia Bass, our travel agent, told me that of all the places she's vacationed in the world, Hawaii is her favorite." The wife is smiling, but still shaking her head. Well, while she's deciding, let's discuss who to interview if you plan to offer expert testimony in your speech.

You may find it helpful to turn to experts or authorities when researching your speech topics. If your subject is drug abuse, your attention turns to the medical doctor and the drug abuse therapist. If your subject is inflation, your attention turns to the economist. If your subject is engine repair, your attention turns to the auto mechanic. The source of expert testimony changes with each topic.

There are two ways you can support your views with the expert testimony of others. You can quote them word for word, or you can paraphrase what they have said in your own words. You can paraphrase the expert's testimony if the material is longer than a couple of sentences or to simplify the statement in an accurate manner. The shorter the quotation, the greater the impact it will have on your audience.

Because the information you are presenting is not yours, you must *give credit* where credit is due. You must orally document the testimony by telling the audience who said it, where you got the information, and the date of the testimony. It may be stated as simply as, "In the April 2007 issue of *National Geographic,* James McBride states, . . ." or "Dr. Richard Talcott, in the May 2007 issue of *Astronomy*, expresses his belief that . . ."

You can add more credibility to your expert, especially if your authority is not well known to the audience, by presenting some background information before you give his or her testimony. For example, with the first quotation from James McBride, you could preface his remarks by adding that McBride is the "author of numerous books and articles on the subject. . . ." Keep in mind that your documentation and background information on your expert have more impact if you present them *before* you give the testimony.

Visual Aids

The old Chinese saying, "one picture is worth a thousand words," holds true in public speaking as well. The final category of supporting material is *visual aids*. Visual aids can improve your speech by focusing the attention of your listeners, making your ideas easier to understand, and helping your listeners remember what you said.

This is our husband's final attempt to convince his wife to vacation in Hawaii. He will use a series of visual aids: "Honey, just look at these recent photos Sylvia took on her last vacation to Hawaii. Look at the beautiful water. Doesn't the sand look clean? Can you imagine yourself on that beach right now?" She finally says "Yes!" The visual aids did the trick! She's going to Hawaii. But we're not, so we need to examine different visual-aid forms.

The various forms of visual aids include the speaker himself, a chalkboard, objects, models, drawings and sketches, charts, and electronic media. Let's examine each of these forms of visual aids in more detail.

The *speaker himself* can be a very powerful visual aid. Not only do dress and appearance help provide the audience with a strong visual message and a means of evaluating the overall message of the speaker, but body movement, gestures, and facial expressions also can play an important role in helping the audience visualize the speech.

For example, the speaker's body can demonstrate how to move when skiing, dancing, or kicking. His hands and gestures can show how to massage a neck, hold chopsticks, or throw a football. His face can display a range of emotions that can help the audience visualize a scene from a story or anecdote. Don't be afraid to act out or demonstrate portions of your speech that can be appreciated and understood only when they are seen by the audience.

A *chalkboard* or whiteboard is another readily accessible visual aid that may help the audience visualize portions of your speech. Chalkboard use is best for impromptu speeches, when the speaker has no preparation time to construct a prepared drawing or chart. The disadvantages of chalkboard use are many. Often, the speaker will speak to the chalkboard and not the audience. And the speaker's body will partly obscure much of what is being put up on the board. The chalkboard should be used only as a last resort. If you prepare properly for your speech, you will have adequate time to construct a prepared drawing or chart that will prove much more valuable to the audience.

The *object itself* is an excellent visual aid. Showing the audience the actual computer, quilt, vase, or surfboard that is the topic of your speech leaves little to misinterpretation. Often, however, the actual object is impractical to bring to the classroom or auditorium.

A *model* makes a helpful visual aid. A model is a representation that serves as a manageable copy of the object itself. If you were giving a speech on airplanes, A-frame cabins, or the water molecule, a model could serve as an effective visual aid. One thing to remember about models is they don't have to be works of art. One speaker spent more than $40 having a plastic model of a jet engine constructed, when a balloon would have done just fine. Make sure that your model is large enough for your audience to see and that it gives your audience a rough idea of what you're talking about.

Drawings and sketches are perhaps the easiest of all visual aids to construct. Now, you might be thinking, "I'm no artist," and skip the rest of this paragraph. But hold on for a moment. As in model construction, your drawing or sketch doesn't have to be a work of art. With a few felt-tip pens, a compass, a straight edge, and some patience, you can create a drawing or sketch that can add clarity and dimension to the speech.

Keep your drawings simple. Don't overload the audience with unnecessary details when a stick figure sketch would suffice. Make your drawings, sketches, and lettering large enough so that the people in the back row will be able to see them. After you're done with the first draft of the drawing, move as far away from the drawing as the back row of your audience will be and give it a glance. If the drawing can be seen from there, fine. If not, it's back to the drawing board for a larger version.

The colors used in your drawing or sketch should stand out at a distance. Colors such as black and red on white cardboard are easily seen. Pink and yellow on a white background cannot be seen. Use a 2 × 3-foot white poster board (the kind you buy at stationery stores for three or four dollars) for drawing your sketches; they stand up better on easels than sheets of regular paper do.

Charts permit the speaker to present a wealth of information in very little space. Word charts, number charts, steps in a process, organizational flowcharts, and maps add important visual dimensions to any speech. Line graphs, pie charts, and bar graphs can also be used to present statistics so that large amounts of data can be seen at one glance.

When constructing a chart, keep it as simple as possible. The lettering and numbering should be large enough to be seen by everyone in your audience. Using letters and numbers so small that only the speaker can see them is a common mistake made by those speakers who forget the chart is for the audience to see, not for the speaker.

> *Many public speakers can talk for hours without any notes-or knowledge.*
> —MELVIN BELLI

PowerPoint is an excellent software program that can be helpful in designing and constructing much more elaborate visual aids and multimedia presentations to go along with your speeches. This relatively simple-to-use computer-assisted graphics program allows you to design and combine highly professional looking charts, graphs, slides, photographs, and video clips. You might consider enrolling in a computer applications class or workshop that teaches you how to use this program. When you decide to use a computer-generated presentational program such as PowerPoint, keep these suggestions in mind:

1. **Be brief.** Computer-generated presentational programs should be used to enhance your speech, not replace it. Limit your computerized presentation time to no more than 15 percent of your total speaking time. A helpful rule of thumb is to present one slide for every two minutes of speaking time.

2. **Be simple.** Keep your presentations simple. Allow your program's design wizards to help you select the designs, colors, and print type. Don't reinvent the wheel each time you speak.

3. **Be consistent.** Use consistent lettering, transitions, and bullets throughout your presentation. Too much variety can be distracting to the audience.

4. **Be focused.** Use one to three words per bullet. Don't use more than five or six bullets per slide or you'll lose your audience. Limit each slide to one thought or idea. You don't want your audience to spend the entire time reading. This is a speech, not a book.

5. **Be prepared.** Practice your speech with your computerized program. Mark the places in your note cards where you will use your computer slides. Time your practice sessions so that you'll be within the time limits.

6. **Be flexible.** As you practice your presentation, be flexible enough to edit your presentation if it's running too long or too short. Omit certain slides if you think they're unnecessary or don't contribute to the presentation. Change the font, font size, color, or background patterns if they're distracting or unsatisfactory. You're the boss!

7. **Be ready.** Set up any equipment you'll need well before your speaking time. Test the computer program, check the room lighting, and test anything else you might be using for your speech.

8. **Be forewarned.** In the event of computer or electrical failure, be prepared to give your speech without the computerized visual aids. Unlike poster boards, computer programs depend on properly working computer and electrical sources, so be forewarned that electrical disasters occasionally do happen.

9. **Be generous.** Remember that you can print out graphs, tables, lists, outlines, and more from your computerized program for distribution to your audience. It can be helpful for your audience to have some hands-on material to take home and refer to long after your presentation is complete.

Finally, the use of *electronic media*, such as video playback recorders, overhead projectors, and slide projectors, can also be considered when planning the visual-aid portion of your talk. When you consider their use, remember that electronic media may not be appropriate for some speeches. If you have only five minutes to get a group of people to vote in tomorrow's election, electronic media may not be the best approach to convince your audience, because five minutes do not give you adequate time for preparation. On the other hand, if you're trying to convince a group of teenagers to not drink and drive, and you are given adequate preparation time, a video of a fatal car accident scene may have an impact on your audience that words cannot provide.

After considering the advantages and disadvantages of using electronic media, it would be wise for you to practice with the device ahead of time. When you practice your speech, include the use of the machine. There's nothing more embarrassing than trying in front of an audience to figure out how a machine works.

Suggestions for Using Visual Aids.

If you decide to use any visual aids in your speech, here are some recommendations you may find helpful:

1. **Devote Time to the Process.** If you decide to use any visual aids in a speech, set aside adequate time to design, construct, and practice using whatever aids you select. Too often, speakers will decide on a visual aid as almost an afterthought the morning of the presentation, not devoting enough time to its design and construction. The results can be embarrassing, both to the speaker and the audience. So if you decide to use visual aids, begin early in the speech process and give your visual aids the time and energy they deserve. Your audience will appreciate your efforts, and so will you.

2. **Make the Visual Aids Large Enough.** When designing and constructing your visual aid, keep your audience in mind—especially those seated at the back of the room or auditorium. If it's possible, visit the room you'll be speaking in and stand at the very back and look at the podium. How large will your visual aid have to be so that it will be seen easily even by people seated way back there? Bring a friend, a newspaper, and a large red marking pen. Have your friend hold up an unfolded newspaper at the podium and see how much of it you can make out from the back of the room. Then have your friend write your name with five-inch letters with the large red marker on one of the newspaper sheets and see if you can make out the name from where you're standing. If you can't, have your friend repeat the process with larger letters until you can see the letters easily. Remember to take your friend out for dessert afterward. It's always good to take care of those who take care of you!

3. **Make the Visual Aids Simple.** Visual aids should clarify or reinforce a point you are trying to make. The goal is for the audience to see and understand your visual aid within 3–5 seconds. Not 30–40 seconds. Just 3–5 seconds. You don't want to overload them with too much visual information. Here, less is more. Decide what it is you really want to emphasize with each visual aid and design it with that in mind. Don't clutter your visual aid with 15 statistics, 20 bullet points, or 25 photographs. Very few people will be motivated enough to look at them, and even fewer will remember anything you showed. Save yourself and your audience time and effort: focus on what is essential, and keep your visual aids simple.

4. **Limit the Number of Visual Aids.** Your visual aids should not become the primary focus of your presentation. A speaker during a three-minute Introduction Speech will quickly be overshadowed by her well-intended, 35 fully animated PowerPoint slides, with all the bells and whistles. Limit your visual aids to no more than 15 percent of your total speaking time. So in a five-minute speech, the time devoted to using visual aids should be about 45–60 seconds. Remember, you are the speaker, so don't get lost behind a mountain of visual aids.

5. **Show Your Visual Aids Only When You're Talking about Them.** Keep your visual aids hidden from the audience until you want to display them. Novice speakers will often set up and display all of their visual aids before they begin their introduction. Although this can be a relief to the speaker, it is usually a distraction to the audience. Who could pay attention to the speaker's introductory remarks when faced with a 3 × 5-foot picture of an injured family in an automobile accident or a list of the 15 most common mistakes made on a first date? Keep your visual aids out of view until you need them. Then you will receive the audience's undivided attention.

6. **Maintain Eye Contact.** The most common mistake made by speakers using visual aids is that they lose eye contact with their audience when focusing on their visual aid. The speaker will read word for word what is displayed on the chart or screen, talk to the visual aid, stare at the object he is speaking about, or simply gaze at his chart as he tries to remember his next point. Above all else, maintain direct eye contact with your audience. Do not look at or talk to your visual aid. Your lack of eye contact can communicate a lack of interest in your audience. (The same can hold true with your romantic interest!) So above all else, keep what's most important in sight.

7. **Don't Pass Your Visual Aids Around.** Even though you'll be tempted to let your audience handle your visual aids, DON'T! Even if they're begging on bended knees. If you do, it will mark the beginning of the end for your presentation. You'll lose their attention. Even the people not holding your pet lizard, the silk floral arrangement, or your collection of 55 square-dancing magazines will still be watching the others fondle your treasures with envy, waiting for their turn to come. No matter how mature or sophisticated your audience appears, they're kids at heart, and you'll lose them once you turn them loose with your visual aids. Maintain control and the audience's attention.

8. **Practice with Your Visual Aids.** Always practice and time your speech using the visual aids you've prepared. This means that your visual aids are already

completed and ready to go before you begin your timed practice sessions. Remember to keep the visual aids out of view until you are ready to discuss them. Speak to your imaginary audience and NOT to your visual aid. This part of your practice is vital to a successful speech. Don't talk to or look at your visual aids during your practice sessions. Keep your eyes on the imaginary audience. Whatever you do in practice is what you'll do during your actual speech, so keep your eyes on the audience. And as you evaluate your practice speech times, determine if you need to trim some of your visual aid segments. Often, visual aids will take longer to use than you might imagine before you practice, so keep track of your times.

9. **Have a Great Life Anyway.** No speaker or speech is perfect. Take this to heart as you use your visual aids in your speech. Things happen to us all. That's life. So don't scream, frown, apologize, or even sigh if something goes wrong with your visual aids when you present the speech to a live audience. Charts fall off easels, the 55 square-dancing magazines may scatter all over the floor, and your PowerPoint file might freeze. When things like that happen, pause, take a breath, and smile. Pick up the chart, gather the magazines, or just gently kick the computer and keep the show going. Audiences will appreciate your calm, gracious response to these minor mishaps. Remember: it's only a speech, and you'll have a great life anyway.

5.2 Where to Look for Speech Information

Now that you have an idea of what to look for when you're researching your speech, we need to spend some time discussing where to look for this information. There are four primary areas to explore: your own experience and knowledge, library resources, electronic resources, and interviewing.

Your Own Experience and Knowledge

Most people rush off to the library when they are faced with the prospect of researching a speech topic. And by doing so, they overlook one of the richest sources of speech information—their own experience and knowledge.

If you sit quietly for a moment or two and scan your prior experience and knowledge of the speech topic you've selected, scenes from the past, bits and pieces of knowledge from old lectures or conversations, and anecdotes from personal experience will run through your mind. Each one potentially provides unique and interesting information for the content of your speech. A woman giving a speech on parenting may remember stories about her parents, movies that depicted the struggles and rewards of parenting, a sitcom that revolved around raising children, and an anecdote or two about raising her own children. This information from past knowledge and experience serves as an original and colorful source of speech information.

Just to be is a blessing.
Just to live is holy.
—ABRAHAM HESCHEL

The brainstorming technique can be utilized here when surveying your past experience and knowledge. Simply jotting down every related experience and piece of knowledge—no matter how small or trivial—will provide a springboard from which you can begin your research.

Library Resources

The library might not be your first choice for exciting places to visit on a Friday evening, but it does serve as one of the most rewarding sources of speech information. Every library, regardless of size, usually provides sources of information such as those below that you will find helpful in researching your speech.

The library's *computer* or *card catalog* indexes all of the library's information by author, title, and subject. This catalog is your primary guide to the books in the library. If you are unfamiliar with its operation, ask the librarian on duty for assistance.

Magazines and *periodicals* are another source of information for your speech. The *Reader's Guide to Periodical Literature* will be your most valuable resource for locating magazine and periodical articles that are related to your speech topic. The advantage of magazine or periodical information is that it is generally more current than information in books and encyclopedias. The *Reader's Guide* indexes the articles of more than 130 U.S. journals on a wide range of topics. In addition, you may wish to consult other indexes such as the *Education Index* for topics related to education or the *Index to Behavioral Sciences and Humanities*.

Quotation books provide another rich source of information for your speech. *Bartlett's Familiar Quotations*, a reference book containing more than 1,500 pages of quotations on every topic imaginable, is one of the most popular collections of quotations. One-third of the book is an index to help you find a suitable quotation on just about any topic. Your library should have a copy of *Bartlett's*, along with several other similar reference works. A quotation often provides an ideal beginning or ending to your speech.

Your library should have one or two of your local daily *newspaper indexes*, in addition to the *New York Times Index*. Although newspapers don't always provide the most scholarly writing on a given topic, the articles can be a source of recent and local information for your speech. After you've taken a look around your local library and maybe even talked with a librarian, you can now turn your efforts to electronic resources in your search for speech topic material.

Electronic Resources

Having ready access to the Internet from home, school, and cell phone, you might be tempted to begin your speech research with search engines such as Google, Yahoo, or Bing, but this approach can often decrease your effectiveness in gathering relevant information. By using these popular Internet search engines, you can easily become overwhelmed by the shear number of websites generated, the biased and false information presented, and the number of reputable sources that are excluded or overlooked. That's why it's usually a good idea to begin your speech research with your college, school, or local library's database.

Library Database.   To begin your search of electronic resources, use your library's database or portal, such as ProQuest, EBSCOhost, or InfoTrac. These are commercial databases containing sources of information that have been selected and edited by experts to provide quality research material. ProQuest provides indexes and archives of hundreds of sources of information such as newspapers, periodicals, and dissertations. Its contains more than 125 billion digital pages. EBSCOhost provides more than 300 full-text and secondary databases, which include full-text journals, magazines, books, monographs, reports, and other publication sources. InfoTrack College Edition offers more than 20 million articles from nearly 6,000 reputable sources, with articles added daily. No matter which commercial database your school, college, or local library offers, you can be certain that the sources of information are selected and edited by experts and the material you collect from them is credible.

Virtual Libraries.   From the convenience of your own computer, you can access a rich collection of informational sources from virtual libraries. With the click of your mouse, you can enter into these Internet libraries and browse their collections of books, periodicals, magazines, journals, directories, and newspapers. Here are four of the more comprehensive virtual libraries: Virtual Library (www.vlib.org), Internet Public Library (www.ipl.org), Digital Librarian (www.digital-librarian.com), and the Library of Congress (www.loc.gov/rr/index.html). Even if you don't have a topic to research, these virtual libraries are fun to explore from the comfort of your own home.

The Internet.   After you have searched your library's database and toured a virtual library for your speech topic research, you can also access a broader-based collection of information sources on the Internet using web search engines. A search engine is designed to search for information on the World Wide Web and presents its results as a list of web pages, information sources, images, open directories, and a variety of other different types of files. There are a number of helpful search engines available to you, but remember that no search engine will find all of the available sites that are on the Internet, and many search engines allow business sites to purchase top 10 rankings on their search results. Unlike your library's commercial database, a search engine's information results are not screened, selected, and edited by experts, and so it can occasionally list biased, misleading, or false information. Here are a some of the best search engines available:

> Google (google.com)
> Bing (bing.com)
> Alta Vista (altavista.com)
> HotBot (hotbot.com)
> Lycos (lycos.com)
> Yahoo (yahoo.com)

Key-Word Search Guidelines.   Your Internet researching will be more effective if you follow some simple guidelines. First, avoid using general or vague subject terms when you search for information. Terms such as "car," "love," and "disease" will result in far too many hits from your commercial database or search engine. Using Google's search engine, the term "car" results in 941,000,000 hits, which is much more than you can skim in an hour.

Second, use specific terms in searching for supporting speech material. Instead of using the term "car," try the more specific key word that relates to your speech topic such as "Porsche," which results in 81,400,000 hits. An even more specific term, such as "Boxster," gives us only 3,200,000 hits, eliminating all those millions of web pages that don't contain information related to your speech topic, Porsche Boxster. How's that for a time-saving suggestion?

Third, use Boolean operators to increase your search effectiveness. Boolean operators are words or symbols placed between the key words of your topic search, such as AND, OR, NOT, +, and −. These words and symbols can narrow or expand your key-word searches. Use AND to narrow your topic search. "Boxster AND engine" eliminates all those web pages that don't contain information about both the Boxster and engine. You can expand your search by allowing results that contain alternative terms by using OR between words. "Boxster OR Carrera" will result in web pages that contain either the Boxster or Carrera models of Porsche. NOT restricts your search by excluding certain terms or words, such as "Boxster NOT Carrera." This restrictive search will give you web pages that contain Boxster but not Carrera. Finally, + and − placed directly in front of your key word indicates the inclusion or exclusion of that term, such as "+engine −Carrera."

Fourth, you can use your Help pull-down menu or Advanced Search button on your search engine to access more advanced filters or search criteria. In addition to many of the Boolean operator functions listed in the preceding paragraph, you can narrow your search by language, file type, domain ranking, region, copyright usage, results per page, numeric rankings, and so on. The more you can narrow you search, the more effective your electronic research will become. Think small.

Evaluating Electronic Source Material.   Now that you've begun searching electronic source material for your speech, here are three criteria you can use when selecting information. First, is the author of the web article or document clearly identified? Is he or she an expert in the field? Are his or her credentials and qualifications provided? Second, many documents on the Internet are published by organizations, rather than specific authors, so you must evaluate the credibility of the particular business, agency, or interest group whose article you are considering. And finally, you must take into account the timeliness of the document you are evaluating. A good rule of thumb is to consider only those articles that have been published in the past three years. If any web article fails one of these criteria, don't use it. There are too many other more credible and reliable documents from which to choose.

> *Education is not a handful of facts, but knowing how and where to find them.*
> —HERBERT SPENCER

Interviewing

The final source of speech information we will discuss is the *interviewing* of experts. Although many speakers are reluctant to ask for an interview from a local expert, the rewards of doing so can go beyond those of simply giving a well-researched speech. Many a friendship, both professional and personal, and many a job have blossomed because of a 15-minute interview.

For a given speech, don't interview more than one or two experts, because the interview process involves more time and effort than you might imagine.

The first step in conducting an interview is to decide with *whom* you want to talk. If your speech is about sleeping pills, you may want to speak with a pharmacist or a physician. If your topic is automobile engine repair, you may want to talk with an auto mechanic who specializes in engine overhauling. Or if your speech is on the planet Jupiter, you may want to interview an astronomy instructor at a local college or university.

The second step is to *request an interview*. Whether you request an interview in person, over the telephone, or in a formal letter, keep your request brief and friendly. Let the person know who you are, that you are researching a topic for a speech in his or her field of expertise, and that you would like a 15-minute interview at his or her convenience (not yours). If the person cannot or will not grant an interview, thank him or her for the time and try the next candidate. If he or she agrees to the interview, great!

The third step is to write a list of *questions* for the interview itself. This should be done only *after* you have researched the topic from your own knowledge and experience and have conducted your library search for material. This prior research will enable you to ask more enlightened, specific, and articulate questions.

The fourth step is the *interview itself*. Be punctual. Nothing is more annoying to your interviewee than for you to arrive late to a meeting that you requested. Dress up for the interview. Don't arrive in a tank top and old jeans. Show some respect. And stick to your time limit of 15 minutes. You can cover a lot of territory in that period of time, so long as you stick to the task at hand. Bring your list of questions and a pen to jot down noteworthy remarks. At the end, thank the interviewee.

Finally, after you've returned from the interview, take a moment to write a brief *thank-you card or letter* to the person you interviewed. The few minutes and the cost of the stamp will add that touch of class that few interviewers ever consider.

5.3 How to Record Your Speech Information

Now that you have a better idea of what to look for and where to look for it, let's briefly discuss how to record the information you will be using.

In your research, you will find a variety of examples, quotations, statistics, and comparisons that you will want to collect. You may not use all of the information, and you may not even know the order in which you will present it. So, you will have to find some way of recording all these data. People have used everything from professional calligraphy paper to the clean side of a McDonald's hamburger wrapper to record their speech information.

The best material to use for recording your information is the 4 × 6-inch index card. You can purchase a pack of 50 cards at any office supplies store or drug or stationery store for a couple of dollars. Index cards are recommended because sorting and rearranging your material is much easier when each piece of information is recorded on a separate index card, as opposed to one large sheet of paper.

> *Knowledge is knowing a fact. Wisdom is knowing what to do with it.*
> —OLIVER WENDELL HOLMES

When recording your research material on the index card, write the author's name on the upper left-hand side, followed by the title of the book, magazine, newspaper, periodical, or website address. Also include the date of the publication. For information from the Internet, indicate the most recent update of the article being presented.

If you are using information from an interview you have conducted, give the interviewee's name and professional background and the date of the interview. Your documented information (statistic or quotation) can now be written in the middle of the card. A finished note card should look something like this:

> Randy Fujishin
> *Natural Bridges*, 2011.
>
> "You either enlarge or diminish others with every interaction."

How much information should you research for your speech? A helpful rule of thumb is to gather about three times the actual amount of evidence you will present. For a six-minute speech, you would devote two minutes of actual speaking time to your documented evidence—statistics, expert testimony, and quotations. So, given the "three times rule," you would want to gather enough evidence to fill six minutes of speaking time, knowing you will select only two minutes of material for the actual speech. It's always a good idea to gather more information than you'll need so you can choose the most relevant evidence for your particular audience.

Regarding the number of sources you should consult, present at least three different sources of information. Three is the minimum. Fewer than that would not ensure sufficient depth or breadth of research.

A final word of caution would be to begin your research as soon as possible. Most people tend to procrastinate and let things slide to the last minute. But tardiness in your research will only increase your anxiety and wreak havoc on your sleep. Don't wait until the night before you are scheduled to speak to begin your research. That will only make you old before your time.

5.4 Helping the Audience Understand Your Evidence

It's been said that "People don't care how much you know. They want to know that you care." In many respects, this holds true for your audience when it comes to presenting evidence in your speeches.

Though it is necessary to present an adequate amount of evidence in your speeches, don't overdo it. Include only the most informative and compelling evidence you could find, but not all of the data you collected. Remember: you're not competing in a debate tournament; instead, you're giving an informative or persuasive speech to an interested audience. So invest some effort into the way you present your evidence.

Your audience will be more receptive to and more likely retain your evidence if it is presented in a way that's easy to follow and understand. To accomplish this goal, you can use the "Evidence Three-Step" technique. These simple three steps for presenting a piece of evidence will help your audience understand and remember the testimony or statistic. Let's look at this technique.

Evidence Three-Step

Step 1: Cite the source.
Step 2: State the evidence.
Step 3: Restate the evidence.

Step 1: Cite the Source

The first step is to cite or document the evidence you are presenting. You want to establish the credibility of your information first so that your audience will be more receptive and willing to consider the evidence. State the author's name, the source, and any other pertinent background information you feel will be helpful.

"According to Randy Fujishin in his book, *Natural Bridges*, . . ."
"Dr. Vijai Sharma, in his Mind Publications blog, states that . . ."

Step 2: State the Evidence

The second step is to state the evidence. Keep your evidence short and to the point. There's no need to go on and on with expert testimony or statistics. It's more difficult for you to remember, and you run the risk of losing your audience's attention. Keep it short. Restrict your expert testimony to 20 words or less if possible. You can memorize a brief quotation, and note cards won't be necessary. Here are examples of a short quotation and a brief statistic.

"You either enlarge or diminish others with your communication."
"Over 90% of people report some degree of stage fright when they face the prospects of a public performance."

Step 3: Restate the Evidence

The final step is to restate the evidence *in your own words*. The purpose of this third step is to provide the evidence in words that your audience will understand and appreciate. Often, evidence is stated in technical or specialized language, which can be difficult for your audience to grasp. Your goal is to bring the expert testimony or statistic to a level that every member of your audience can understand and appreciate. So restate your evidence in simple language. This will show that you care about your audience. Here are two examples of restatement.

"*In other words*, the author is saying that every time you interact with another person, you either make that person feel a little better or worse than they felt before they talked with you."

"*Another way of understanding Dr. Sharma's statistic is* that in this class of 30 students, 27 of us will experience some level of stage fright or anxiety as we prepare for our first speech."

Now let's look at one example using the entire "Evidence Three-Step" technique:

"(1) According to Randy Fujishin in his book, *Natural Bridges*, (2) "You either enlarge or diminish others with your communication." (3) *In other words*, the author is saying that every time you interact with another person, you either make that person feel a little better or worse than they felt before they talked with you."

When you restate the expert testimony or statistic in your own words, the audience will more clearly understand and appreciate your evidence. More important, they will know that you cared enough to go that extra step.

COMMUNICATION ACTIVITIES
PERSONAL ACTIVITIES

1. **What happened on the day you were born?**
   Have you ever wondered what was going on the day you entered the world? Here's a fun research project. Go to the library and look up a *New York Times* newspaper published on the date you were born (month, day, and year). You may have to go into the back of the library and use the microfilm machine, but be of good cheer. It will be well worth your efforts. Who says research is boring?

2. **Whom do you trust?**
   Make a list of three magazines, newspapers, or other publications you trust in terms of the reliability of their information and reporting. Would you have listed these three publications 10 years ago? How about 10 years from now? What publications would you not accept as being reliable or truthful?

3. **Whom would you have dinner with?**
   If you could interview (over dinner) anyone (either living or dead) for three hours, who would it be? That's any human being who has ever lived or is now living! Why did you select this individual? Would you have interviewed him or her 10 years ago if you were given this fantasy choice? How about 10 years from now? What do you think you would learn during the interview?

CLASS ACTIVITIES

1. **Your dream home speech**
   Take a moment and pretend you have just inherited $5 million. You can live anywhere in the world. Where would you choose to live? Pick a specific location (for example, the city of Hilo, Hawaii, as opposed to "somewhere in the Pacific"). Once you've decided on a specific place, go to the library and see if you can locate three sources of information on your dream home location. After reading about this place, does it still hold its appeal? What did you learn about this place? What did you learn about yourself? Prepare, practice, and present a three- to five-minute speech discussing three interesting facts or facets about this dream location. Your speech should include an introduction, body, and conclusion.

2. **Overcoming-my-fear speech**

   There's a good chance at this very moment, in the back of your mind some-where, that you're fearful or worried about something. It might be a small lump on your neck, the possibility of a relationship breakup, or anxiety over being late on a credit card payment. No matter what your fear or worry is, make a research project out of it. Think of one or two people you could talk to or inter-view who are experts, or at least experienced, in your area of concern. Whom did you interview? What did you learn about your fear? What actions can you take to eliminate, decrease, or accept this fear? Prepare, practice, and present a three- to five-minute speech about three insights you discovered about this fear. Your speech should include an introduction, body, and conclusion.

3. **Intercultural speech**

   Select a culture, other than your own, that you would like to learn more about. Research at least three written sources, and interview one individual from the culture you selected. Prepare, practice, and deliver a three- to five-minute speech presenting three interesting facts you learned about this culture. Your speech should include an introduction, body, and conclusion.

Chapter 6

LISTENING TO OTHERS
BEING GOOD TO THE SPEAKER

LEARNING OBJECTIVES

After reading this chapter, you should be able to:

6.1 Explain the listening process

6.2 List some barriers to listening

6.3 Explain some bridges to listening

6.4 List some benefits of listening

W ho would have thought that a public speaking course could improve one's love life? But that's exactly what Nikkil discovered even before he delivered his final speech.

Nikkil enrolled in an evening public speaking class to advance his career as a software engineer. He also thought it might help him with his English, since he and his young family had immigrated to the United States only a few years ago. But Nikkil soon discovered that public speaking offered other benefits he never dreamed possible.

One night after his children were asleep, his wife, Misha, surprised him by saying, "Nikkil, I've noticed that you don't interrupt the kids as much as you used to. And I think you're a lot more open to what I have to say too."

"It's funny," he said. "But I think my speech class has changed me. My instructor says that the greatest gift we give to one another is to listen with respect and an open mind."

"I like that," smiled his wife.

"I've also learned to follow a speaker's ideas, test the reasoning, and analyze the content of a speech, but it all begins with respect and an open mind."

"Well, whatever you're learning, it's made a difference in our relationship," Misha said as she hugged her husband.

"I think so too."

Who would have thought?

One of the most important skills you will learn in a public speaking class has little to do with what you say or how you say it, but rather, how you listen. Now, you might be thinking, "I already know how to listen." But this assumption might not be true. In fact, very few of us have ever been taught to listen effectively.

From your childhood, your assumption was most likely that you knew how to listen—you were born with the skill to listen, just as you were born with the ability to cry and eventually babble out a string of words to the delight of your parents. This assumption was reinforced by important people in your life. After impressing your parents with your speaking skills, it wasn't long before

> *No one can develop fully*
> *without feeling understood*
> *by at least one person.*
> —PAUL TOURNIER

they were shouting, "Haven't you been listening to me?" Your teacher would be ordering you to "Listen up!" And a friend was soon complaining, "You need to listen to me for a change." Each of these statements or questions assumed that you actually knew how to listen. But in reality, very few of us did.

Both as a speaker and as an audience member, effective listening is critical to your success and enjoyment of public speaking. So let's begin by looking at the basics of the listening process.

6.1 The Listening Process

In our daily lives, we spend more time listening than we do speaking, reading, or writing. Of all the communication skills, listening is the one we use most often. Studies show that we spend 45 percent of our communication time listening and only 30 percent speaking, 16 percent reading, and 9 percent writing. And not too surprisingly, studies also suggest that we remember only a fraction of what we hear. Listening is important, and we don't do it very well. So how can we improve our listening?

Let's begin by defining listening. *Listening* is the process of receiving, attending to, and assigning meaning to aural stimuli. In other words, it's the process of making sense out of the sounds we hear. This process can be better understood by examining the five steps of listening: receiving, attending to, interpreting, evaluating, and responding.

Receiving

The first step in the listening process is that of *receiving* or hearing sounds from the environment. Hearing is limited to the physiological process of receiving and processing these sounds. At any given moment, you can be hearing the words of a speaker delivering a speech, the hum of the air conditioner, the muffled whispers of the people around you, and the rumblings of your own stomach. All of these sounds and more are bombarding your ears at the same time, all competing for your attention.

Attending To

The second step is selecting or *attending to* primarily one of the sounds from the many you are receiving and disregarding or filtering out all the others. For instance, you might choose to focus your attention on the words of the speaker in class and filter out the sounds of people whispering, the rattle of the air conditioning, and even the rumblings of your stomach. Listening requires, as does life, that we choose from the many and focus on

> *Take a tip from*
> *nature; your ears aren't*
> *made to shut, but*
> *your mouth is.*
> —MALCOLM FORBES

the few. Whether it is objects, possessions, goals, friends, or a spouse, you must choose from the many. The purpose of life is not to attend to everything, but only those few things that you find meaningful.

Interpreting

Once you've selected the focus of your attention, the third step in the listening process is *interpreting* or assigning meaning to the sounds you've selected. When listening to a speaker, you must determine the meaning of the words or encode what the speaker is attempting to communicate in the speech. In addition to the actual words themselves, you will also weigh the speaker's verbal cues, such as tone of voice, vocal variety, and rate of speech. Interpretation will also involve your sense of sight and considering the nonverbal behavior of the speaker. All of these considerations are necessary for effective message interpretation.

Evaluating

The fourth step of listening is *evaluating* the message you have heard. Not only are you required to understand what the speaker is attempting to communicate, but you must also think about the message in more critical terms that include evaluating the reasoning used, the accuracy of the information given, and the credibility of the evidence presented. Listening is more than just understanding what the speaker has said; it involves the evaluation of the speech content as well. This evaluation process can also involve judging the qualifications and credibility of the speaker. Did the speaker sound and appear honest, sincere, and trustworthy? This fourth step in the listening process is often the most difficult to learn and develop, but it's essential to becoming an effective and responsible listener.

Responding

The final step in the listening process is *responding* to what you have heard. You might not always agree with or accept what the speaker is saying, but you can communicate that you are listening and understand what is being said. Eye contact, smiling, and nodding can communicate interest, encouragement, and agreement. Frowning, shaking your head from side to side, or long glances at your watch can convey disagreement or boredom.

You can also respond to the speaker's message by asking questions at the conclusion of a speech, engaging in a discussion with the speaker after the event is over, or even following the speaker's invitation to enroll in a class, donate to a political party, or volunteer at a charitable organization. One of the most significant responses you can have to any speech is to remember the message after the applause has finished. Since the vast majority of what you hear is soon forgotten, a message that is remembered, perhaps for a lifetime, is a successful message indeed.

6.2 Barriers to Listening

Listening is a difficult process, especially given the requirements placed upon the listener in the public speaking setting. Here are several common barriers to listening in this setting.

Abundance of Messages

The first barrier to listening is the abundance of messages that bombard us every day—messages crying out to be heard, such as sounds from your iPod, your cell phone, television, conversations, business meetings, phone messages, phone conversations, and the list goes on. There are just too many things to listen to even when we're listening to a speaker giving a presentation.

External Noise

External noise or interference from outside sources is the second barrier to listening. Some examples of external noise are traffic, barking dogs, machinery, and the music from our neighbor's stereo. These external noises make listening difficult. In the public speaking class, external noises can come from other students whispering next to you, a loud air conditioning fan, or people talking right outside the classroom windows.

Rapid Thought

The third barrier we experience is rapid thought. We can understand an individual's speech up to 500 words per minute, while the average person speaks approximately 125 words per minute. With all of this spare time on our hands, our thoughts can drift; we can think about our response to what is being said or just daydream. Our rapid thought can be a barrier to listening.

Judgmental Frame of Reference

We often have a judgmental frame of reference when it comes to listening to others. Questions that flood our minds as we listen to others are focused on our evaluations of what is being shared. Does this subject interest me? How does this affect me? Do I agree with what is being said? In public speaking, this judgmental frame of reference can be a barrier to effective listening because it can easily make us tune out the words of the speaker if we are uninterested in, disagree with, or don't like the topic he or she is presenting. This is one of the most common barriers to effective listening.

Short Attention Span

Another common barrier to effective listening is a short attention span. In addition to devoting less attention to topics we find uninteresting, disagreeable, or distasteful, we are also conditioned to expect and respond to rapidly changing messages provided by our technology. The cell phone, especially with text messaging, is a tool that permits and encourages an endless barrage of rapid-fire exchanges from a variety of individuals from the moment we get up until the moment we sleep. Instant messaging, e-mail, and chat rooms also make your computer, laptop, or smartphone another example of technology that enables lightning-quick interaction and exchanges of messages. Even television helps reduce our short attention span by its endless split-second cuts between the actions and conversations of those who entertain us.

These miracles of technology keep us connected and entertained in ways that were inconceivable just decades ago. But there is a price for this never-ending connection, and that price might be our inability and unwillingness to simply sit still for a few minutes and listen to another human being speak without feeling the desire to tap out a message or shout out a response. This ability to sit still and simply give someone our undivided attention is becoming a rare skill in this ever-changing world of ours.

Effort

The final barrier to effective listening is that listening requires effort. As you learned earlier in this chapter, effective listening requires that you invest effort in five specific tasks—receiving, attending to, interpreting, evaluating, and responding to the speaker's message. Each one of these factors demands that you place your attention and energy into these important undertakings and put aside other competing needs and desires. It's often easier to drift off and think about those activities you'd prefer to be doing or people you'd rather be with, or maybe just zone out and drift into a comfortable nothingness. But as an audience member, you have a responsibility to choose to be present, attentive, receptive, and responsive. All of these activities require your effort. But remember that your efforts to listen can increase your knowledge, widen your scope of understanding, and bless the speaker in ways you can't begin to imagine. You don't learn anything new when you're talking. But when you're listening—really listening—your life can change for the better. It's worth the effort.

> *Man's inability to communicate is a result of his failure to listen effectively.*
> —CARL ROGERS

6.3 Bridges to Listening

As we've seen, there are many barriers to effective listening. But there are actions you can take to improve your listening skills and actually bridge the gaps and shortcomings that would normally prevent you and the speaker from connecting in a meaningful way. Let's now turn our attention to building bridges to successful listening.

Prepare to Listen

The first thing you can do to be an effective listener is to prepare to listen before the speaker even begins to talk. If you know the topic of the speech ahead of time, you might want to briefly research the topic. Nothing big or in depth, but enough to know the basics of the topic. This is where the Internet is helpful. Just Google the topic and scan the web articles for basic information that you find helpful or interesting. It's surprising how much you can learn about a topic with just a few minutes of research. Your preparation in this area can also benefit you in following, analyzing, and even discussing the presentation after the speaker has concluded.

Another way you can prepare to listen is to arrive at the auditorium or classroom early so you can find a seat in the front. The closer you are, the easier it will be to hear and see the speaker. Avoid the back and the sides of the room, since noise and activity from outside the room through windows and open doors can be distracting. Turn off your cell phone and any other electronic devices you may have. And whatever you do, don't text one of your friends during a speech. That's not only distracting to the speaker and to those seated near you, it's rude. And if someone seated near you talks on a cell phone or begins texting, politely and quietly request that he or she stop. The speaker and those seated around you will thank you. Be courageous in your courtesy.

Keep an Open Mind

Even before the speaker begins speaking, remind yourself to keep an open mind. Be gentle as you receive the speaker's message. One of the primary barriers to listening is our tendency to evaluate others. And this evaluation begins before the speaker even says a word. We observe the way the speaker walks to the podium, the clothing she wears, the expression on her face, the way she stands, and even the amount of time she takes before she utters her first word. By the time the first sentence is finished, we normally have formed some initial judgments about the speaker.

To provide a bridge of connection for the speaker, suspend your evaluation a little longer than normal. Put the transmission in neutral for a short period of time. Just like watching a sunset, simply observe and take in the scenery. Receive the speaker's initial words openly, without asking questions of yourself such as, "Do I like the way the speaker looks?" "Is the speaker's voice pleasant?" "Would I dress like that?" or "Do I agree with the speaker's opening remarks?" Be willing to be spacious as you listen. Give every speaker the respect, openness, and support you would desire.

Support the Speaker

This might sound strange, but as an audience member, you are in a position to do more than just listen openly to a speaker; you can also support the speaker's attempts to communicate with you. This doesn't mean that you have to agree with the speaker's message. It does mean, however, that you can focus your attention on the speaker, smile your acknowledgement of his efforts, and nod occasionally with statements you agree with or find interesting. You don't have to stand up and cheer, but you can support any speaker with your eye contact and smile. You'd be surprised at the large number of audience members who don't support a speaker in any observable way, even when they agree with what he is saying. So put some effort into consciously supporting every speaker. Your efforts will be noticed and appreciated by the speaker. In fact, your support might be remembered by the speaker long after his words have fallen silent.

> *The first duty of love is to listen.*
> —ERICH FROMM

Identify Specific Purpose and Main Points

The purpose of public speaking is for the speaker to communicate a message to the audience. As an audience member, your willingness and ability to identify the specific purpose and main points of a speech are among your primary responsibilities as you listen to the speaker's words.

Your first goal is to discover the specific purpose or theme of the speech. Usually the speaker will state the specific purpose in the introduction of the speech. The title of the speech often provides the central idea or purpose of the presentation. Whether the specific purpose is clearly stated or implicit in the body of the speech, your goal as a listener is to ask yourself the question, "What is the central idea or specific purpose of this speech?" This should be your focus of attention, especially during the introduction of the speech.

Once you've identified the specific purpose, you should try to recognize the main points of the speech. These are the three or four main ideas or reasons the speaker uses to develop the body of the speech in an attempt to inform or persuade the audience. The main points are usually previewed in the introduction and reviewed in the conclusion. In the body of the speech, the speaker might also identify each main point by stating transitions that are clearly pointed out or numbered. For instance, the speaker might say, "Now my second point is . . .," or "The third reason is . . ." Numbered transitions make the identification of main points easy.

In the event that there are no clearly stated transitions, you can ask yourself questions such as, "What am I supposed to know, think, or do because I listened to this speech?" "What are the main categories of information the speaker is presenting?" or "What are the main reasons the speaker is providing?" You can also ask, "What supporting material or information is the speaker giving for each point?" to discover details and examples that develop the speech.

Recognize Nonverbal Cues

You will listen more effectively if you attend to the nonverbal cues of the speaker, because the messages given by the speaker can be communicated as much by the speaker's tone of voice, facial expressions, and body movement as by the words themselves. In fact, many times we tend to rely more on the nonverbal cues of the speaker than the verbal content when we interpret the communication of others. The speaker's nonverbal cues should match and reinforce her verbal communication. If the speaker is telling her audience that they'll enjoy volunteering as a Big Sister, her tone of voice and facial expressions should reinforce her words. She should be smiling and speaking with enthusiasm and conviction. But if she's speaking with a frown on her face and in a monotone voice, you might question her sincerity and conviction. A speaker's nonverbal cues will provide important information that you must interpret and weigh as you listen.

Take Notes

Another important way you can build a bridge to better listening is to take notes on the speech. Note taking can be an active way to become more involved in the listening process. Here are some guidelines for effective note taking.

First, limit your note taking to only the important points of a speech, such as the specific purpose, main and subpoints, and significant or interesting details of the speech. Don't feel obligated to write down every word of the speech. Second, use your own words. Don't get hung up on trying to get the exact wording or phrasing. Paraphrase and summarize what you think the speaker is attempting to communicate. You'll recall the information more readily if you write it down in your own words.

Third, use some form of outlining or bullet point organization when taking notes. Use one word or short phrases for the bullet or outline points. It saves time when writing and is visually easier to comprehend and recall when reviewing your notes later. Fourth, if you fall behind in your note taking, skip a few lines and resume taking notes on what the speaker is currently saying. You can always go back and fill in the missing information if you can remember it. If not, don't worry. You can't remember everything. But it's important to follow the speaker and not get left behind. Just the main points, remember? You don't want to spend your entire time as a listener with your head buried in your notebook. Enjoy the speech. See the speaker. Pay attention and show your support and appreciation by maintaining eye contact, smiling, and nodding your head in acknowledgment every once in a while. There's more to life than taking notes.

Identify Personal Benefits

The final way you can become a more effective listener is to be personally invested in the speech. That is, ask yourself questions such as "How can this speech topic make me a better person?" "How will this speech improve my life?" or "How can I use this speech to be beneficial to others?" Fundamental questions such as these will enable you to become more involved in the speech and in the speaker, because you will frame the event as an opportunity for self-improvement and improving the lives of others. This might be the highest calling of every speaker—to make this life and this world just a little better because of an attempt to communicate a message of significance to the audiences. And as an audience member, your highest calling might be to discover how any speech might make you a better person.

> *The most basic of all human needs is the need to be understood.*
> —KARL MENNINGER

6.4 The Benefits of Listening

Now that we've examined the process of listening, let's explore some of the benefits of listening that you will experience in the public speaking classroom. Some of these benefits include learning about new topics, appreciating others, evaluating speeches, becoming a better speaker, and being good to others.

Learning about New Topics

One of the most obvious benefits of listening in a public speaking course is learning about a vast array of topics that will be presented by the other students in the class. Not only will you be given the opportunity to share topics that interest you, but 20 to 30 other people will be given the same opportunity to share their interests and passions as well. In a sense, it's like attending a wonderful potluck meal every time your public speaking class has speeches, getting a taste of what other folks like to cook up and enjoy in their lives. The topics will surprise, fascinate, and even inspire you. Their speeches might make you cheer, shed a tear, and maybe even motivate you to try an activity you would never have dreamed of doing just minutes before. To live a good life, we need to continue to learn new things and venture forth boldly as we get older. So keep an open mind and heart to the topics presented by others. They just might be some of the finest gifts you'll receive during this season of your life.

Appreciating Others

Not only will you be given the opportunity to learn about new topics, you also will be given the chance to meet and appreciate new people. You might not have thought about this benefit when you enrolled in your public speaking course. Most likely, you were focused on the uncertainty and anxiety you imagined such a class might arouse in you. Yet one of the most surprising and deeply pleasing benefits of listening to other people share their interests and passions is the appreciation, camaraderie, and even friendly affection you will experience toward many of the other speakers in class.

Evaluating Speeches

Your ability to critically evaluate speeches is another benefit you will receive from listening to speeches. That doesn't mean you'll become mean spirited and criticize every speaker who delivers a speech. Instead, you will be able to examine and analyze the reasoning, information, and evidence presented in a speech. It's one thing to know if you're bored or engaged, or persuaded or unconvinced as you listen to a speech. But it's quite another thing to know the reasons a speech held your attention or motivated you to action. Your ability to know what to look for and how to analyze what is being said will give you the knowledge and confidence that your responses to speeches are based on more than just your emotional reactions to the speaker's delivery. Instead, your responses will be based on the critical evaluation of sound reasoning, reliable information, and trustworthy evidence. This ability to effectively evaluate what you hear will serve you well for the rest of your life.

Becoming a Better Speaker

Not only will you learn about new topics, have a greater appreciation for other people, and sharpen your analytical skills, but you will also become a better speaker yourself by listening to other speakers. Paying careful attention to the delivery, content, and organization presented by the other students in class will enable you to incorporate these same strengths into your own speaking. We become better skateboarders by skateboarding with those who are more skilled than us. We become better tennis players by playing tennis with those who can show us a thing or two. The same holds true for public speaking. Just by watching more skilled and talented speakers, we are influenced, encouraged, and even inspired to do better ourselves. That's why it's usually a good idea to spend time with friends whose character and faith you admire, whose generosity and warmth you appreciate, and whose maturity and trustworthiness you respect. You become like those you associate with over time, so select your friends

> *There are no gifted or ungifted. There are only those who give and those who withhold.*
> —MARTIN BUBER

carefully. In their attitudes, beliefs, and behaviors, you could be catching glimpses into your own future.

Being Good to Others

Just as a speaker can have an effect upon the audience, the audience, in turn, can influence the speaker. This fact is one of the most important lessons an audience member can learn. As a listener, you can make a difference in how the speaker feels about his presentation and even how he feels about himself long after the speech has ended. You can be good to the speaker.

You might not think of yourself as having a great deal of influence over a speaker when you're sitting in the audience. But you certainly do. If you doubt your power to influence the speaker, try smiling really big the next time you catch the eye of the speaker and see what happens. Flash your smile four or five times during the speaker's presentation and see the result. Most likely, you'll get an almost confused smile from the speaker in return. You might even get a smile of appreciation, especially if the rest of the audience isn't being supportive or responsive.

Another way you can have a positive influence on a speaker is to offer verbal and nonverbal encouragement before she goes up to speak. If you're sitting next to the speaker, you can pat her on the shoulder when she gets up to speak or give her the "thumbs up" sign if she's seated farther away. You can always say something positive and encouraging if you're within speaking range, such as "Do a great job!" or "You'll do fine!" as the speaker approaches the podium.

You can also be good to the speaker after the speech has been delivered. As the speaker returns to her seat, you can say, "I loved your speech!" or "You did a fine job!" It's also an encouragement to shake her hand or pat her on the back if she's taking her seat next to you. As an audience member, you can be good to a speaker before, during, and after the speech. Most of the time, the audience politely listens to each speaker and offers mild applause, but you can offer more. You can be good to any speaker by choosing to invest extra effort to acknowledge, encourage, and cheer the speaker on. Many listeners regard their role of an audience member as passive and receptive, but you can enlarge the role of the listener to include acknowledgment, support, and even inspiration to the speaker. You can choose to be good to others.

COMMUNICATION ACTIVITIES
PERSONAL ACTIVITIES

1. **Effective listeners you know**
   On a sheet of paper, identify three individuals whom you consider effective listeners—people who withhold evaluation and let you share your ideas and emotions. List specific behaviors that each person has demonstrated. If possible, thank each of the individuals for his or her positive contribution to your life.

2. **Communicating in other cultures**
   Ask an individual from a different cultural background about his or her listening behaviors and attitudes. How do these behaviors and attitudes differ from your

own? How are they similar? How did you feel about communicating with a person from a different cultural background about his or her listening behaviors and beliefs?

3. **Seeing your communication improvements**

On a sheet of paper, list three specific ways you can improve your listening. How do you feel about each behavior? How can each improvement change your impact on the speakers you will listen to in the future?

CLASS ACTIVITIES

1. **Reporting audience behavior**

Have one student stand in front of the class and simply report verbally what the audience is doing at the moment. Observations such as, "I see you smile," "I see you nodding your head," and "I hear you laughing" will make the student aware of the audience without having to memorize a speech or be concerned about effective delivery. The purpose of the activity is to encourage the speaker to pay attention to the audience. Have five students volunteer to stand and report audience behaviors for only 60 seconds each. As a class, discuss your thoughts and feelings about this activity.

2. **Cheering on the speaker**

Have one student stand in front of the class and give a short 60-second impromptu speech about one achievement he or she has experienced. As the speaker talks, have the audience spontaneously cheer, clap, or shout something positive to the speaker. Have five different students volunteer for this activity. As a class, discuss your thoughts and feelings about this activity.

3. **Listening to a loved one**

Take your mother, father, or friend out for dessert (you buy of course) and ask questions about life, love, and their pursuit of happiness during this lifetime. The goal of the time together is for you to be a good listener. Focus your attention on listening, not telling your own story. Paraphrase important points and keep the focus on the speaker. Remember, you're the listener. What was it like to focus your efforts and energy on listening to someone you love? What was his or her response to your improved listening?

Chapter 7

DELIVERING YOUR SPEECH
BEING YOURSELF

LEARNING OBJECTIVES

After reading this chapter, you should be able to:

7.1 Explain three characteristics of good delivery

7.2 Summarize the elements of good delivery

7.3 Explain some guidelines for speech practice

7.4 Discuss the speaker evaluation list of questions

7.5 Explain the concept of delivery between speeches

7.6 Identify seven ways to use social media to increase delivery effectiveness

7.7 Explain how to take the opportunity to view your speech

Mike enrolled in a public speaking course during his first semester at the University of California at Santa Barbara. As a freshman, he was surprised to discover that the majority of students in the class were seniors who had avoided the public speaking course until their final year of college.

There was one senior in the class named Ron, who spoke with authority. Mike would sit mesmerized by the sound of this voice. Ron would stand behind the podium, almost motionless, with only the slightest twist of the wrist or a subtle tilting of his head to accentuate a point or ease the audience into his next thought. What confidence! What command! Mike now had a role model for speaking.

As he practiced his third speech of the course, Mike spent hours trying to lower his voice to match Ron's deep, resonant musical notes. As he practiced his talk, his body wanted to dance, as it had during the first two speeches, but Mike restricted his movements, so he could match Ron's subtle and almost aloof gestures and posturing. As he practiced, Mike became more and more excited. His practice was paying off. He was speaking and moving just like Ron. It was working.

Mike's third speech, however, was a bomb. He didn't really know what had happened that morning in class when he got up to speak. His voice was deep like Ron's. His posture was motionless like Ron's. And his gestures were as subtle as any Ron had presented. In fact, Mike felt like he was Ron! But something wasn't right.

It wasn't until after class that Michelle, one of the other students, came up to Mike in the hallway and said, "I liked the 'friendly' Mike more." That's all she had to say. Michelle liked the "friendly" Mike more. She liked the old Mike, and not his imitation of Ron.

Mike took Michelle's comment to heart, and two weeks later he delivered his next speech in a more relaxed and conversational tone of voice. He talked and moved naturally. He was being himself and not acting like somebody else. And it felt right. This was one of the most important lessons Mike learned in his public speaking class—to be himself by speaking naturally.

7.1   Characteristics of Good Delivery

The content of your speech is what you say. Delivery is how you say it. Delivery is the overall "who" that you present to the audience, not the "what" that you say. Delivery is more than just the volume, rate, and pitch of your voice and the way you enunciate words. It includes your appearance, posture, body movement, hand gestures, eye contact, and facial expressions. In other words, *delivery is all of the nonverbal communication you express to your audience when you speak.*

> *Naturalness and simplicity are the truest marks of distinction.*
> —SOMERSET MAUGHAM

The adage "It's not what you say, but how you say it" merits serious reflection, especially in light of current research. Studies have shown that nonverbal communication has a greater impact than verbal communication when we receive and interpret messages. One such study asserts that only 7 percent of our emotional response to another person is determined by the verbal component of what is said, whereas 93 percent of our response is shaped by the speaker's nonverbal behavior!

What does this mean to you as a public speaker? Obviously, it suggests plenty. The most thoroughly researched and well-organized speech will have little impact on an audience if the speaker's delivery lacks a conversational quality, a desire to communicate, and speaker naturalness.

Enlarged Conversational Quality

The majority of impressive professional speakers you have observed in person or heard on radio or television were speakers who probably sounded more like formal orators whose voices boomed rather than whispered, whose gestures painted grandiose scenes, and whose bodies illustrated every phrase. Often, these speakers were addressing large audiences, and such delivery might have been appropriate for the occasion. But for our public speaking purposes, the most effective speaking style is an enlarged conversational quality.

An *enlarged conversational quality* of speaking means talking with the same naturalness and quality of voice you would use when speaking with another person, only enlarged just a little. To do this, you increase the volume of your conversational tone of voice so people in the back of the room can hear you, and you expand your gestures and movements a bit so all the audience can see them. The primary goal of using an enlarged conversational quality is that your audience will get the feeling that you are talking to them in a natural fashion, not talking at them with calculated and rehearsed gestures.

How can you speak with an enlarged conversational quality when your body stiffens, your hands freeze, and your voice tightens even at the thought of addressing an audience? The most useful way to achieve this enlarged conversational quality while planning and practicing your speech is to imagine that you are talking to just *one* person.

See this person in your mind's eye as you prepare the wording of your outline and practice the delivery of your talk. Try practicing your speech with the mental image of someone you feel safe with. You don't need a photograph of the individual, only the mental image. If you can do this successfully, you will begin to acquire the correct conversational tone.

Desire to Communicate

It's been referred to as "speaker directness," "speaker presence," "focus," "love for the audience," and "immediacy." We'll simply refer to it as the speaker's *desire to communicate*. This desire to communicate is the feeling the audience senses when a speaker really wants to be there sharing her message. The audience knows the speaker really desires to communicate with them. She wants to be there, and not somewhere else. The speaker is not forced to talk; she wants to talk.

With this desire to communicate, the speaker also communicates an awareness of and a sensitivity to her audience. The speaker's eyes are focused on the audience, not on her notes. She is aware of the audience's feedback and is sensitive to their responses. They get the sense that she sees them, feels them, and is with them in body and spirit.

This sounds like a description of the behavior of someone who loves you—the immediacy, the focus, the concern, and the sensitivity. No, you're not required to fall in love with your audience; however, you are encouraged to forget yourself and focus your attention, your thinking, and your energy on being there with your audience and showing your desire to communicate with them.

Ideally, you are a speaker who wants to be there sharing with the audience. They may soon forget most of your words, but they will remember you and your desire to communicate.

Speaker Naturalness

There's an old Jewish proverb that wisely asks the question, "If you can't be yourself, who can you be?" A common and disturbing problem that prevents us from living a free and healthy life is our inclination to try to act, think, and be like someone else— awkward attempts to be someone we are not. Granted, imitation is one of the basic tools in learning, whether for language acquisition or writing style. But as a template for living, it can be hazardous.

When Mike was trying to imitate Ron, he was uncomfortable and awkward. For 18 years, Mike had spoken like Mike. He had talked and behaved in a manner that was natural for him and no one else. Mike was comfortable with the way he communicated. His voice may not have been as deep as Ron's, but it was friendly and warm. His gestures may not have been as smooth as Ron's, but they were expressive. And his body movement wasn't as controlled as Ron's, but it showed his enthusiasm and desire to communicate.

Over the years, Mike has improved the quality of his voice, the smoothness of his gestures, and the movement of his body. And so will you. But Mike is funda-mentally the same speaker he was back then. The big difference now is that Mike has come to appreciate and develop his own natural speaking style. He isn't trying to be someone else. And neither should you.

> *The only time you touch the hearts of your audience is when you're being yourself.*
> —BURL IVES

No one else in the world speaks exactly as you do. And no one else in the world feels, acts, or thinks exactly as you do either. Your individuality is what makes you, you. That's what makes life so stimulating and excit-ing—the differences, not the similarities. Perhaps your individuality or naturalness is the most "precious possession" you can share with another person.

As you speak to your audience, let them see the real you. Don't hide behind the voice of someone else. Don't disguise the rhythms of your gestures. And don't conceal your body's true dance. The audience has you for only a few minutes of their lives; let them hear the real you, not someone else.

"If you can't be yourself, who can you be?"

7.2 Elements of Good Delivery

Now that we've examined the three characteristics of good delivery, we can look at its specific elements. Those elements include your body, gestures, eye contact, facial expressions, breathing, and vocal characteristics.

Body

Your body communicates a great deal about you to others. The first thing your audi-ence will notice about you is your overall appearance as you step up to the podium or take center stage. Your appearance in terms of dress and grooming will have a signifi-cant impact on an audience.

A speaker's attire can enhance or detract from the effectiveness of the presenta-tion. Somewhat formal dress can often increase a speaker's credibility with an audi-ence, whereas flamboyant, shabby, or enticing attire can actually distract, annoy, and even anger the audience. You don't necessarily have to suit up in a tux or evening gown, but you should carefully and thoughtfully consider the audience and the occa-sion and dress accordingly.

Grooming should also be an important consideration when preparing for your talk. A hot shower and just a splash of cologne or perfume will not only enhance your appearance but also make you feel better about yourself.

Once you're up there at the podium, your audience will check out your overall *posture*. Before you begin speaking, *pause at least three seconds to center your weight evenly on your two feet*. Don't lean on one foot more than the other. Equal weight, that's what we want here. And your feet should not be spread more than shoulder's width. A little less would be fine. Keep your back straight, and square your shoulders to the audience. Don't aim a shoulder at the audience—square those shoulders.

Let your hands hang at your sides freely as you take your three-second pause before speaking. A common error made by novice speakers is that they don't pause and get set before speaking. They simply run up and begin talking nervously even before they reach the podium. That sends a loud message to the audience. It says the speaker is nervous, anxious, and literally out of control. Take those three seconds to center yourself. It will pay off for the remainder of your talk.

When an individual faces an audience, the normal response is to freeze—not move. But a rigid, motionless delivery style would be monotonous to watch for even a short period of time, and it will only serve to make you, the speaker, more tense and nervous. *Body movement* has been shown to attract the attention of an audience. You don't need to do cartwheels across the stage or backflips off the podium, but there are some body movements that are helpful in sustaining audience interest and emphasizing important points.

Speaking of podiums, try moving away and speaking from the side of the podium to communicate a more informal speaking style. This more informal and natural speaking style is beneficial in most speaking situations. If the audience can hear your voice without the use of the podium microphone, step away from the podium when you're speaking. This will give you more room for body movement and gestures.

You might also find it useful to walk two or three short steps to your right or left when you state a main-point transition or stress an important phrase in your talk. This is called *walking into your points*. This walking movement recaptures the audience's attention and visually reinforces the transition from one point to another. Walk slowly when you do this. Don't rush. Stroll slowly into your next point.

If you want to get more intimate with your audience, walk a few steps in their direction. Be careful not to fall off the stage, but stroll toward the audience. This movement works really well when you're giving the punch line to a joke or the climactic ending to a story. You can do just the opposite—that is, walk away from the audience—when you want to voice strong emotion. Just a few steps back is all you need.

A final word on body movement. Too much movement, unrelated movement, or repetitious movement can distract an audience. Use your body movement to direct attention and emphasize points during your talk. Use it carefully.

Gestures

Your *gestures* consist of your hand and arm movements during your speech. Use gestures to emphasize and express important ideas and emotions. The normal tendency for a beginning speaker, when facing an audience, is to cement her hands to the sides of the podium, clutch her hands either in front or in back of herself, or freeze them at her sides. This too can only serve to increase the speaker's anxiety. There are two excellent practice techniques you can use to loosen up your hands and arms.

The first one we'll call the *silent hula technique*. Just as a Hawaiian hula dancer does, you can practice

> *Movements are as eloquent as words.*
> —ISADORA DUNCAN

communicating passages or sections of your speech *without words*, using only your hands and arms to express the thoughts and feelings. It sounds silly, but it gets your mind off the words of the speech and refocuses your attention on your gestures. You'll be pleasantly surprised at how your hands come alive once you forget about the words and concentrate on the message.

The second technique for loosening up your hands and arms is called *catching rain*. Catching rain is exactly what it sounds like. Stand with both hands comfortably outstretched in front of you, with your palms up and your elbows at your sides. Then begin to recite your speech. The only rule with this practice technique is that your hands and arms cannot fall beneath your waist. As you speak, you will notice your arms will begin to move by themselves as you talk! It's like they have a life all their own. Small movements at first, but then more pronounced as you get into your talk. Who knows why it works. But once your mind is occupied with your mental chatter, it forgets about the hands and arms, and the body takes over. Sounds weird. But give it a try.

Eye Contact

The manner in which eye-contact behavior is interpreted varies from culture to culture. But in U.S. culture, you are expected to have direct eye contact if you are to be perceived as interested, honest, and credible. If not, you run the risk of being seen as uninterested, reticent, or even devious. When you speak to an audience, this principle holds true also.

Direct eye contact with your audience serves a variety of positive functions for the speaker. First, it establishes contact with the audience. How can a relationship be established if you don't even see them? Second, eye contact holds the attention of the audience. You don't need to look into the eyes of every one of your audience members to keep their attention, but spread your eye contact around the room. Look at the front, the back, and the sides. Don't get stuck on one section of the room. Avoid looking at your notes, the floor, or the ceiling. Third, eye contact is the best way to receive feedback from the audience. Do they look bored? Are they interested? Are they confused? All of these questions can be answered quickly and silently by glancing around the room. Finally, eye contact suggests honesty. The adage, "A person won't look you in the eye if he or she is lying," seems to be true in public speaking as well.

Facial Expressions

Research has found that once a relationship has been established, the face is the area at which most people look to observe and evaluate the emotional responses of another person. As a public speaker, your facial expressions are important in your communication. Although many of the audience members in the back rows may not be able to see your expressions in detail, all of your listeners will develop a sense of how you are feeling and who you are by your facial cues. In addition to your eye-contact behavior, your ability to use your mouth and face to emphasize, stress, and illustrate emotions cannot be overlooked.

Facial expressions and habits are one of the most difficult movements to change or modify, primarily because we are so unaware of them. Like the sound of our voice, our facial expressions have a life all their own, a life outside of our conscious aware-ness. We simply cannot see our face as we go about our daily life. Sure, we can view it in a mirror, a photograph, or even on videotape, but those are indeed brief moments. So our faces are literally strangers to us.

If you want to try something really unusual, stare at your face in a mirror for five minutes without looking away. No distractions. No one else in the room. Just look at your own face for five minutes. See what happens. The image in the mirror becomes almost unrecognizable after a few moments of studying the detail of your own face. Who are you, anyway?

Here's one specific suggestion for your facial expressions while you give your speech. Smile. This suggestion may sound trite, and yet it needs repeating. You need to smile. Did you know it takes less muscle effort to smile than to frown? No wonder we get so exhausted when we're frowning during our bad moods.

Smile during the first three seconds you're in front of your audience, as you get your posture centered. Even if you are going to present a very somber topic, you can still invest three seconds for smiling. It'll relax both you and your audience. You'll discover when you smile during this initial phase of the speech that you're more likely to loosen up and express a variety of emotions during the remainder of your talk.

> *Never bend your head.*
> *Hold it high. Look the*
> *world straight in the eye.*
> —HELEN KELLER

But what if you're not a smiler by nature, or you happen to be depressed that day? Fake it! Yes, fake it! Life's too short. You owe it to your audience to be "up" for your talk. You can frown for the rest of the day. But give your audience the best you have. This is not therapy; it's your speech, your gift to the audience. Make it a good one!

Breathing

An entire book could be written on the importance of breathing, but we're going to spend only three paragraphs stressing its pivotal role in making you an effective speaker. For starters, if you didn't breathe once during a five-minute speech, you'd most likely pass out, and maybe even die. How about that for being important? You could go through an entire five-minute talk and never once look at one person, give one ges-ture, state one transition, or wear a stitch of clothing, and not much would happen to you. Maybe speaking naked would cause something to happen, but overall, nothing much would. Yet without breathing for those five minutes, you die. It's that simple.

More than 2,000 years ago, Lao Tzu said, "It is not wise to rush about. Con-trolling the breath causes strain." Did you know that when you're frightened or anx-ious, you hold your breath? When you're speaking before an audience, you have a tendency to hold your breath. You see it in just about every beginning speaker. The rapid rate of speech. The run-on sentences, punctuated occasionally by huge gulps of air. Remember, even when you're under extreme stress, your body knows enough not to kill itself.

What can you do to breathe properly when speaking to an audience? Three things, really. First, begin breathing in deep, even breaths about a minute or two before you are called to speak. Don't hyperventilate and pass out. Just slow, deep, even breaths. Second, while you're smiling and centering your posture during the first three seconds in front of your audience, draw in three deep breaths while you're doing your "one thousand one, one thousand two, one thousand three." This will give you air to begin your speech. Third, breathe after each long sentence during your speech. Breathe from the stomach, not from the throat. Inhale with your stomach. Pause often during your speech. Pause long enough to inhale deeply and exhale completely. This will seem like an eternity when you're up in front of all those people, but it will save you. It will save not only your life but your speaking style as well.

Vocal Characteristics

There are six aspects of your voice worth mentioning here. Vocal characteristics are made up of rate, volume, pitch, inflection, enunciation, and vocal variety.

Your speaking *rate* is the speed at which you talk. It's generally measured in number of words per minute. The average speaking rate is about 110 to 130 words per minute. Some people speak more slowly, others more rapidly. If you speak too slowly, you run the risk of losing the attention of your audience. If you speak too quickly, you make it difficult for your audience to understand you. In addition, an extremely rapid rate of speech can annoy or irritate an audience. Find a rate of speech that is comfortable for you, but don't feel that it is best to stick to this speed. One of the marks of an experienced speaker is the ability to vary the speaking rate. The most common error is for the beginning speaker to speak too rapidly. In that case, you should pause more after long sentences and phrases and take deep breaths. Another helpful aid is to occasionally mark in red the word "SLOW" on your note cards.

> *The human voice is the most beautiful musical instrument.*
> —JUDY COLLINS

Volume is the loudness of your voice. In public speaking, you have to speak loudly enough so that your listeners in the back row can hear you without straining. If the people in the back appear to be having difficulty, stop your talk and ask them if your voice can be heard. Speak louder if they can't hear you. A soft voice not only makes it difficult for the audience to listen to your speech, but it also can be interpreted as a sign of reticence, weakness, or fear.

If you discover that you need to develop more volume in your speaking, you might try practicing the *backyard yelling exercise*. You'll need a friend for this one. Anyone will do. Have your assistant sit in a chair in the backyard, in the parking lot of your apartment house, or anywhere you have 30 feet of free space where you won't get hit by traffic. Pace off about 30 feet between you and your assistant. Begin your speech. If your friend cannot hear you, have him raise his hand for you to increase your volume. Increase your volume, even if you feel as if you're screaming. Your assistant will lower his hand when he can hear you. This goes back and forth until you reach a volume that is loud enough for your assistant to hear from 30 feet. If you can pass this test, you'll be heard in any room.

Pitch refers to the highness or lowness of your voice. It can be thought of as the placement of your voice on a musical scale. Each individual has a natural pitch level. The movement of pitch either upward or downward from this natural pitch level is known as *inflection*. Inflection is used to give emphasis to certain words or phrases. A speaker who never varies her pitch (inflection) is said to speak in a monotone fashion. A monotone voice is a boring voice after a few minutes.

One way to get inflection into your voice is to emphasize important words in your sentences. Read aloud the sentence that follows while emphasizing a different word with each reading. Begin with the emphasis on the first word, and read the sentence. Then read the sentence again, with the emphasis on the second word. Repeat the process until you've read through the sentence seven times.

I would love to see you again.

The meaning of the sentence changes with each different reading, doesn't it? Inflection is a powerful verbal tool in speech emphasis, and it is one of the most effective cures for a monotone delivery.

One last method for changing a monotone voice is called the *singing exercise.* You simply sing your words as you practice your speech. In a standing position, deliver your speech by singing every word. Make up a melody as you go along. Don't sing to the melody of a song you know. Just let the words and melody flow. It may feel foolish initially, but who cares? The point is to break your monotone habit.

Enunciation consists of articulation and pronunciation. *Articulation* is defined as the ability to pronounce the letters of a word correctly, whereas *pronunciation* is the ability to pronounce the entire word correctly. There are three common causes of articulation problems: sound substitution, slurring, and the omission of sounds.

> *I have found that if you love life, life will love you back.*
> —ARTHUR RUBINSTEIN

Sound substitution happens often in speaking. Many of us say "budder" instead of "butter," or "dat" instead of "that." In the first case, we substituted the sound of "d" for "t," and in the second example, we substituted the sound of "d" for "th."

Slurring is usually caused by a rapid rate of speech or a running together of words. We often say "I'll getcha a hot dog," instead of "I will get you a hot dog." Be aware of slurring your words when you speak.

The final cause of articulation problems is the *omission of sounds.* We sometimes say "flowin'" instead of "flowing," or "singin'" instead of "singing." Don't get lazy when you pronounce your words.

The final characteristic of your voice is *vocal variety.* Vocal variety refers to the variance or range you give to the rate, volume, and pitch of your speech. You'll recall that inflection is the variance or change in pitch. This gives your voice vocal variety. Variance in your volume and rate also plays an important role in keeping your speech interesting and lively. Vocal variety in your pitch, volume, and rate prevents a monotone speech delivery, and nothing puts your audience to sleep faster than a monotone voice.

7.3 Speech Practice

No one is born with public speaking skills, no matter what you think. The outstanding speakers are those individuals who invest countless hours of practice time improving their skills. Nothing comes without a price.

This book isn't worth a penny if you don't actually take the time and effort to practice the skills that we have been discussing up to now. The choice is ultimately yours. It's always yours. When you practice your speech, consider these guidelines for a productive practice session.

Complete Your Outline before You Practice

Begin your practice sessions only after you have typed your final outline. Read through your outline a number of times so you become familiar with the content and structure. Then make your 4 × 6-inch note card of main points and key words so you can quickly refer to it during your practice sessions.

Choose a Private Practice Site

Select a room in your house or apartment that will give you adequate space to walk three or four steps in any direction. Don't practice in your car during a rush-hour commute. Select a real room that is free of interruptions and distractions such as telephones, children running around, a noisy television, or even Grandma knitting quietly in the corner. After you've selected the room, set up three chairs, side by side, to represent your audience. You should be standing about eight feet away from the chairs, facing in their direction. Remember to have about three or four steps of clear space all around you so you can walk into your transitions.

Practice in a Standing Position

There are people who practice their speeches in a prone position, in a sitting position, and even in the lotus position. But you will be standing when you deliver your speech to your audience, so you should be standing when you are practicing. If you won't practice from a standing position, you might as well just squirt lighter fluid on this book right now and set a match to it. Please practice your speech in a standing position. Anything short of this is a sin.

Loosen Up before You Begin Practicing

As you stare at the three chairs representing your audience, get a mental picture of one of your favorite people in the world sitting in the chair on your left. Don't worry about the chair on your right. As you visualize that person, begin your deep breathing. Breathe for a minute or two with your eyes open. Deep, even breaths from your stomach. Shake your hands vigorously at your sides. Keep breathing. Roll your head to the right a couple of times and then to the left a few more times. Sing a song or just talk gibberish for a minute or so, starting out with a low volume and then going up in volume until you almost reach a shouting intensity. Keep this up until you feel like you're loose and ready to go.

Practice in Small Increments Initially

Practice your introduction all the way through two or three times until you get it right. Then move on to your first main point. Practice it by itself two or three times until you're satisfied with your command of the material. Then move on to the second main point. Continue the process until you've completed the conclusion. Just one section at a time. Small increments for now. Once you've moved through the entire speech, section by section, go back to the introduction and first main point, and see if you can get through both of those parts combined. Try it again

> *There is no such thing as an insignificant improvement.*
> —TOM PETERS

until you feel satisfied. Then add the second main point to your cluster. Then add the third main point. And finally the conclusion. There, you've got the entire speech.

Time Your Speeches

A stopwatch is a wonderful aid when timing your speeches, but any watch with a sweep second hand will do. Time your small-increment practice sessions. You should be able to figure out roughly how long each section should be. As you practice and check your time, you might have to add a little here and cut a little there. But that's what this is all about. When you are comfortable with each section, time the entire speech and edit your talk so that it's within the required time limit. With timed practices, you should know within 30 seconds either way how long your final presentation will be. Now that's preparation!

Practice the Entire Speech Five Times

At one practice session, practice your entire speech two times. A few hours later or the next day, practice your speech another two times all the way through, referring to your note cards only when necessary. On the morning you are scheduled to speak, practice your speech only once all the way through. And that's it. No more practice. If you practice your speech too often, you run the risk of sounding memorized. Five times, no more.

Don't Practice in Front of a Mirror

You won't be speaking into a mirror when you deliver your speech, so don't practice with one. Mirrors have a tendency to confuse the speaker. They can distract more than help. So don't even think of practicing in front of one.

Record Your Practice Sessions

If you're really serious about conducting practice sessions that are worthwhile, invest $30 and pick up the cheapest audiocassette recorder you can find and record your five full-speech practice sessions. This takes a little guts and some money, but there's nothing quite like it for evaluating your performance and progress. Don't practice with a videotape unit just yet. It'll overwhelm you with visual stimuli, and you won't be focusing on your speech patterns. Save the videotape for later speeches. For now, just the audiocassette, okay? When listening to your recording, check for naturalness, the desire to communicate, and an enlarged conversational quality. Also check your voice for proper volume, rate, pitch, and vocal variety. Did you have too many verbal pauses, such as "ah," "um," and "you know"? Observe your energy level. Did you sound enthusiastic or dead? See how helpful this $30 recorder can be in your speech practice regimen?

Evaluate Your Speech

Before you deliver your speech to an audience, evaluate one of your practice speeches for content, organization, and delivery. Your practice speech can be videotaped for your viewing, or have a friend watch your practice session. Either way, have your friend complete the evaluation form on the following page, or complete it yourself. Don't limit yourself to the objectives contained in the list. Feel free to add your own points. The important thing is for you to critically evaluate your speech before you present it to your audience.

Speech Day Checkout

On the day of your talk, practice your speech one time all the way through. Take a hot shower and dab on your cologne or perfume. Smell good for yourself, if for nobody else. Don't eat a heavy meal or really greasy food three hours before you're scheduled to talk. It'll make you sleepy. And no alcohol anytime before you speak. Arrive early to the auditorium or room so you can get a feel for the layout, the atmosphere, the podium, and the microphone setup. Also, find out where the restroom is, a telephone if you need it, and where you will be sitting before you speak. Do all this *before* people begin arriving. As your speaking time nears, try to keep to yourself. This is not the time for idle chitchat. Keep to yourself and begin breathing deeply and evenly from your stomach. Glance over your key-word note card once more. Wait quietly until your name is announced. Then slowly get up from your chair, breathing evenly and deeply. You're now ready to walk to the podium. Aren't you glad you practiced? Have fun. And remember to breathe from the stomach, deeply. . . , evenly. . . .

Be Gentle on Yourself

No matter what happens, be gentle on yourself. It's only a speech! A hundred years from now, it won't matter all that much. What really counts is your decision to attempt a speech. Go get 'em.

7.4 Speaker Evaluation

CONTENT
Topic appropriate to the audience?

Topic specific enough/limited in scope?

Adequate development of main points:

    Human-interest material?

    Statistics/expert testimony?

    Statistics/expert testimony documented?

Vivid, descriptive language?

Visual aids clarified/developed points?

Audience questions answered effectively?

ORGANIZATION

Introduction

    Attention getter?

    Purpose of the speech stated?

    Preview of main points?

    Goodwill established?

Body

    Transitions clearly stated?

    Internal transitions?

    Recap of each point before transition?

Conclusion

    Summary of main points?

    Final-thought device?

Delivery

    Appropriate dress for occasion?

    Get set before speaking?

    Straight posture?

    Relaxed, natural body movement?

    Direct eye contact?

    Expressive gestures?

    Fluid, articulate speech?

    Adequate volume?

    Adequate vocal variety?

7.5 Your Delivery between Speeches

Academy Award-winning actor Tom Hanks once observed, "Anyone can be nice when the spotlight's on, but what happens when the lights go down?" In this chapter, we've examined ways to improve your delivery—how you communicate nonverbally during a speech. But it's also important to raise the questions, "What do you communicate to the other students between your speeches?" "How do you act before and after your 5- or 10-minute speech?" "Are you nice 'when the lights go down' and your speech is but a memory?"

Some speakers will spend enormous amounts of time and energy trying to improve and perfect their public speaking delivery skills, yet pay little or no attention to their behavior in class before and after they deliver their speech. As we conclude this section on speaker delivery, let's reflect for a few moments on what nonverbal communication messages you give to others before and after your speech.

Do you attend class regularly? Or do you miss every third or fourth meeting? Do you arrive to class on time or even a few minutes early? Or do you rush in late more times than not? Do you smile at others before, during, and after class? Or do you frown or smirk as you glance around the room? Do you listen attentively when the instructor talks or students speak? Or do you read your notes from another class, check your cell phone messages, or whisper to your neighbor? Do you encourage speakers nonverbally during their presentations by maintaining eye contact, nodding, smiling, applauding, and asking questions after the speech? Or do you check out and stare out the window, play with your pen, or fall asleep? Do you encourage and compliment others in class? Or do you roll your eyes, give disgusted sighs, and moan about every assignment? Do you interact with others briefly before and after class in supportive and friendly ways? Or are you the last one in and the first one out of the room? In other words, are you enlarging or diminishing to others by your behavior before and after you deliver your speech?

Sure, you can learn to be pleasant, positive, and poised when the spotlight is on you, but what do you communicate to others when the lights go down and you return to your seat? During the 50 hours of a semester class, less than one hour of your time is spent speaking in front of the audience. What do you communicate during the other 49 hours? Are you enlarging or diminishing? That's a delivery question worth considering.

7.6 Using Social Media to Increase Delivery Effectiveness

Social media can provide you with a variety of ways to make your speech more relevant, your interactions with your audience more rewarding, your information more accessible, and your speech available to the world.

Advertising Your Speech

Social media is an easy yet effective way to advertise your speech as well. If you're speaking at an event that is open to the public, you can communicate the details to your followers on Twitter or your friends on Facebook. You can provide the name of the event, speech topic, location, date, and time of your presentation. Be sure to include any other helpful information such as special considerations for the occasion, dress code, admission price, and parking cost.

Welcoming Your Audience

In addition to welcoming your audience in person, you can tweet a welcome to your followers or post a welcome to your friends on Facebook. It's always a nice touch to receive a brief message of welcome a few minutes before you are being introduced. If you're giving the speech to a public speaking class, make sure you send your message before the class is scheduled to begin. No matter where you give your speech, a welcome on social media will bring a smile to the faces of your audience as well as bring one to your own. Go beyond what is expected.

Interacting With Your Audience

If your speaking event has the ability to scroll a live social media comment feed behind the speaker, you can check to see if the audience has any questions or comments that you might want to address. This gives you the opportunity to be more sensitive and flexible, modifying if necessary the direction of your speech to more appropriately meet the interests or needs of your audience. Sometimes it's fun just to see insightful or humorous comments flashed upon the screen or television monitor beside you.

However, the live feed does come with some drawbacks. It can be a distraction to both the speaker and audience. Inappropriate comments can detract from your speech and the speaking occasion. And in some instances, the live feed can compete directly with the speaker, serving to upstage the presenter. But if used properly, by both speaker and audience, a live social media feed can be impressive and memorable.

Sharing Your Materials

One of the most generous uses of online media is to share the content of your speech with others. After delivering your speech, you can post links to your PowerPoint presentation, notes, or other material you presented during your speech. By making your material available online, your audience won't need to take notes. What a gift to the audience and to the speaker. It frees everyone up to focus on the speech. Remember to post your material in PDF form so that your material cannot be modified. You might also consider labeling or watermarking your name discretely on every page of your PDF document, picture, or PowerPoint page to discourage plagiarism or copyright infringement. You can also provide your e-mail address or domain name on the first page of your document so people can contact you.

Sharing Your Speech

YouTube is one of the easiest and most effective ways to share your speech with the world. Have one of your friends record your speech on their mobile device and upload the presentation to YouTube. Before your audience's applause ends, your presentation can be broadcast to the world. Just think of it: your grandmother in Ohio or an interested viewer in Hong Kong will be able to view your speech in all its glory.

Learning from Your Speech

In addition to posting your speech online for enjoyment, enlightenment, or fame, YouTube can also provide an opportunity for soliciting feedback on the effectiveness of your content, organization, and delivery. If you're enrolled in a public speaking class, your instructor or fellow students can view your speech and give informed and helpful feedback to improve your speaking skills.

Thanking Your Audience

One final way you can use social media is to thank your audience for attending your speech. You can tweet a brief thank you to your followers or post a thank-you to your friends on Facebook. You can even e-mail a thank-you to your audience members if you have their e-mail addresses. It's amazing how impactful a simple message of thanks can be. Show gratitude in all that you do.

7.7 Take the Opportunity to View Your Speech

If you're fortunate enough to have your public speaking instructor or someone at your speaking event record your speech, count your blessings! Here are some suggestions that will help you get the most from your viewing of your speech.

Actually View the Speech

Don't chicken out. View your speech! Even when speakers are given the opportunity to view their speeches, they will often skip the opportunity. Be strong. See what your audience sees.

View the Speech Alone

Before you push the Play button, however, find a place where you can watch your speech alone.

This is no time for family members or even a best friend to be by your side as you watch. They can throw everything off balance. You'll be more concerned with their responses to your speech than with your own responses. So watch the speech by yourself. Here are some helpful suggestions when viewing your presentation.

View the Speech WITHOUT Sound the First Time. Turn off the sound on the playback monitor before you hit the Start button. Yes, TURN OFF THE SOUND. This might sound strange, but an initial silent viewing, without the distraction of your voice, will provide greater psychological and emotional freedom to actually see what's on the screen.

It's quite an experience. Don't judge, evaluate, or even think. Just close your mouth, open your eyes, and observe during this first viewing. Watch the entire speech. No notes. No judgments. Just keep your eyes open until the speech ends.

View the Speech WITH Sound the Second Time. Now you're ready to view your speech WITH sound, so turn up the dial on the sound control. Grab your notepad and pencil and push the Play button a second time.

It's different with sound isn't it? Your voice will most likely sound higher than you imagined because the voice you "hear" when you talk is lowered somewhat by the density of your head. No fooling. The stuff in your head actually lowers the perceived pitch of your voice, so remain calm if you don't sound as deep and wonderful as you thought. Hang in there. You'll get used to your voice after a minute or two.

Look for 15 Positive Things

As you watch and listen to your speech this second time, take notes on all of the positive behaviors you see and hear. Look for what you're doing well. Seek out the positive. Look for what's working. Our natural tendency is to immediately see our weaknesses and the negatives. But that's not your goal. Your goal is to write down at least 15 positive things you notice about the content, organization, and delivery of your speech.

Here are a few positive things you can begin your list with, just in case you have difficulty seeing what you did well:

You showed up.
You dressed for the occasion.
You faced the audience.
You spoke.
You spoke loud enough to be heard.
You spoke on a topic.
You remained at the podium and didn't run out of the room.
You stood on your feet and didn't fall over.
You kept your eyes open.

These behaviors might seem too obvious or even a bit silly, but they will help you focus on the positive. In fact, begin by looking for the obvious. Look for the little things. Give yourself credit. After jotting down a few of these behaviors, write down other behaviors you see and hear that are listed in your instructor's speaker evaluation form or in the speaker evaluation form offered earlier in this chapter.

What about your weaknesses or the behaviors that you want to improve? Sure, there's always room for improvement. But limit the number of behaviors you want to correct or improve to only one or two per speech.

Of course you might have more than one or two behaviors that are in need of improvement, but don't overwhelm yourself with negatives. Limit your list of improvements to one or two and no more. This limited focus will not only provide you with a manageable number of goals to work on for your next speech, but, more important, it will also concentrate your attention on the positive and not the negative. That's a good suggestion for viewing your speech, as well as living your life.

COMMUNICATION ACTIVITIES
PERSONAL ACTIVITIES

1. **Loosening up**

   Find a large room, an empty meadow, or a deserted beach. Take off your shoes and socks (and anything else you feel comfortable removing) and simply dance for 60 seconds without thinking about dancing. Use your legs, hands, arms, head, butt, nose, and fingers. Just let your body move and dance. If you try this four or five times with an open mind and heart, you'll be amazed at how loose you become. Let go of all those tapes in your head demanding that you grow up and act your age! Whose voice is that, anyway? Just let go and have fun. Like being a kid again, huh? What was that like? How do you feel? Would you do this crazy dance again?

2. **Seeing an old friend**

   If you have access to a videotape recorder, record one of your speech practice sessions. Tape at least five minutes of one practice. Then replay the video *without sound*. It's important that you don't have sound. Without the sound, your body will "talk" to you. Look at what your body says. Watch all of you—the face, gestures, body, arms, legs, fingers, and eyes. What does this body tell you? How does this body move? Is this body happy? Sad? Stiff? Loose? What's going on with this body? Does it make a difference when you add sound? How does it feel when you black out the video portion and simply listen to your voice? What did you learn about yourself?

3. **The body in other cultures**

   Ask an individual from a different cultural background what his or her people's attitudes and behaviors are in regard to their bodies. Do they value and attempt to demonstrate expressive gestures when speaking? How do they feel about eye contact? Is it encouraged or discouraged? Is a conversational tone of voice appropriate for public speaking or is a more formal style valued? What do they see as unusual or inappropriate nonverbal communication behavior?

CLASS ACTIVITIES

1. **Group practice: expanding your delivery**

   Divide the class into groups of five or six students. Each student will be given an opportunity to practice a speech (that he or she has already outlined) using the silent hula, catching rain, and singing exercises presented in this chapter. For 30 seconds, each student will stand in front of the group and perform the silent hula as he or she presents (nonverbally) the introduction to a speech. After the entire group has completed the silent hula, each student will practice the catching rain technique for 60 seconds while delivering the first point of his or her speech to the group. And finally, each group member will sing 60 seconds of his or her second point. No fair talking! Only singing will count. What was this like to experiment with and expand your delivery skills? Be prepared to share your reactions to this group activity in class.

2. **Getting rid of the "ahs" and "ums"**

   "Ahs," "ums," and all other verbal pauses are really apologies for silence in this culture. It's as if we're embarrassed to have any silences in our speech. We need to apologize for not having something to say immediately, so we fill in the silence with "ahs" and "ums." Verbal pauses are distracting when they dominate our speech patterns. If you have trouble with them, try this exercise with a friend. Stand up in front of her and deliver your practice speech. When she notices you saying a verbal pause ("ah" or "um" or anything else), she simply smiles and raises her hand briefly. This signals to you that you have done it again—given an apology for silence. She doesn't have to verbally interrupt you. She only raises her hand. This is also her signal to you that it's okay to pause and think about what you're going to say. When you first try this, you'll find that your partner's hand will be going up quite a bit. But after a while, if you permit yourself to pause before you speak, her hand will be raised less and less. Share your reactions to this activity in class.

3. **Spending five minutes in silence**

   For a period of five minutes, each student is to roam about the classroom and attempt to communicate with five fellow students WITHOUT USING

WORDS OR NOTES. In other words, every student in class will attempt to communicate nonverbally with five other students (about 60 seconds with each person) using posture, body movement, gestures, hand motions, eye contact, and facial expressions. No one is permitted to speak during the entire time. After the five minutes is up, return to your desks and discuss the experience. What was it like to communicate without words or notes? How might this experience help or improve your speaking delivery when you speak to an audience? What did you learn about yourself?

4. **Out-of-class speaker evaluation**

   Observe an out-of-class speaker and evaluate his or her effectiveness using the speaker evaluation form in this chapter, one provided by your instructor, or one you designed for this assignment. Observe a speaker in a formal speaking situation, such as a minister, politician, author, after-dinner speaker, or special occasion lecturer. Take notes as the speaker is talking, using your evaluation form as a guide. Write a report discussing the strengths and weaknesses of the speaker. Share your observations and insights with the class.

Chapter 8

INFORMING YOUR AUDIENCE
TEACHING OTHERS

LEARNING OBJECTIVES

After reading this chapter, you should be able to:

8.1 Explain the three goals of informative speaking

8.2 List some designs for informative speaking

8.3 Offer some suggestion for language use in informative speaking

8.4 Identify the types of informative speeches

8.5 Discuss ten ideas for the question-and-answer session

8.6 Explain the public speaker self-image scale

During the day, Building 7 at Campbell High School serves as the classroom for nearly 110 boys and girls in five auto mechanics and body repair classes. Each period, this large airplane hangar of a room echoes with the sounds of banging and clanging, buzzing and pounding. The students enroll in auto shop to learn the basic skills for a future trade or, more likely, because they didn't enjoy the math and science classes during their first two years of high school. Regardless of their motives, they all rush through the tall sliding metal doors of Building 7 when the bell sounds, laughing and shoving as they scurry to their next class.

Six nights of the week, Building 7 lies dark, empty, and silent until 7:20 the next morning, when the auto shop teacher, Mr. Carl, unlocks the tall, silver sliding metal doors and flicks on the fluorescent lights, signaling the start of another noisy day in auto shop.

But tonight, Building 7 is transformed into a place of empowerment—a place where 11 women are learning to master their own lives in a small way and overcome some fears. These women are standing around the engine compartment of a 1987 Toyota Corolla, as Mr. Carl shows them how to change the oil and filter.

In a few moments, each woman will return to her car and begin the process of changing her own oil and filter as Mr. Carl walks among the students, answering their questions, correcting their mistakes, and congratulating their successes.

For the past six years, Mr. Carl has been teaching the adult education course entitled "Easy Car Maintenance for Women," and nearly 200 women have learned to maintain their own cars thanks to his instruction. The students grow to love this quiet, slow-talking, 74-year-old retired auto mechanic, who wears a white shirt and red bowtie under his dark blue Sears coveralls. They love the way he asks them about their kids during the 8:00 break, the way he pats them on the shoulder when they finish changing their oil, and the cookies he bakes himself for the one-night-a-week course. They grow to love this old man whose hands are scarred from years of working with tools, yet whose eyes sparkle in the fluorescent light.

Mr. Carl was once asked why he worked as a part-time teacher at an age when others are content to sit in retirement. "For over 50 years, I've worked as an auto mechanic," he replied, "and nearly all that time was spent in silence under car hoods. When I retired eight years ago, I felt the need to pass on my trade to others. I felt this strong desire to share my knowledge and skills with people before I died."

Through Mr. Carl's teaching, 200 women in and around the city of Campbell won't have to pay to have their oil and filter changed because they now possess the skill and knowledge to do it themselves. More important, these women can share their knowledge and skills with others and, thus, pass on the legacy of Mr. Carl.

> *Our highest calling is to pass our knowledge from generation to generation.*
> —W. S. GILBERT

Like Mr. Carl, your role as a public speaker will often be that of a teacher. You may not see yourself as a teacher like Mr. Carl, yet one of the primary responsibilities of a public speaker is to inform the audience: to impart knowledge; to show the audience new skills; to share information that is important, interesting, and maybe even life changing. With your words alone, you may literally change the lives of the audience by sharing information that is truly meaningful and enlarging.

Now, you will most likely not be giving speeches every day of your life, but the ever-increasing emphasis on information in our world will demand greater skills in your ability to send and receive information. Although some of this information will be delivered in written form, much of it will be orally transmitted.

How do you inform others? How do you give directions, describe a scene, demonstrate a process, explain a concept, define a word, or tell a story? These areas of communication involve sharing information with others. Those who can inform others effectively will experience greater success in their professional and personal lives than those who cannot. Although this chapter focuses on your public speaking skills, you will find its application useful in your daily interactions with others as well.

8.1 Goals of Informative Speaking

As an informative speaker, you face quite a challenge speaking before any audience. Some audiences are more receptive than others; and yet, each member of your audience needs to have his or her interest aroused, to understand what you are saying, and to remember the information after you've finished speaking. These are the three primary goals of any informative talk: to stimulate interest, increase understanding, and assist retention.

Stimulate Audience Interest

Your first goal of informative speaking is to arouse the interest of your audience. Without the successful completion of this first goal, the other two goals will not be accomplished. The old saying, "There are no uninteresting topics, just uninterested listeners," affirms the need for you to get your audience aroused.

An experienced instructor once advised a first-year teacher, "Forget all that stuff they taught you in graduate school. The first requirement of a good teacher is to keep the students awake. Everything else is secondary." The same holds true for public speaking. If your audience's interest is not adequately stimulated, the prospects for a successful speech are dim indeed.

If you present your information in ways that make it *relevant* or personally useful to your audience, you are more inclined to arouse and maintain their interest. This is where audience analysis really pays off. Study your audience's demographics, interests, knowledge, and attitudes before selecting the materials you will present and determine how you will adapt that material to your specific audience.

Make the information relevant to where they are, not where you are. Bring your information close to where the audience lives. Drop it right in their laps. Present

> *To the degree you are helpful is the degree to which you will be happy.*
> —KARL REILAND

your material in ways that will make your audience realize, "I didn't know it affected me in that way." If you're talking about the importance of healthy eating habits to a group of young college students, make it relevant to them by describing how the accumulated effects of eating processed and fried foods will make life miserable for them in the future. Explain how increased risks of cancer, heart disease, diabetes, and other diseases multiply when their diet is saturated with these foods. Ask them how they will feel when their bodies fail and they can't do the things they take for granted today. Ask them if that's the future they want to have. Make your topic hit home for your audience. Make it relevant.

If the information in your speech is *new*, the audience is more apt to pay attention. This principle of newness is seen in the marketing of products on your grocery store shelves. The words *new* and *improved* are splashed across the labels of hundreds of products annually. It seems that marketing research discovered that if consumers perceived that a product was "new," they would be more likely to buy it. For your speaking purposes, new information will not be difficult to find, so use new information when it's appropriate.

There are some topics that are well-worn subjects of discussion, such as weight loss, exercise, or smoking. These topics are often met with disinterest by many. But you could present one of those topics in a different light or from a slightly different angle to give it freshness. For example, a talk on computers could be presented so that the audience could see their application for possible dating or mate selection, employment assistance, or vacation rental help, rather than the usual spreadsheet and word-processing functions.

Information is more likely to stimulate audience interest when it is *startling*. When we are startled, we are emotionally shaken, and all of our attention is focused on dealing with the source of that surprise. To hear a warning from the speaker that skin cancer is on the upswing in the United States may arouse our interest. But to hear that some scientists predict that in 20 years, one out of every three adults will experience some form of skin cancer by the time he or she reaches middle age will have a startling impact on the audience.

Increase Audience Understanding

The second goal of informative speaking is to present the information in a way that will be understood by your audience. Simple language, clear organization, examples, and visualization are four ways you can help your audience understand what you are saying.

The first way you can increase understanding is to use *simple language* when you speak to an audience. Aristotle once advised, "Think as wise men think, but speak as the common people speak." Some years ago, one of the foremost authorities on U.S. economics taught at the University of California at Berkeley. She had authored several books on economics and had testified before Congress on numerous occasions, discussing our nation's economic woes. This expert was intelligent, gifted, and accomplished. But when she spoke in her Economics 2 course, the majority of her students didn't understand half the words she used. The students left her lectures feeling confused, frustrated, and often cheated. Here she is, "Ms. Economics Expert," and she couldn't speak in a style they could understand. What a waste of time! Abraham Lincoln cautioned, "We should speak so the least intelligent in the room can understand our words, then everyone will understand."

A speech that is *clearly organized* will help your audience understand what you have to say. The newspaper-writing adage to "tell them what you're going to tell them, tell them, and then tell them what you told them" works with public speaking audiences as well. Remember the preview of main points, main-point transitions, and the summary of main points?

We need to remember that speaking is different from reading. The reader can *see* the various headings and subheadings, and can see the paragraph structure on the printed page. But the listener cannot. He must rely on *hearing* the words of the speaker. Make your speech easy to understand by previewing the points, stating clear transitions, and reviewing the points.

The third way you can increase understanding is to use *examples* and *stories* in the development of your speech. Providing examples is one of the most concrete ways of helping your audience understand the ideas, concepts, and feelings you are trying to communicate. Every main point or concept you are trying to share with your audience should be accompanied by an example, be it brief or detailed. Stories are useful in developing a point you are trying to have the audience understand. The advantage of telling stories is that they have a definite beginning, middle, and ending, and they usually captivate the audience's attention more effectively than shorter forms of examples. Another advantage is that a story is far easier to master and share with an audience than a list of statistics and facts. And the audience will most likely remember a well-told story long after the statistics and quotations have been forgotten.

> *To be conscious that you are ignorant is a great step to knowledge.*
> —BENJAMIN DISRAELI

The fourth way you can help your audience understand what your speech is about is to have them *visualize*. Visual aids are worth the effort they require because the dividends they pay in helping your audience see and understand what you're discussing are great. You can also have your audience visualize without the use of physical props. Many things you talk about cannot be adequately described on paper, such as the distance to the nearest star, the weight of the earth, or the speed of light. These concepts can be visualized when you have the audience "see" them in terms of something more familiar. For example, a speaker may describe the information storage capacity of one microchip as equal to the amount of information that could be stored in 100 full-size books.

Assist Audience Retention

The third goal of informative speaking is to help your audience remember what you have said. Now don't get your hopes too high. Studies in listening and retention clearly suggest that we don't remember all that much of what we hear. Immediately after we listen to a lecture, we generally retain only 50 percent of the material presented. And within two weeks, we can remember only 25 percent of what was said. There is some recent research that would lead us to believe that the actual figures are much lower.

What can you do to help the audience remember what you said? Unfortunately, much of it is out of your hands. *Retention* is determined to a large extent by the listener's motivation, interests, training, psychological state, physical health, life circumstance, stress level, work schedule, interpersonal conflicts, and numerous other competing demands.

But there are still some specific things you can do to increase the probability that the audience will retain some of the information. The use of repetition, association, acronyms, one-sentence sayings, and handouts can all help your audience remember your talk.

Repetition is a useful tool in your attempts to help your audience remember what you said. You can use it to repeat a thought. "This is so important, let me repeat that idea for you one more time," or "I need to say it again." Your preview and summary of main points in the introduction and conclusion of your speech are a form of repetition. You can also repeat the main point you are completing before going on to your next point by saying, "Now that we've looked at America in the 1970s, we can move on to our second point, and that's how America looked in the 1980s."

The use of *association* is a powerful tool for helping people retain information. Its purpose is for the listener to associate one thing with another. Usually, you have a listener associate a known quantity with an unknown quantity. For example, suppose you are trying to describe the workings of a jet engine to an audience of sixth-graders. You might want to say that the jet engine pushes out air and forces the plane forward, just as a balloon is thrust forward when you blow it up and let it go. You hope that the kids can make the association between the engine and the balloon. If you can use association in your speech, your audience will more likely remember your talk.

An *acronym* is a word formed from the initial letters of groups of words in a set phrase. The acronym is a very creative and effective technique when you want your audience to remember the main points of your speech. For example, if you presented a speech on acceptance skills in communication, you could use the acronym "MOM" to help the audience remember the three main points, which are "*M*ingle, *O*penness, and *M*irroring." Acronyms are a simple way of having your audience retain the main points of your speeches. Here's another example. Recently, a young woman gave a talk on three aspects of communication. They were (1) talk is cheap, watch behavior; (2) attitude is more important than aptitude; and (3) perception is communication. To help the audience remember her three points, she had them recite the word "TAP," which represented the first letters of the first words of each principle: "T" for "Talk," "A" for "Attitude," and "P" for "Perception." After she gave the speech and was getting into her car in the parking lot of the auditorium, a young man came up to her, smiled, and said, "TAP, talk, attitude, and perception. I remembered your speech." He smiled and walked on. He didn't say anything else, simply that, and kept walking. But he had remembered the main points of her talk. Use a simple acronym, and your listeners will remember your speech, too.

A fourth method for getting your audience to remember your talk is the use of a *one-sentence saying* that summarizes the theme or central idea of your speech. The sentence can be one you construct yourself, a quotation, a proverb, a verse from a poem, a title from a movie or book, or anything else that is no longer than a sentence and is easy to remember. If you use the one-sentence technique, state the sentence in the introduction, the transitions to each main point, and the conclusion.

> *The more you say, the less people remember. The fewer the words, the greater the profit.*
> —FENELOR

For example, a speaker gave a speech entitled "Premarital Sex and You" to high school students at a summer retreat. In the speech, the young man addressed the social, psychological, and physical wounds that premarital sex could inflict on the lives of those high school students. The one sentence the speaker used as the theme for the talk was simply "Going to bed can cost you plenty." He must have used that sentence 10 times in the speech. "Going to bed can cost you plenty." Your one-sentence saying can have a powerful impact on the audience's retention of your message. Keep your message simple, and keep your audience focused so that they'll remember.

The final thing you can do to help your audience remember your speech is to prepare a *one-page handout* highlighting the important points of your talk. You can simply outline the key points and include suggested readings. Leave some space between your key ideas on the handout so the listeners can jot down notes or things to remember. If you invest the extra time and energy these handouts require, the payoff can be significant, because the listeners have something in their hands to help them remember your speech.

8.2 Designs for Informative Speaking

There are three basic designs or strategies for constructing an informative speech that we'll be examining next: exposition, description, and narration. Most informative speeches use a combination of two or more of these designs in their construction.

Exposition

The first approach to informative speaking is exposition. *Exposition* means to expose or explain. Therefore, the main goal of exposition is to inform your audience. Exposition is used to explain a process, concept, or idea to others. You've used this form of informative speaking before when you've given directions to your home, told a story, described a restaurant, or defined a word. There are three forms of exposition: definition, demonstration, and analysis.

Definition.   The first form of exposition is *definition*. If you want to give your audience a clear idea of what you're talking about, they will have to understand the words and concepts presented in your talk. It's important that you define words or concepts that may be unfamiliar, vague, or abstract to your listeners. When you define a word or concept, use simple language. If possible, use your own words to define the term. Try to avoid dictionary or technical definitions because they tend to sound stiff and lifeless to the listener. The definition is the fundamental building block of all informative speaking. Without an understanding of your words and concepts, your audience will be lost in your speech. There are three ways that you can make your definitions clear to your audience: example, comparison, and etymology.

When you define a word by *example*, you use examples to clarify the word or concept. An example is something that is used to illustrate a point. To define by example is especially helpful when you are trying to clarify a vague or abstract word. When using examples, you can use the actual object, such as showing a fighting saber when talking about samurai swords. Or you can give a verbal example of brotherly love as you define a certain aspect of the abstract term "love."

Comparison can also be used to define a word or concept by comparing the word to something that is known to the audience. If you can relate a new word or concept to something that is already understood by the audience, you will be more successful in getting your message across. A speaker trying to define the concept of balancing on a surfboard might compare it to walking on a railroad track or riding a skateboard.

The third form of definition uses etymology. Often, it is useful to trace the origin and development of a word in your attempts to give clarity. This is called *etymology*—the study of the origin and development of words. A speaker once traced the word "sarcasm" to its original Greek term *sarkasmos*, which means "to rend or rip flesh." The original Greek definition gave her audience a much more descriptive picture of her term.

Demonstration.   When attempting to inform your audience about a process, the second form of exposition, demonstration, works well. *Demonstration* enables you to actually show the audience how something works or how something is made. The use of demonstration can also involve the participation of your audience. For example, if the subject of your speech is emergency water safety techniques, and you are demonstrating the technique used for relaxing a muscle cramp in your leg, you could have the audience members rub their own legs to get a feel for the technique, or you could demonstrate it yourself.

A demonstration speech would be appropriate if you were going to speak on topics such as making sushi, repairing a lamp, cutting hair, using a vacuum cleaner, checking for skin cancer, or binding a book. Some of these topics would lend themselves to audience participation, whereas others would not. Consider the choice carefully before you invite audience participation.

Review the suggestions on visual-aid usage discussed in Chapter 5 if you will be using demonstration in your speech. If you are going to demonstrate a process or show how something works for your audience, here are some additional suggestions to consider when constructing and delivering your talk.

Cluster the steps of your demonstration into a maximum of three or four main points. Even the simplest of processes requires a multitude of mini-steps for its completion. Your goal is to cluster these mini-steps into three or four major clusters or categories. For instance, the seemingly simple process of tossing a salad contains a number of steps that would confuse an audience if you were to present each one as a main point. Instead, cluster these steps into three main points, such as "gather the materials, prepare the ingredients, and toss the salad." Other cluster designs, such as "Plan, Do, Finish," and "Gather Materials, Do the Process, and Clean Up," are useful when trying to put your process into some recognizable form. Clustering your steps provides clarity of organization for your audience and ease of handling for you.

Another way you can help your audience understand and remember your demonstration is to *preview and review main points in the introduction and conclusion* of your speech. Remember that you need to lead your audience by the hand and clearly orient and review the process. If

> *We create our reality with our language.*
> —SHUNRYU SUZUKI

you want to be really organized and impressive, number the steps in your preview and summary of main points, so it sounds like, "The first step is to gather the materials, the second step is to mix the ingredients, and the third and final step is to bake the cake."

The final suggestion for demonstrating a process is to include *dead-time talk*. When a speaker is actually demonstrating the slicing of the vegetables, the carving of the wood, or the mixing of the ingredients, there is a tendency on the part of the speaker to focus on the process and not talk. In other words, the audience is watching the process, and the speaker is not saying a word. That's okay if the silence lasts a few seconds, but 20 or 30 seconds of silence could make your audience feel uncomfortable. This dead time should be filled with some discussion. When you are demonstrating a process in a speech and you have 20 or 30 seconds of possible dead time, share a brief anecdote about the first time you ever did the process or a humorous incident that happened to you when you were doing this process. This dead-time talk not only fills the silence, but it also adds color and substance to your talk.

Analysis. The third form of exposition is analysis. *Analysis* is the breaking down of an idea, concept, or event into its various parts to get a clearer picture of how something operates or functions. The review of a play or movie, the structure of the federal government, an evaluation of the strengths and weaknesses of a proposal, and the development of the space program are topics for which you could utilize analysis in your presentation.

When presenting to an audience topics that could possibly be difficult to understand—such as a budget report, an organizational flowchart, or a newly implemented time management program—dividing the concept into its component parts for closer examination is always beneficial.

Description

The second approach to informative speaking is description. *Description* makes use of sensory information to verbally paint a clear picture of what you're talking about without the use of visual aids. The categories of description that you can use are size, shape, weight, color, composition, and age.

Size can be described in terms such as "big" or "small" or "large" or "tiny," but these terms are subjective and relative. They can mean different things to different listeners. It's much better to be specific when describing size to your audience. A speaker can describe a cut on the arm as a "large cut," but that description does not paint the same picture as another description with specific dimensions. A cut that is described as "eight inches in length, half an inch wide, and two inches deep" paints a picture that would make even the sturdiest of listeners squirm in their seats.

Shape can be described in geometric forms, such as square, triangular, round, spherical, and rectangular. "His face was square with a cone nose," "The racetrack is oblong," and "Her house looked like a rectangular box" are examples of using shapes to describe objects.

The *weight* of an object, like its size, can be described in a subjective and relative fashion, such as "light," "heavy," "featherweight," or "hefty." A more precise way to describe an object's weight is to report it in ounces, pounds, and tons. Instead of saying that "the man was heavy," you could describe the man as "weighing 500 pounds, or one-quarter of a ton."

Color is the fourth category of description you can use when painting a mental picture of the object you are describing. The obvious labels of "black and white" and "red and green" help give the audience a clearer picture of what you're communicating. It's useful to link the color to a common object that is familiar to the audience's experience, such as "red as a cherry," "blue as the ocean," or "black as a moonless night."

The *composition* of an object provides further detail to the picture you are painting. Composition refers to the makeup or construction of an object. "His legs looked like plucked chicken skin," "The lake was as smooth as glass," and "His hair was matted down like oiled feathers" are examples of composition.

A final category of description is *age*. The usual descriptors of "new" and "old" are helpful in painting a picture of an object. But once again, more specific descriptions of age, such as months, years, and centuries, provide more vividness. To describe the sofa as "being in our family for over 50 years" gives us a better appreciation for its age than to simply describe it as "an old sofa."

Narration

The third form of informative speaking is *narration*. Storytelling is the oldest form of passing information from one generation to another. Before the written word, myths of the creation, stories explaining life's mysteries, and rituals that bound tribes and cultures together were passed on in the form of stories. Century after century, these stories were handed down through the generations.

> *We have stories to tell, stories that provide wisdom about the journey of life.*
> —SAUL RUBIN

In public speaking, storytelling or narration can be used as a powerful means of clarifying an idea or concept for your audience. Equally important is the ability of a story to stick in the listener's memory long after the story has been told. When you use narration in your speech to describe an important concept or idea, you might consider these suggestions:

Your story should illustrate your point. Don't include a story in your speech just because it's your favorite. Your story must illustrate, demonstrate, or clarify a point you are trying to make with your audience.

Know your story. You should be so familiar with your story that you could tell it without the use of notes. Know the correct pronunciation of all the words, names, and places in the story. You should know your story so well that you become the story.

Become the various characters. When reciting dialogue, use the voices of the various characters in your story. This may feel awkward at first, but it will present a better story to your listeners if you sound like the "old woman," the "frightened boy," or the "mean old king." Your nonverbal behavior can also be a way of taking on the personality of the various characters. Use the posture, walk, gestures, and facial expressions of the different characters so that your audience can also "see" the story you are telling.

Time your story during your practice sessions. It often takes longer to tell a story than you would expect. You get caught up in the characterization, the detail, and the emotions of the story, and before you know it, your speaking time is up. Time your story when you practice your speech. You may have to cut a little here and there to get the story to conform to the time requirements.

8.3 Language Use for Informative Speaking

Before we outline the basic types of informative speeches, we need to mention some additional recommendations for the effective use of language in your presentations. The message sent isn't always the message received, and the following suggestions will help you in your attempts to communicate clearly with your audience in all types of public speaking.

Simple Language

Many beginning speakers feel the need to impress an audience with highly elaborate, ornate, or complex language. So instead of saying, "The group members were residents of Spain," a speaker might say, "The group members were denizens of Spain." "Denizens" sounds fine, but who knows what it means? The speaker, in her attempt to sound impressive, increases her chances of losing her audience. Use language that is simple and readily understood by your audience. Avoid using technical language or jargon that is foreign or unfamiliar to your audience. If you must use specialized vocabulary, define the words clearly and simply so that your audience can understand what you mean. Finally, when using acronyms, make certain that you explain what each letter represents. For instance, "AA stands for Alcoholics Anonymous," or "CPR stands for cardiopulmonary resuscitation." You might assume your audience knows what the letters stand for, but if you're wrong, you've just lost more of your listeners along the way.

Specific Language

Avoid using vague or abstract language in your speeches. Overused words and clichés should also be avoided. If you use language that is vague or overused, the audience isn't challenged, and they may begin to drift off to other things in the room besides you. You don't want that. So use words that are as specific and concrete as possible. Instead of saying, "The woman planted some flowers in her yard," you might want to use more specific words: "The woman planted purple tulips, yellow roses, and red geraniums in her yard." Do you notice the difference? Which scene do you see more vividly? Remember to use specific words in your language.

Active Language

Use strong, active verbs in your speeches. Avoid using weak verbs such as *is, was, will be,* and *are.* Instead of saying, "It is my feeling that … ," you can more forcefully announce, "I feel …" Which of the following two statements sounds more assertive: "This matter needs *to be* brought before the board of directors" or "This matter *demands* the attention of the board of directors"? Your choice of verbs will make a critical difference in the movement, urgency, and flow of your speeches. Will your language put the audience to sleep or take them for a roller-coaster ride?

Personal Language

Language that is personal in nature will have a greater impact in reaching your audience than more formal or distant language. The use of personal pronouns such as *I, you, us,* and *we* will help bring you closer to your audience. Their use can make the audience feel that you are interested in them and understand their concerns and desires. Notice the difference between these two sentences: "Americans need to get a physical exam once every two years" and "You need to get a physical exam once every two years." The first sentence is directed to 290 million people. The second sentence is delivered to only one person. Language that is personal will bridge that gap between you and your listeners.

Guiding Language

Another way you can use language more effectively in helping your audience understand and remember your speech is to use language that guides them in, around,

> *The limits of my language mean the limits of my world.*
> —Ludwig Wittgenstein

and through your presentation. Transitions are the best devices the speaker can utilize in guiding and directing the listener. External transitions are complete sentences used to signal movement from one major part of the speech to another. Between the main points of your speech, external transitions are essential in directing the listener from one point to another. "Now that

I've discussed the history of the radio, let's move to my second point, and that's the innovations after World War II." This transition even recapped the previous main point ("Now that I've discussed ...") before signaling movement into the second point of the talk. Internal transitions are those words and phrases that signal movement between the smaller parts of a sentence or main point.

Internal transitions such as *and, also, but, however, although, because, on the other hand, for example, therefore,* and *finally* all signal relationships between the smaller parts of sentences or main points. Use internal transitions to keep your thoughts connected to one another and your listeners connected to your speech. Transitions are the verbal bridges that show the relationships between your points and thoughts, and they keep you linked to your audience.

Unbiased Language

In this world of cultural diversity, your task as a public speaker is to demonstrate respect for your audience by using language that does not demean or insult the listeners. You are to use language that isn't perceived as belittling or hurtful to another person or group of people because of their race, ethnicity, age, class, gender, or disability. The use of unbiased words in your speech can encourage an audience to be more open to your thoughts and ideas, even though they might hold different positions on that same topic or issue. By using language that honors and respects the audience, your speech can encourage receptivity to your ideas, open discussion, and even promote a willingness for the audience to modify or change their opinions because you used words that honored and respected them. The use of unbiased language can increase your credibility as a speaker because it displays your awareness and sensitivity to the many differences among your audience. Here are a few specific ways to avoid bias in your speeches.

Stereotyping occurs when you assign characteristics to people solely on the basis of their class or grouping. When you say that athletes are poor students, Asians are shy, old people are grouchy, or politicians are corrupt, you are stereotyping all members of that category of people or ethnic group. As speakers, we must avoid any use of stereotyping a class or group of people. Instead, talk about specific individuals without reference to any particular group to which they may be associated. In our examples, you can be more specific by saying, "Bill was a poor student," "Jill Yamamoto seemed reticent during our discussion group," "My grandfather often gets angry," and "Senator Mitch Foster was convicted of perjury." Notice how the statements were about specific individuals and not groups of people?

The traditional use of the pronoun "he" and the noun "man" is another common way a speaker can demonstrate bias in the language of a speech. When speakers use "he" or "man" to refer to both males and females, these words can elicit masculine images and feelings in the minds of the audience. This is known as *gender bias*. One easy way to avoid gender bias is to simply say "he or she," or "women or men" when no gender-specific reference is desired. This acknowledges both male and female and doesn't emphasize one gender over another. A second way to avoid gender bias is the use of plurals. Instead of stating that "A teacher uses all of her skills to reach her students," you could use plurals and change the sentence to, "Teachers use all of their skills to reach their students." A final way to avoid gender bias is to replace words or phrases that contain man or woman with gender-neutral terms. For instance, replace words such as "fireman" with "firefighter," "chairman" with "chairperson," "cleaning woman" with "office cleaner," and "mankind" to "humanity." The use of gender-neutral terms avoids bias and promotes greater equality in the minds of your audience.

Positive Language

Ultimately, you want to have a positive effect on your audience. Not only do you want them to understand and remember your message, but you also want them to perceive you as a credible speaker, someone they can trust and respect. You may even want them to like you. We're only human. In addition to the obvious recommendations of using appropriate language (no swearing or vulgarity) and avoiding emotionally loaded words or terms (don't refer to Texans as "rednecks" while addressing the Texas Republican Convention), you should be complimentary to your listeners whenever you can. Begin your talk by thanking the audience for the invitation to address them. Research the audience or group so you can mention in your speech one or two things they've accomplished recently. And end with a final appeal that is in accordance with the group's goals and objectives.

Above all, you want to have an enlarging impact on your listeners. They should feel that their time with you was well spent, and your positive language and attitude will help to guarantee this goal.

8.4   Types of Informative Speeches

Now that we've examined the goals and designs for informative speaking, let's turn our attention finally to the various types of informative speeches. The three primary informative-speech designs are expository, descriptive, and narrative. Sample main-point structures for each of the various types of speeches to inform follow.

Expository Speeches
Definition Speech

Specific Purpose: To define three aspects of success.

  I.   The first aspect is personal fulfillment.
  II. The second aspect is intellectual stimulation.
  III. The third aspect is social contribution.

Demonstration Speech

Specific Purpose: To demonstrate the three steps required in baking cookies.

  I.   The first step is to gather your materials.
  II. The second step is to mix the ingredients.
  III. The third step is to bake the cookies.

Analysis Speech

Specific Purpose: To describe the three branches of the federal government.

    I. The first branch of the federal government is the legislative branch.

    II. The second branch of the federal government is the judicial branch.

    III. The third branch of the federal government is the executive branch.

Descriptive Speeches

Describing a Person

Specific Purpose: To describe three characteristics of George Washington.

    I. The first characteristic of Washington is that he was very intelligent.

    II. The second characteristic of Washington is that he possessed a brilliant military mind.

    III. The third characteristic of Washington is that he was a persuasive speaker.

Describing a Place

Specific Purpose: To describe three Lake Tahoe attractions.

    I. The first attraction is Lake Tahoe's beautiful lake.

    II. The second attraction is Lake Tahoe's campgrounds.

    III. The third attraction is Lake Tahoe's hiking trails.

Describing an Event

Specific Purpose: To explain the Denver Broncos' Super Bowl journey.

    I. The first stage was the preseason training.

    II. The second stage was the regular season.

    III. The third stage was the Super Bowl playoff postseason.

Narrative Speeches

Personal Experience Narrative

Specific Purpose: To relate my aircrash adventure in Montana.

    I. I was flying to Montana in a Piper Cub airplane.

    II. Inclement weather forced the plane to crash in the foothills of eastern Montana.

    III. I survived six days before being rescued by forest rangers.

Historical Narrative

Specific Purpose: To explain the bombing of Pearl Harbor.

    I. The Japanese planned the attack for two years.

    II. The surprise attack was devastating in terms of loss of lives.

    III. The attack forced the United States into World War II.

8.5 Question-and-Answer Session

When presenting an informative or persuasive speech, you may find it helpful to hold a brief question–and–answer session after you conclude your presentation. Questions from the audience allow you to provide specific information that might not have been covered in your speech. It's also a great opportunity to interact with your audience in a more flexible and intimate way, letting them see another side of you. Here are a few suggestions that will make your question–and–answer session more effective.

1. **Prepare for Questions.** As you prepare and practice your speech, be thinking of questions the audience may ask. Make a list of possible questions that address difficult to understand or controversial aspects of your presentation. You might even have a friend or colleague listen to your speech and suggest questions that your audience might ask. It's always good to be prepared.

2. **Announce the Question-and-Answer Session Before Your Speech.** You might have the person introducing you announce that a question–and–answer session will be held after you conclude your speech. If you don't have someone introducing you, you can state in your speech introduction that you'll answer any questions after your speech. This gives the audience members time to formulate their questions as you're speaking.

3. **Model the Questions.** After you conclude your speech, model the manner in which you want the questions asked by raising your hand and saying, "Now I'd be happy to answer any questions you may have." By raising your hand, you are demonstrating how you'd like the audience to ask their questions, so it won't be a free-for-all with people speaking all at the same time. Take control from the beginning.

4. **Restate the Questions.** Restate each question to the entire audience after the question has been asked. Begin your response with "The question was …" and repeat the question. By doing so, you ensure that the entire audience hears and understands the question. When you restate the question, speak to the entire audience and not just the individual who asked the question. Remember, you're addressing the entire audience and not having a dialogue with one person.

5. **Use the 25/75 Percent Rule.** When you're answering the question, look at the person who asked the question 25 percent of your speaking time, and maintain eye contact with the rest of the audience the other 75 percent of the time. Don't get into a conversation or debate with the individual. Keep your remarks and eye contact primarily focused on your audience.

6. **Keep Your Answer Short.** Your answer should be as brief as possible. A sentence or two at the most. Avoid a yes or no response, but don't give a second speech either. The question was raised by one person in your audience and not on the minds of the entire audience. So keep your remarks short and sweet. Just answer the question and move on.

7. **Admit You Don't Know.** If you don't know the answer to a question, be honest and say so. Don't make up an answer or ramble on and on about the fact that you don't know. Simply say, "I don't know the answer, but I'll be happy to research the answer and get back to you if you'll give me your e-mail address after the speech." Short and sweet.

8. **Smile.** Above all else, be friendly and pleasant as you respond to questions. Speak slowly, maintain eye contact, be enthusiastic, and smile. Above all else, smile. The effectiveness of your question and answer session will be judged not on your knowing all the answers to the questions, but by your willingness to be of service to your listeners. Be friendly as you attempt to serve your audience. Remember to smile.

9. **Control the Audience**. Don't let one individual dominate the question-and-answer session by asking too many questions or giving a speech of his own. If a person is asking too many questions, address the individual directly by saying, "You've asked a number of questions already. Does anyone else have a question?" If an individual is making a long-winded statement instead of asking a question, ask, "Do you have a question for me?" If the person continues talking you can say, "We can dialogue about this matter after the session is over. Does anyone else have a question?"

10. **Conclude the Question-and-Answer Session.** Know when to quit. If the audience is getting restless, falling asleep, or sneaking out of the room, it's time to conclude the question-and-answer session. Limit the questions to five at most. The majority of your audience won't be heavily invested in listening to your responses to questions they didn't ask. So keep the session short. Five to seven minutes at most. Be kind and let the audience go on with their lives. Simply announce, "Well, it seems that there are no more questions, so once again, thank you for coming and have a wonderful rest of the day." Don't you wish all the events in your life could end this nicely?

8.6 Public Speaker Self-Image Scale

Now that you've had some experience presenting two or three speeches to an audience, it might be interesting to assess the image you have of yourself as a public speaker. Earlier in this book you responded to the Speaker Apprehension Self-Assessment Scale before you actually began your journey as a public speaker. Take a few moments now and respond to this Public Speaker Self-Image Scale. Read and respond to each statement from your current perspective as an experienced speaker.

As a public speaker, I see myself ...

1. focused more on the *audience's* needs and concerns, rather than my own.

1	2	3	4	5
Strongly Disagree	Disagree	Neutral	Agree	Strongly Agree

2. confident that I will demonstrate natural, enthusiastic delivery.

1	2	3	4	5
Strongly Disagree	Disagree	Neutral	Agree	Strongly Agree

3. confident that I will present a relevant and interesting speech.

1	2	3	4	5
Strongly Disagree	Disagree	Neutral	Agree	Strongly Agree

4. confident that I will present a clearly organized speech.

1	2	3	4	5
Strongly Disagree	Disagree	Neutral	Agree	Strongly Agree

5. confident that I will feel relaxed when I deliver a speech.

1	2	3	4	5
Strongly Disagree	Disagree	Neutral	Agree	Strongly Agree

6. confident that I will successfully respond to questions from the audience.

1	2	3	4	5
Strongly Disagree	Disagree	Neutral	Agree	Strongly Agree

7. confident that I will enjoy delivering a speech.

1	2	3	4	5
Strongly Disagree	Disagree	Neutral	Agree	Strongly Agree

Add up your total score for the seven questions and reflect upon your responses to these statements. A higher score can indicate greater confidence than a lower score. What changes in your self-concept as a public speaker do you notice? What areas of growth and improvement do you see? What areas still need some attention and effort? Realize that with any skill, the more practice and experience you possess, the more confident and relaxed you will be performing that skill. Public speaking is a skill that provides you with many life benefits, so take opportunities to put your speaking skills to use and watch how your confidence will soar. Good for you.

SAMPLE INFORMATIVE SPEECH OUTLINE
SILENT RETREAT CENTERS

Specific Purpose: To inform the audience about silent retreat centers.

Introduction

A few years ago, I found myself getting frustrated over little things at work, angry with family and friends, and miserable about my busy, frantic lifestyle. I felt I needed a change. Then a friend recommended that I go to a silent retreat center for two or three days and let the silence speak to me. I did go, and it made a world of difference. Today, I'd like to explain what a silent retreat center is, what it does, and how to find a silent retreat center.

Body

I. First, I'd like to explain the purpose of a silent retreat center.
   A. A silent retreat center gives you a vacation from a busy, noisy world.
      1. Rita Winters, in her book, *The Green Desert*, explains that "the purpose of silent retreat is to leave the noise of the world and discover the peace in silence."
      2. Story about my first time at a silent retreat center.
   B. Silent retreat centers are provided by a variety of religious groups.
   C. Lodging, food, and quiet are provided for you.
II. Second, what a silent retreat center does for you.
   A. The silence provides you with self-communication.
      1. Sara Park McLaughlin, in her book, *Meeting God in Silence*, tells us that "silence lets you hear your deepest voice."
      2. Story about Thomas Merton's deep listening.
   B. The silence can provide psychological healing.
      1. Richard Foster, in his book, *Freedom of Simplicity*, warns that "the complexity of rushing to achieve and accumulate more in life threatens to overwhelm and harm us."
      2. Story about my sister's silent retreat center experience.

    C. The silence can provide spiritual direction.

III. Third, how to find a silent retreat center.

    A. Making the decision to go to a silent retreat center.

      1. You need to decide to take good care of yourself.

      2. Counselor Dave Pennington explains that "even your decision to treat yourself to a time away from the world is the beginning of a more serene and balanced life."

    B. The Internet is an excellent resource for finding silent retreat centers.

      1. Try www.retreatsonline.com for listings.

      2. Call the center and speak with someone before making a reservation.

    C. Things to take to the silent retreat.

      1. Comfortable clothing.

      2. A journal.

      3. Reading material.

      4. A gentle attitude.

Conclusion

Today, I've shared with you the purpose of a silent retreat center, what it does for you, and how to find a silent retreat center. It's my hope that if you're feeling a little stressed with life, frustrated with friends and family, and miserable about a lifestyle that is spinning out of control, you might consider making a reservation at a silent retreat center. Thomas Merton once said that "one's deepest journey passes through silence." I hope you begin your journey soon.

References

Foster, R. 1998. *Freedom of Simplicity*. San Francisco: HarperSanFrancisco.

McLaughlin, S. 2004. *Meeting God in Silence*. Carol Stream, II: Tyndale Publishers.

Pennington, D. Mar. 3, 2004. MFC Therapist, San Jose, CA. (408) 767–1111.

Retreats online. Jan. 3, 2005. Retreat homepage [www document]. http://retreatsonline.com/guide/silent.htm.

Winters, R. 2004. *The Green Desert*. Cumbria, Britain: Crossroads Carlisle.

SAMPLE KEY-WORD OUTLINE

Introduction

Frantic life story

Silent retreat: is, does, find

Body

I. What silent retreat is

    Vacation (Winters reference 1)

    Variety of groups

    Lodging, food, quiet

II. What silent retreat does

    Self-communication (McLaughlin reference 2)

    Psychological healing (Foster reference 3)

    Spiritual direction

III. How to find silent retreat
Decide to attend retreat (Pennington reference 4)
Internet search
Things to take

Conclusion
Silent retreat: is, does, find
Merton quotation

COMMUNICATION ACTIVITIES
PERSONAL ACTIVITIES

1. **The best teacher**
Who was the best teacher you have had in your life? What did he or she teach? What did this person teach you about yourself? What did you like or appreciate about this teacher? Can you identify any specific techniques or approaches in the person's informative speaking that you felt were especially effective in helping you learn? Can you identify any specific delivery characteristics that captivated and held your attention? Which of these delivery and informative-speaking techniques might you use in your own personal speaking? Have you ever written this teacher a thank-you note for his or her contribution to your learning?

2. **What do you teach others?**
Although you may not realize it, you are always teaching those around you by your example. Children in the neighborhood, your family members, those at work, and your friends observe your actions over time. It's not really what you say that's important. It's what you do. What does your behavior say about you? Do you keep promises? Are you punctual? Are you enlarging? Do you listen without interrupting? Do you encourage? Can you keep a secret? Do you touch? Are you there when others need a friend? What does your behavior teach others about you?

3. **Teachers in other cultures**
Ask an individual from a different cultural background about his or her culture's attitudes and behaviors toward teachers. Are teachers valued? Are they respected? How are they paid? What are the primary teaching methods? How do students interact with their teachers? What classroom attitudes and behaviors are different from ours? How are they similar?

CLASS ACTIVITIES

1. **Group discussion: Brainstorm informative speech topics**
Divide the class into groups of five or six students. Each group is to brainstorm a minimum of 30 possible topics for informative speaking. What topics are of interest to the group? Remember not to evaluate or judge any of the suggestions

offered by the group members. After the group has completed its list, review the list and discuss which topics might be of interest to the entire class. Which topics might not be of interest? Why? Be prepared to share your group's list with the class.

2. **Explanation speech**

   Prepare, practice, and present a three- to five-minute informative speech explaining a word, concept, theory, or idea. Develop each of your three main points with documented information and examples. Include any visual aids that might be helpful. Your speech should contain an introduction, body, and conclusion.

3. **Demonstration speech**

   Prepare, practice, and present a five- to seven-minute demonstration speech showing how something is made or how something works. Use the cluster method of arranging the main points of your speech. Develop each of your main points with documented information and examples. Include any visual aids that might be helpful. Your speech should contain an introduction, body, and conclusion.

4. **Tribute speech**

   Prepare, practice, and present a five- to seven-minute tribute speech honoring someone who is important in your life. The purpose of this speech is to share three wonderful things about this individual with your audience. A tribute speech can be used to honor someone at a birthday, retirement party, anniversary, or eulogy. Your speech should contain an introduction, body, and conclusion.

5. **Informative speech**

   Prepare, practice, and present a five- to seven-minute speech on a topic that would be of interest to your audience. Research this topic thoroughly after analyzing your audience. Develop each of your main points with documented information and examples. Include any visual aids that might be helpful. Your speech should contain an introduction, body, and conclusion.

6. **What it's like to ... speech**

   Prepare, practice, and present a five- to seven-minute speech describing what it's like to be or do something—for instance, what it's like to be the oldest child, divorced, a twin, a police officer, an Asian American, an artist, a mechanic, or to parachute from an airplane. Research this topic thoroughly after analyzing your audience. Develop each of your main points with documented information and examples. Include any visual aids that might be helpful. Your speech should contain an introduction, body, and conclusion.

Chapter 9

PERSUADING YOUR AUDIENCE
CHANGING OTHERS

LEARNING OBJECTIVES

After reading this chapter, you should be able to:

9.1 Summarize the basics of persuasion

9.2 List and explain Aristotle's three persuasive proofs

9.3 Identify some types of persuasive speeches

It's the silence of the place that Michelle loves most. Nestled in a secluded corner of rolling hills and occasional oaks, the small monastery has served as a retreat center for people of all walks of life for more than 50 years.

As you wind up the two-mile dirt road from Highway 1 to the monastery grounds, you're awed by the ever-increasing expanse of ocean below, the rugged slant of the Santa Lucia mountain range falling into the sea, and the silence—that powerful silence. And it was one particular speaker's love of the monastery's silence that finally convinced Michelle three years ago in a communication course to sign up for an overnight retreat.

It was in her public speaking class that Michelle heard an older student deliver a persuasive speech convincing students to visit the Camaldolese monastery for two days of silence. Like the other students in class, Michelle was told that such a visit would quiet her mind and relax her body. The speaker provided a number of statistics and a few expert opinions to support her points.

But it was the speaker's third point about the silence and how it soothes the soul that finally moved Michelle from reluctance to willingness, from skeptic to believer. It was the speaker's description of a silence so powerful, so foreign, so healing that one is gradually transformed by the experience. And sometimes in the process, one is even moved to tears as the sounds of civilization are silenced and the voice of heaven whispers.

> *Speech is power to persuade, to convert, and to compel.*
> —RALPH WALDO EMERSON

A few days after hearing the speech, Michelle made the call to the monastery south of Big Sur, and she has continued to make the call every six months since to venture into silence and once again hear the voice of heaven whisper.

We are bombarded daily by persuasive appeals to purchase this product, contribute to that charity, or subscribe to this belief. We in turn try to convince someone to babysit our kids, ask the boss for a raise, or request the neighbor to turn down his stereo. Daily, we must deal with hundreds of persuasive events, whether we are conscious of them or not. Your ability to convince others and motivate them to action will, to a large extent, determine the quality and destiny of your life and the lives of those around you.

9.1 Basics of Persuasion

Persuasion is the process of trying to get others to change their beliefs or behavior. Unlike informative speaking, for which the goal is the sharing of information, persuasion is aimed at going a step further—changing others. This process of changing—and not simply sharing—is the focus of this chapter.

Three Purposes of Persuasion

In persuasive speaking, there are three purposes we can attempt to achieve with an audience, although most persuasive appeals utilize a combination of all three. The persuasive purposes are to reinforce an already-held belief, change a belief, and motivate to action.

The first persuasive purpose is to *reinforce an already-held belief*. This is the goal of our persuasive appeals if we're speaking on such topics as "Everyone Should Vote" or "The Cure for AIDS Must Be Found." These are beliefs that are held by the majority of any group, and your speech will be directed to reinforcing or strengthening those beliefs.

A second persuasive purpose is to *change an audience belief*. This would be your goal if you were speaking on such topics as "We Should Ban Air Conditioning in Cars" or "We Should Have a Flat Tax." These beliefs are not held by the majority of your audience, and your goal in these instances would be to change their beliefs.

The final persuasive purpose is to *motivate to action*. This would be your goal if you were speaking on such topics as "Contribute Money to the Red Cross" or "Attend This Evening's City Council Meeting." The primary purpose in speeches like these is to get the audience members to actually do something.

Whether your goal is to reinforce a belief, change a belief, or motivate the audience to action, it should be clearly indicated in your proposition.

The Proposition

In persuasive speaking, the specific purpose, purpose statement, or goal statement is called the proposition. The *proposition* is the desired effect you want to have on your audience. What exactly is it that you want your audience to believe or do? Many persuasive attempts are doomed from the beginning because the speaker does not know exactly what she wants from the audience. A properly constructed proposition can ensure this clarity and specificity.

A proposition must be limited to one sentence. The intent and goal of the persuasive speech must be contained in that sentence. How do you want the audience to respond? If you want to strengthen an already-held belief, you must phrase your proposition accordingly. For example, "to strengthen the audience's belief that everyone should take regular vacations" and "to reinforce the audience's belief that child abuse is a terrible crime" are two propositions that attempt to strengthen already-held beliefs.

> *It is terrible to speak*
> *well and be wrong.*
> *—Sophocles*

You can phrase your proposition to reflect a desire to change the audience's beliefs. For instance, "to convince the audience that we should not permit freedom of the press" and "to convince the audience that we should abolish home mortgage interest deductions on federal income tax" are two propositions that seek to change audience beliefs.

Finally, you can phrase your proposition to motivate your audience to action. Propositions such as "to persuade the audience to volunteer as a Big Brother or Big Sister" and "to motivate the audience to donate blood at the annual company blood drive" are seeking to get the listeners to do something.

A poorly phrased proposition will hinder your efforts to organize and deliver an effective persuasive appeal. Make certain that your proposition contains a clear and specific purpose and goal. When you are constructing your proposition, consider the following three suggestions:

> **Your proposition should meet an audience need.** Your proposition will be more likely to succeed if you consider the needs of your particular audience and design your proposition around those needs. If a person has a need for a computer, he will be more likely to receive a message on computers. If a person needs employment, he will be more likely to receive a message on employment opportunities or interviewing techniques. Your ability to analyze and consider audience needs will be valuable when deciding on your proposition.
>
> **Your proposition should be reasonable.** To ask that each member of your audience donate $10,000 to a charitable organization or that they jog 10 miles a day is probably asking for more than most people are willing to give. Your proposition should be phrased with a reasonable goal in mind. It's the old "foot-in-the-door" technique; you begin by asking for something small and reasonable, and then you build your argument or persuasive appeal to include more comprehensive objectives. Remember: in all things, moderation.
>
> **Your proposition should be simple.** The more complex your proposition is, the more likely you are to confuse your audience. A multiple proposition can even have a counterproductive effect on your listeners. The proposition "to persuade the audience to rethink their current belief that milk is good for them, to believe that natural juices provide greater benefit to their overall physical and psychological health, and to invest in a one-week vacation at the Nirvana Health Food Resort" would not only be overwhelming in terms of evidence required, but it also would place too much *demand on the audience* in terms of the sheer amount of persuasion asked for. A more manageable proposition might be "to convince the audience to drink natural juices" or "to persuade the audience to drink less milk." Keep it simple.

9.2 Aristotle's Three Persuasive Proofs

Now that we've examined the persuasive purposes and the proposition, we can introduce the three persuasive proofs. More than 2,000 years ago, Aristotle divided all persuasive effort into three categories: ethos, logos, and pathos. *Ethos* is the ethical appeal or credibility of the speaker. *Logos* is the logical appeal. And *pathos* is the emotional appeal. We now examine how each of these three dimensions of persuasion can help you change and motivate others.

Ethos (Speaker Credibility)

Aristotle believed that the most important component of persuasion was the perceived credibility of the speaker or her ethical appeal. Is the speaker someone who can be trusted? Someone who has our best interests at heart? Someone who sounds like she knows what she's talking about? These and related questions shape our opinion of a speaker and will directly affect our response to her appeal. Ethos is the perceived credibility of the speaker. Ethos, or speaker credibility, consists of the speaker's competence, goodwill, and character.

The speaker's expertise or experience is called *competence*. We will generally listen to and believe a speaker we perceive as trained, knowledgeable, and experienced in a given subject or discipline area. A physician's knowledge, training, and experience all contribute to her overall competence in the field of medicine. The expertise of the knowledgeable professor makes him more believable than a professor who displays a poor command of the material. Your competence as a speaker can be enhanced by speaking on topics you have previous experience with or training in. You can also increase your perceived competence by providing your listeners with evidence and research from experts in the subject area you are discussing.

The second component of ethos is *goodwill*. We will generally believe people we like. Goodwill is the dimension of the speaker that deals with interpersonal warmth, friendliness, and enthusiasm. One of the reasons we like puppies is that they show friendliness and boundless energy toward us. If a speaker is cold, aloof, and condescending, our usual response is to reject that person. Some research suggests that the perceived goodwill of the speaker is the most important of the three elements of credibility.

> *Example is not the main thing in influencing others. It is the only thing.*
> —ALBERT SCHWEITZER

How can you increase your sense of goodwill? First, show enthusiasm. Speakers who talk in a lifeless monotone, as if they were delivering a funeral eulogy, are generally received in similar fashion. Be enthusiastic in your nonverbal communication! Show some life! What goes around, comes around. Second, be friendly *toward your audience*. Use a speech style that is warm and friendly. Be personable. Smile. And third, use humor when appropriate. There's something about well-received humor that increases liking and attraction.

The third component of ethos is the speaker's character. *Character* is the overall makeup of a person. It's what the speaker is made of. Honesty, integrity, and trustworthiness are major elements of a person's character, and if the speaker seems to possess these traits, we are more likely to believe him than if he does not. An audience member must feel that she can trust and respect the speaker before she will be persuaded by that speaker.

What, then, can you do to be perceived as possessing an honest and trustworthy character? Here are some suggestions. First, be truthful. Don't exaggerate points. Present your views fairly. Second, share your motives with the audience. Tell the audience why you are taking the position you are taking. Even if they disagree with you, they will appreciate your candidness. Third, establish common ground with your audience. An audience will more likely feel better about you if you possess similar beliefs, values, attitudes, and experiences. Finally, dress appropriately. Your audience bases much of their evaluation of you by the manner in which you dress.

Increasing Speaker Ethos   Speaker goodwill and character are two of the traits of ethos. You can increase your level of goodwill toward your audience and develop your character in the process by focusing your attention and efforts on your audience rather than on yourself.

Here are some ways you can increase your ethos as you prepare for and deliver any speech. The first three suggestions are not readily visible to your audience, but their impact will influence how you think and feel and, thus, how you deliver your speech. The remaining suggestions visually demonstrate your goodwill to your audience as you speak.

Research your audience. Before you speak, gather as much information about your audience as you can. Interview the speaking event contact person, conduct a site visit to the group or organization, or e-mail an audience survey in order to gather relevant information that will make your upcoming speech tailored to their interests and needs.

Consider your audience. In the weeks and days prior to your speaking event, focus your attention on your audience. Consider how you will be providing them with information that will make their lives better. Remember that you either enlarge or diminish others with your words. So think about the audience every day for a few minutes. Meditate on your audience. Pray for your audience if you're so inclined. Your time and effort will be worth it.

Connect with your audience before you speak. You might want to add a personal touch if your audience is small (20 to 30 people) by contacting them directly through e-mail, social media, or a good old-fashioned letter. This requires considerable effort, but it's worth it.

I've spoken at small conferences of 40 to 50 attendees where I've sent personal, handwritten letters to each individual one week before I was scheduled to speak. It was a lot of work to write a couple of sentences of welcome and good wishes to each audience member, but you would not believe the warm and enthusiastic welcome I received even before the audience was seated in the conference room. Reach out and touch someone before you speak.

Dress up. One obvious way you can increase your credibility with the audience is to dress up a little more than you normally would. That doesn't mean a suit and tie or an evening gown, but you should be one of the best-dressed people at the speaking event. You are the speaker for goodness' sake. Act like one, ... I mean, dress like one.

Arrive early and mingle. Arrive at the speaking event 30 minutes earlier than you are expected. This gives you time to check out the speaking room or auditorium before the audience arrives. It's also a good to locate the drinking fountain, restroom, and emergency exit in case the audience really dislikes your speech. Plus, you'll have a few minutes alone to collect yourself, breathe, and focus your attention and spirit in the right direction.

Be respectful in your delivery. As you are delivering your speech, be respectful of your audience. Use encouraging, supportive, and gracious language when addressing your audience. Don't use obscene, vulgar, or disrespectful language. You want to be a speaker who demonstrates the highest standards of ethical and respectful delivery. We're talking about your character on public display when you address an audience. So always take the high road and be respectful in your delivery.

Be the last to leave. Although some speakers want to be treated like royalty and be rushed off stage to their waiting limousine amid the thunderous applause. I would suggest that you stick around, answer questions, and chat with those audience members who honor you with their presence as they line up to shake your hand. In fact, be the last one to leave—after you've helped clean up, thanked the appropriate support folks, and tied up any loose ends with the speaking event contact person. Be the first one to arrive and the last one to leave. Talk about ethos ....

Express your thanks. Remember to write a thank-you note and send it via snail mail (the U.S. postal service) to the group or organization that sponsored or hired you to speak. Also write a separate thank-you card to the contact person who assisted you. Have a grateful heart. It not only builds friendships, but it also builds your character. Public speaking is more than just speaking in front of an audience. It develops and expresses your ethos.

Logos (Logical Appeal)

The second component of persuasion is logos. *Logos* is the logical appeal or the reasoning process presented by the speaker. *Reasoning* is the process of drawing conclusions from evidence. You will recall that evidence takes the form of either statistics or expert testimony. Let's examine the two basic forms of the reasoning process: deductive and inductive reasoning.

Deductive reasoning moves from a general rule or premise and applies it to a specific case. The flow is from the general to the specific, from big to small. An example of deductive reasoning would be

1. Mary is a member of a church. (*premise*)
2. Therefore, Mary believes in God. (*specific conclusion*)

In most deductive reasoning, one of the premises is not stated. This is called an *enthymeme*. Let's look at the reasoning again and include the missing premise:

1. Members of a church believe in God. (*major premise*)
2. Mary is a member of a church. (*minor premise*)
3. Therefore, Mary believes in God. (*specific conclusion*)

When all three steps of the deductive reasoning process are stated, as in the preceding example, it is called a *syllogism*.

Let's see if you can fill in the missing part in the following syllogism:

1. All human beings are mortal.
2. Travis is a human being.
3. Therefore, _____.

(How was that? The answer is "Travis is mortal.")

Try to complete the missing information in this example:

1. All divorced people have been married.
2. _____.
3. Therefore, John has been married.

(Was this one easy for you? The answer to the minor premise is "John is divorced.")

Now, let's see how the syllogism can be used to test the deductive logic of a speech. Suppose that you want to convince your audience that automobile air conditioning units are destroying our atmosphere. The syllogism would look something like this:

Major Premise. Freon gas destroys the earth's ozone layer.
Minor Premise. Most automobile air conditioning units leak significant amounts of freon into the atmosphere.
Conclusion. Therefore, automobile air conditioning units are destroying the earth's ozone layer.

Now that you have constructed the syllogism, you will need to research and present evidence—both statistical and expert testimony—that will prove your major and minor premises to your audience. These can serve as the content for the first two points of your persuasive speech. If you succeed in getting your audience to agree with your major and minor premises, they should accept your conclusion. If used correctly, deductive logic can be an effective persuasive tool.

Whereas deductive reasoning moves from the general to the specific, *inductive reasoning* uses the opposite strategy. It examines specific examples or facts and then draws a general conclusion. Inductive reasoning moves from the small to the large, from the specific to the general.

Suppose you have owned three mutt dogs in your life, and each one of those mixed-breed dogs was friendly, well behaved, and healthy. From your experience and observation of those three specific dogs, you could arrive at the general conclusion that all mutt dogs make great pets. If you read statistics asserting that married couples who communicated regularly stayed married longer than couples who did not, you might conclude that regular communication is an important requirement for a long marriage. In both cases, you moved from specific observations or evidence to a general conclusion.

In the case in which your experience with three different mutt dogs led you to conclude that all mixed-breed dogs make great pets, you were using the inductive reasoning process. In other words, you said to

> *The less men think,*
> *the more they talk.*
> —MONTESQUIEU

yourself that what is true in some instances is true in all instances. This is a common form of inductive reasoning used by speakers.

In the second example of communication and marriage length, you were using *reasoning by statistics*, another form of inductive reasoning. Different pieces of statistical evidence, each pointing to the same conclusion, led to the belief that regular communication is important to a long-lasting marriage. Reasoning by statistics isn't readily accepted by all people, however. There are many who are suspicious of anything that resembles numerical data, and there is some basis for their skepticism. Statistics can be presented and interpreted in a variety of ways that can be misleading. Here are some suggestions for using statistics:

Document your statistics orally. If your audience is not familiar with the statistics you will be presenting, you need to document the evidence *before* you share it with your audience. You should cite the author, source, and date of the research. It can be cited as simply as:

"Dr. Joe Yamato, in his book, *Dangers of Sugar*, published in 2009, warns . . ."

or

"In the article 'Top Swimmers in America,' Terrin Flores reported in the current edition of Sports Illustrated that . . ."

Build the ethos of the source/author. If the author or researcher is not familiar to your audience, you may wish to spend a few moments building the ethos or credibility of the person. Do this *before* you document the evidence. Here's a brief example:

"Terrin Flores has been a sportswriter for 22 years. She has specialized in swimming sports and has interviewed all the biggest Olympic swimming stars in the past 18 years." (ethos building) . . . (pause) . . .

"In the article 'Top Swimmers in America,' Terrin Flores reported in the current edition of Sports Illustrated that . . ." (documentation)

Give an adequate amount of statistics/expert testimony. You should present at least one statistic or expert testimony to prove each main point of your speech. Don't go overboard, however. You can reach a point of diminishing returns, and an avalanche of statistics and expert testimony can overwhelm an audience. You need to be the judge of how much evidence to present to a particular audience.

Provide quality evidence. Your evidence should reflect the best possible research available. Are the authors credible? Are the sources of the information—books, magazines, periodicals—credible? If the quality of your information is questionable, the impact of your speech is jeopardized.

Provide recent evidence. Present research that is recent. Whenever possible, give research that is no more than five years old. The more recent the evidence is, the more credible it is to your audience.

Provide relevant evidence. Test your evidence to ensure that it does indeed support your proposition or main point. After you have presented a piece of evidence, your audience should not have to ask themselves the question, "So what? What did that evidence have to do with the point he was trying to make?" Make the relevance of your evidence clear.

Restate your evidence in your own words. After you have stated your evidence or your expert testimony, it is important that you pause for a moment and then restate the information in your own words. This gives the audience another chance to be exposed to the data in a different way. Watch how the speaker restates the evidence in the following example:

> "The study indicated that 16 percent of women showed signs of stress, whereas 33 percent of the men in the experiment displayed stress." (evidence) . . . (pause) . . . "What this means is that twice as many men as women exhibited stress in the test." (restatement)

Translate your evidence into a picture. Sometimes the evidence you present is difficult to envision or comprehend. In such instances, it is important to translate or interpret the evidence in terms that are more readily understood or visualized by your listeners. Notice how the translation of the statistic provides a clearer picture. "The NASA space capsule weighs 120,000 pounds. That's the equivalent of 48 Toyota pickups!"

Other Forms of Reasoning.   There are three other forms of reasoning we should briefly mention because they are often used in persuasive appeals logic. They are reasoning by analogy, reasoning by causation, and reasoning by definition.

> *Reasoning by analogy* is a reasoning attempt that shows that similar circumstances produce similar conclusions. This is a special form of reasoning by generalization. Suppose that Company A went bankrupt last year, and you show that the circumstances of Company A were similar to those of Company B. From that, you could assert that Company B will also go bankrupt. Because its circumstances are similar, it will suffer a similar fate. Another example of reasoning by analogy is, "You're just like your brother, and you'll end up in jail just like he did." Pretty grim, huh?
>
> *Reasoning by causation* assumes that every cause has an effect. When two things occur together frequently, we often assume that one caused the other. Let's say that every time you go swimming, you get a headache. After a while, you might conclude that the swimming caused the headache. The *independent variable*, the swimming, causes the *dependent variable*, the headache. You need to be careful, however, about drawing such conclusions. Is there always a relationship between the two variables? Does the independent variable always precede the dependent variable? And could there be other variables (*confounding variables*) involved that you're not aware of, such as after swimming you always drink three warm glasses of brandy to ward off the cold? That could cause a headache for anyone. Be careful when you draw a conclusion when reasoning by causation.
>
> And finally, *reasoning by definition* is another form of logic that needs to be mentioned. When a situation has all the characteristics that are usually associated with a term, we can then use the term to describe the product of those characteristics. That is reasoning by definition. For example, if Joe's Diner has delicious food,

great service, and reasonable prices, we can say the restaurant is an excellent one. Because good food, great service, and reasonable prices are all characteristics of an excellent restaurant, we can apply that term to Joe's Diner. Once again, be careful when using this form of logic. Sure, Joe's Diner satisfies those three criteria presented, but what about the sanitation of the kitchen, the location of the restaurant, and the overall atmosphere of the place? Be careful with this form of reasoning also.

> *Statistics are no substitute for judgment.*
> —HENRY CLAY

Pathos (Emotional Appeal)

Do you always base your decisions on sound reasoning and well-researched evidence? Where to vacation? Which car to buy? Where to go to dinner? Whom to invite to your party? Where to live? Whom to marry? Should you have children? Should you stay married? These and thousands of other questions confront you during your lifetime.

How do you make these decisions? Do you decide on the basis of advice from others, as you consider their credibility or ethos? Perhaps you base your decisions on logical reasoning and thorough research by emphasizing logos or logical proof. Or do you base your decisions on your "gut feelings," relying primarily on how you feel emotionally about an issue? Most people probably use a combination of all three in decisions of magnitude or importance, but research has shown that much decision making is ultimately based on emotional responses, personal tastes, needs, and desires.

The third and final persuasive proof is what Aristotle referred to as pathos, or emotional appeal. *Pathos* appeals to the listener's needs, desires, and wishes. Whereas logos, or logical appeal, aims for the listener's head, pathos directs its efforts toward the listener's heart. In addition to providing logical reasoning, supported by sound evidence, and presenting yourself as a credible speaker, you must appeal to the emotions of your audience in your persuasive speech.

Hierarchy of Needs. Because emotional appeals deal with an individual's psychological needs, we should begin with an examination of the various needs. An introduction to this area is Abraham Maslow's *hierarchy of needs*, a psychological model of need structure depicting the lowest-level physical needs to the highest-level actualization needs.

The lowest level of the hierarchy is our *physical needs*, such as our need for food, water, air, sleep, and physical comfort. Our most basic requirements to get adequate oxygen to breathe, food to eat, and water to drink are often taken for granted, unless we are drowning, starving, or dying of thirst. Our audience will most likely have these most basic needs met, so a persuasive speech based primarily on the satisfaction of this level of need is not usually advised.

The second level on the hierarchy is *safety needs*. Safety needs not only include physical safety, such as freedom from illness, disease, and violence, but they also include having a job, a place to call home, a sense of stability and order, and a lawful environment. Many persuasive appeals can be generated from this level of safety needs.

> *All learning has an emotional base.*
> —PLATO

Belonging needs serve as the third level of needs. These include the need to be loved by a significant other and the need for family and friends. They also include the need to belong to a group of people who share your interests and activities, such as a church, an interest group, a pottery class, and even a motorcycle club. They can also include the need to belong to a political movement, a nation, or even the human race.

The fourth level is *self-esteem needs*. The assumption here is that people need to feel good about themselves. They need to feel they are worthwhile, attractive, capable, and skilled. People will invest a great amount of energy, effort, and money in activities that will enhance their self-esteem. Self-help books, diet centers, graduate schools, promotions at work, meditation retreats, jewelry stores, exclusive designer clothing boutiques, and a thousand other self-esteem-enhancing sources cry out to us. This level of needs is rich in emotional-appeal material.

Self-actualization involves realizing one's highest potential. It is placed at the top level of the hierarchy of needs. We have a need to be the best we can with what we have been given. To be the best parent possible, the best teacher, the best spouse; to write that book we've been thinking about for years; or to learn to fly an airplane.

A woman returned to school after having been away from formal education for more than 25 years. Even though she was at the age when most people retire from work, she wanted to begin her college education to become a chiropractor. After raising three children by herself and saving for her college education, she was ready to accomplish what she had dreamed of for years. This woman was striving for self-actualization—realizing her highest desire, to become a person who helps heal others.

Some of the best emotional-appeal stories you can include in your speech will come from the lives of individuals who have sought to realize their highest potential. When you are researching emotional appeals for your persuasive speech, remember the various needs of your audience members.

Specific Emotional Targets.

You should consider five other areas when preparing your emotional appeals to a particular audience. They are sex, conformity, wealth, pleasure, and personal growth.

Appealing to the motive of *sex* is one of the most popular strategies utilized by the advertising industry. Every other advertisement has an attractive man or woman fondling products from cars to fertilizer. Our desire to be attractive to others makes for a powerful motivational appeal. Beneath the motive of sex is a deeper need for intimacy, belonging, and love. These needs all provide rich areas to explore for emotional appeals.

Conformity is one of the most powerful needs we have. The need to appear and behave like others is a potent motivational force, affecting young and old alike. Often, the appeal can take the form of avoiding nonconforming behavior or being different from everyone else. "You wouldn't want to be the only person in your neighborhood who didn't have attractive landscaping!" and "How would it feel to be the only person who didn't contribute, when all of your colleagues had?" are examples of this technique.

Another specific target that is especially effective with audiences is *wealth*. Wealth not only includes the desire to possess piles of money, diamonds, and gold; it also encompasses an individual's need to earn, save, and invest money. It can speak to a desire to spend money wisely and prevent its loss. Appeals to wealth can prove beneficial in moving your audiences emotionally.

Another motive you should consider is that of *pleasure*. Most people like doing things that bring them happiness, enjoyment, and pleasure. Use appeals that point out or highlight how your proposition will provide them with pleasure.

Personal growth is the individual's need or desire to examine life, explore different aspects of selfhood, and, ideally, make strides toward growing as a human being. The emphasis is on becoming different from what we were in the past and exploring new ways of living and being. The introvert becomes the extrovert, the thinker becomes the feeler, and the bodybuilder becomes the spiritual seeker. The focus is on process and growth. This need to expand, change, and grow is one of the most potent of all personal needs to appeal to in your audience. It was the reason this book was written.

Suggestions for Using Emotional Appeals

When using emotional appeals, consider the following suggestions:

Select appropriate emotional appeals. You must analyze your topic and audience carefully and then research appropriate emotionally appealing material that will support your proposition and appeal to the needs of the audience.

Establish common ground with the audience. An audience will more likely listen to your emotional appeals if they feel you have things in common with them. During the first half of your talk, usually in the introduction, relate to common experiences, values, beliefs, and circumstances that will establish common ground with your listeners.

Use the yes-response. The audience must ultimately agree with your point of view if you are to be successful in your persuasive speech. One effective technique that can lay the groundwork in the beginning for such an agreeable climate is the *yes-response*—a series of rhetorical questions constructed so that the audience is likely to answer "yes." As the audience silently considers each question, they begin to get into a more agreeable state of mind. Listen to the series of questions this speaker uses for a speech on increasing the size of the police force in a certain town as he utilizes the *yes-response*.

"Do you want a town that is free from crime?"

"Would you like to be able to walk the streets at night again?"

"And wouldn't you want to feel safe in your own neighborhood?"

> *Kindness has influenced more people than eloquence.*
> —GANDHI

Use emotional appeal at the end of the body of your speech. If you are going to fully develop an emotional appeal, such as a story or long illustration, do so toward the end of your speech. The final main point in the body of your speech is the most appropriate place to include a detailed story. The first two main points should stress evidence and expert opinion as you present your arguments, but save the final point for material that is especially appealing to the emotions of the audience.

Match your nonverbal behavior with your appeal. Your body movement, gestures, voice, and facial expressions should reinforce the emotional appeals you are using. If your material is sad, look, talk, and move as if you are sad. If the material is joyous, look, talk, and move as if you are joyous. Don't give your audience mixed messages. Use your nonverbal communication to add credibility and impact to your verbal message.

Use pauses in your delivery. One common mistake speakers commit when delivering emotional appeals is forgetting to give the audience time to digest the material. Use pauses after you've delivered a powerful line of dialogue. A two- or three-second pause will give your audience time to consider what you have just said. It places emphasis on your statement, and it gives you time to breathe. Use your pauses as you practice the speech. If you don't practice the speech with pauses, you will forget to use them when the real speech time arrives.

9.3 Types of Persuasive Speeches

Now that we have looked at the basics of persuasive speaking—ethical proof, logical proof, and emotional proof—we can examine the basic main-point outlines of various persuasive speeches. The introductions, conclusions, and subpoints of the following outlines have been omitted.

Speech of Reasons Approach

If your audience has no opinion, is neutral, or is only mildly in favor or mildly opposed to your proposition, you can use the *speech of reasons* approach. This simple method of persuasive speaking is best suited for these audiences.

Proposition: You should exercise regularly.

    I. Regular exercise will improve your physical health.
   II. Regular exercise will improve your psychological well-being.
 III. Regular exercise will improve your chances of living a long life.

Problem-Solution Approach

If you want your audience to consider the adoption of a specific plan or solution to a problem, you can use the *problem-solution* approach. This works best with an audience that has no opinion, is neutral, or is only mildly in favor or mildly opposed to your proposition.

Proposition: You should support the 8 percent federal income tax plan.

    I. The current federal income tax is unfair.
   II. The proposed 8 percent federal income tax will tax all citizens equally.
 III. The proposed 8 percent federal income tax is the best solution to our tax problem.

Criteria-Satisfaction Approach

If your audience is hostile to your proposition, the criteria-satisfaction approach can be effective because it utilizes the yes-response as you have them agree with your criteria for a satisfactory solution. It also seeks to establish common ground with your hostile audience because you stipulate criteria that are agreeable to speaker and audience.

Proposition: You should attend a community college.

   I. You want a college that meets these criteria.
     A. It must offer a wide variety of courses.
     B. It must offer individualized instructional support.
     C. It must be affordable.

  II. The community college meets these criteria.
     A. It offers a wide variety of courses.
     B. It offers individualized instructional support.
     C. It is affordable.

Negative Method Approach

If your audience is hostile, the *negative method* can be especially effective because the structure forces the audience to realize that there is no other option than the one you propose. Your main-point structure eliminates the other options as viable solutions.

Proposition: You should save money for the future.

   I. Your current level of savings is inadequate.
  II. The social security system will be bankrupt.
 III. Your earning power will diminish in coming years.
 IV. The only solution is to save money now for the future.

Monroe's Motivated Sequence

The final persuasive speech pattern is *Monroe's Motivated Sequence*, developed by speech professor Alan Monroe in the 1930s. This is a popular and highly effective persuasive speech pattern for moving audiences to action. It is based on a developmental model of persuasion, each step building on the previous step. This pattern is especially useful if you are seeking immediate action or results from your audience. Monroe's Motivated Sequence has five steps: attention, need, satisfaction, visualization, and action.

Step 1: Gain Attention.   In the first step, you gain the audience's attention and focus it on the specific problem at hand. You can achieve this by audience questions, stories, startling statistics or facts, and visual aids or by making specific references of connection to the audience. If you gain their attention effectively, the audience will be ready and willing to listen to your speech.

Step 2: Establish Need.   In the second step, you make the audience feel a need for change by showing that there is a serious problem to solve. Your audience should feel that something must be done or has to be learned because of the need you presented and developed. This can be achieved with the following three steps:

1. State the need that exists or will exist.
2. Illustrate this need with examples, statistics, and expert testimony.
3. Show how this need affects your specific listeners.

Step 3: Satisfy the Need.   Once you have gained the audience's attention and proved a relevant need that is personally important to them, you are ready to propose a way to satisfy this need. It is in this satisfaction step that you present your solution to the problem. This is the most important step in the sequence—providing your audience with a solution to reinforce or change their attitudes and beliefs or motivate them to action. Be as specific as possible when you propose the attitude or belief you want them to adopt or the course of action you want them to take.

Step 4: Visualize the Need Satisfied.   After you have presented your solution to the problem, you strengthen the audience's beliefs and feelings by having them actually see or visualize how your solution will benefit them. You are now moving your audience from the present into the future. One way you can achieve this is to describe what the positive future will look like if your proposal is adopted. Use specific examples and illustrations when describing this brighter future. Another way you can achieve a similar result is to describe a worse future if they fail to adopt your solution to the problem.

> *The great end of life is not knowledge, but action.*
> —THOMAS FULLER

Step 5: Ask for Action.   The final step of the motivated sequence is to make a direct request of your audience. You want your audience to move in a specific direction, either in thought or action. State exactly what you want your audience to do or believe, providing specific guidelines as to how they will achieve the desired results. Use strong emotional appeals during this final step. This is the time to be direct, positive, and forceful.

Here's a brief example of Monroe's Motivated Sequence:

   I. **Attention:** A local child is killed by a drunk driver.
   II. **Need:** You or someone you love could be killed or injured by a drunk driver.
   III. **Satisfaction:** Mothers Against Drunk Drivers (MADD) is a national organization that brings attention to this serious problem and supports legislation to get drunk drivers off the road.
   IV. **Visualization:** Imagine our highways without drunk drivers where you and your loved ones are safe.
   V. **Action:** I want you to support MADD with a $10 donation this month.

SAMPLE PERSUASIVE OUTLINE
STOP USING CREDIT CARDS

Proposition: To persuade the audience to stop using credit cards.

Introduction

This past year, a rather traumatic event happened to a good friend of mine—she and her husband were forced to file for bankruptcy due to excessive credit card debt. They lost many of their worldly possessions in the process, and their credit rating was ruined for the next several years. Did you know that Americans currently owe in excess of $540 billion in credit card debt and that the forecast for the future is that this debt will only increase because of our addiction to the mighty credit card? Today, I want you to quit using credit cards because it will save your money, your sanity, and your future. Let's examine each of these powerful reasons.

Body

I. The first reason you should give up credit cards is to save money.
   A. It will eliminate high annual fees.
   B. It will eliminate high annual interest rates.
   C. It will reduce unnecessary spending.
      1. According to Gerri Detweiler in her book, *The Ultimate Credit Handbook*, "Credit card companies recognize human nature and play upon the fact that credit cards make it easy to overextend ourselves."
      2. Story about my friends overextending themselves on credit cards.
II. The second reason you should give up credit cards is to save your sanity.
   A. It reduces your worry over unnecessary spending.
   B. It reduces your anxiety over ever-increasing debt.
      1. Margorie Hillis, in her book, *Orchids on Your Budget*, warns that credit card debt will destroy your peace of mind.
      2. This anxiety can express itself in physical ailments.
   C. It gives you more time to think about more positive things in life.
III. The third reason you should give up credit cards is to save your future.
   A. It can prevent future bankruptcy.
      1. Mike Yorkey, in his book, *Real Solutions for Getting Out of Debt*, explains that "giving up credit cards is a real prevention against future bankruptcy."
      2. Story about Josh Ling being saved from bankruptcy.
   B. It helps maintain excellent future credit ratings.
      1. Sean Mills, credit counselor, says that "living within your budget and not using your credit cards can insure a good credit rating."
      2. List Sean Mills's life goals for your money future.
   C. It can foster a healthy attitude toward future spending.

Conclusion

Today, I've given you three excellent reasons why you should give up using credit cards—it will save your money, your sanity, and your future. So begin your path to financial health and spiritual freedom by actually cutting up your credit cards in a hundred pieces and getting the pieces of your life put back into place. Proverbs warns us that "A fool and his money are soon parted." Be wise and part with those credit cards and not your money!

References

Detweiler, G. 2003. *The Ultimate Credit Handbook*. New York: Jeremy Thatcher/Putman.

Hillis, M. 2010. *Orchids on Your Budget*. London: Virago Books.

Mills, S. Mar. 11, 2009. Credit counselor, San Jose, CA. (408) 767-1112.

Yorkey, M. 2002. *Real Solutions for Getting Out of Debt*. Ventura, CA: Vine Books.

SAMPLE KEY WORD OUTLINE

Introduction

Bankrupt couple story

Eliminating credit cards saves money, sanity, future

Body
I. *Saves money*
   Eliminates annual fees
   Eliminates high interest rates
   Reduces spending (Detweiler reference 1)
II. *Saves sanity*
   Reduces worry
   Reduces anxiety (Hillis reference 2)
   Provides time
III. *Saves future*
   Prevents bankruptcy (Yorkey reference 3)
   Maintains credit rating (Mills reference 4)
   Healthy spending attitude

Conclusion
Eliminating credit cards saves money, sanity; future proverbs quotation

COMMUNICATION ACTIVITIES

PERSONAL ACTIVITIES

1. **The most persuasive speaker**
   Who is the most persuasive speaker you have ever heard? What made this individual so persuasive? How did this person's ethos, logos, and pathos influence or shape your response to him or her? What personality characteristics and delivery skills do you share with this individual? What delivery skills and personality characteristics are different?

2. **A topic or belief you would die for**
   One of the most difficult assignments for the novice speaker is to select a persuasive topic. A method that is helpful in choosing such a topic is to ask yourself the questions, "What (if anything) would I die for?" and "What would I risk my life for?" These two questions could provide some possible topics for your talk. If you discover that you wouldn't die for anything, or at least risk your life for something, maybe you should stick to informative speaking. Persuasive speaking—really good persuasive speaking—usually involves a speaker who is committed to something, stands for something, and is willing to sacrifice for something.

3. **Outlining persuasive main points**
   Select one of your topics or ideas from Exercise 2 ("A topic or belief you would die for") and brainstorm 10 reasons that support this proposition. In other words, give 10 reasons why your audience should accept your particular topic or belief. To help you generate your list of reasons, consider ethical, philosophical, spiritual, economic, physical, and psychological reasons why your listeners would benefit from your proposition. From your list of 10 reasons, select the three best reasons when considering the four categories of audience analysis.

4. **Analyzing a persuasive appeal**

Select three full-page ads from one of your favorite magazines and examine each ad for the kinds of persuasive appeals it is attempting to evoke in the reader. Use Aristotle's three proofs (ethos, logos, and pathos) or Maslow's hierarchy of needs to identify and discuss the persuasive appeals found in each of the three ads you selected.

CLASS ACTIVITIES

1. **Group discussion: Advertising campaign**

Divide the class into groups of five or six. Each group is to design a simple one-page advertisement attempting to get high school seniors to enroll in a public speaking course during their first semester in college. Use any of the information in this chapter to give you ideas as you design this one-page ad. Be prepared to present your ad to the entire class. Your instructor may have each group write and/or draw its ad on an overhead transparency so it can be viewed by all the students.

2. **"I want you to" speech**

Prepare, practice, and present a six- to eight-minute persuasive speech on the topic "I want you to ..." In this speech, you could persuade your audience to visit a place, contribute to a charity, enroll in a particular class, or read a certain book. It's up to you! Research the topic and interview experts in the field you are discussing. Develop each of your main points with documented information, examples, and strong emotional appeals. Include any visual aids that might be helpful. Your speech should contain an introduction, body, and conclusion.

3. **Problem-solution speech**

Prepare, practice, and present a six- to eight-minute persuasive speech discussing a problem of at least countywide importance and presenting a specific solution to that problem. Research the topic and interview experts in the field you are discussing. Make certain that you prove there is a problem and that your solution will solve the problem. Develop each of your main points with documented information, examples, and strong emotional appeals. Include any visual aids that might be helpful. Your speech should contain an introduction, body, and conclusion.

4. **Monroe's Motivated Sequence speech**

Prepare, practice, and present a six- to eight-minute persuasive speech using Monroe's Motivated Sequence (attention, need, satisfaction, visualization, and action). Research the topic and interview experts in the field you are discussing. Develop your main points with documented information, examples, and strong emotional appeals. Include any visual aids that might be helpful. Your speech should contain an introduction, body, and conclusion.

Chapter 10

SPEAKING FOR YOUR LIFETIME
A LIFELONG JOURNEY

LEARNING OBJECTIVES

After reading this chapter, you should be able to:

10.1 Explain the two ways of viewing public speaking

10.2 Discuss impromptu speaking

10.3 Apply the impromptu word list in a practice setting

10.4 Discuss special occasion speeches

10.5 Explain the concept of developing the heart of a speaker

Sylvia glanced around the room as the members of the family reunion committee sat silently staring at the floor. Her Uncle Will had just asked for a volunteer to serve as the master of ceremonies for the upcoming family reunion. It was going to be a weekend affair, with more than 70 family members in attendance. The hotel conference room had been reserved, the caterer selected, and the entertainment committee formed. The only thing left to do was have someone volunteer to serve as master of ceremonies for the Saturday evening festivities.

Uncle Will asked a second time for a volunteer, and again everyone remained silent, motionless. During that moment, Sylvia recalled the words of her public speaking teacher, who said at the end of last semester, "Public speaking is a lifelong skill. When the opportunities arise in your life, choose to speak."

Sylvia's decision to speak did not come easily. She didn't feel like taking on the responsibilities of serving as the MC of the family reunion tribute evening. She didn't feel like getting those butterflies again, as she had in her public speaking class. But Sylvia raised her hand, despite her feelings of anxiety and uncertainty.

Everyone in the room smiled and breathed a sigh of relief when Sylvia volunteered—everyone except for Sylvia. Her journey was just beginning.

10.1 Two Ways of Viewing Public Speaking

Public Speaking: Never Again

Many public speaking students regard their final speech as exactly that—THEIR FINAL SPEECH. Never again will they have to research a speech. Never again will they have to stand before an audience. Never again will they have to experience those butterflies. Never again will they have to give another speech as long as they live. NEVER AGAIN, they reassure themselves.

From this perspective, public speaking can be viewed with anxiety, fear, and even anger, especially if it's a required course. It's seen as a necessary evil, something to be endured. It's a once-in-a-lifetime event. Like the measles—something to be survived and then quickly pushed from our minds and forgotten. NEVER AGAIN.

Becoming a Speaker: A Lifelong Journey

There's another way to view your public speaking experience that is very different from the one just described. Instead of seeing it as an experience to be endured or tolerated, it can be seen as an invitation to a journey that may last your entire lifetime. Rather than a destination to be reached and then forgotten, it can be viewed as the beginning of a process of discovery and enrichment.

Becoming a speaker can be a lifelong journey to discover greater self-expression, gain increased personal power, and achieve a more intimate sense of who you are and where you're going. It can be the beginning of a wonderfully exciting journey that can take you to places you have never seen, put you in touch with people you have yet to meet, and introduce you to parts of yourself you never knew existed. Your decision to continue becoming a speaker—to stand in front of an audience and share a few words in the months and years to come—may make all the difference in your life.

When Sylvia listened to Uncle Will's plea for a master of ceremonies in the opening story, she could have chosen to keep her eyes riveted to the ground like the rest of the family and let the opportunity pass. Instead, she chose to raise her hand and volunteer. She chose to continue her journey to speak in front of others.

When Saturday night rolled around, Sylvia gave a three-minute impromptu speech on the importance of family in this day and age. She introduced each entertainment skit with a funny quotation and concluded the evening's festivities with a brief speech on the importance of staying connected to one another.

By the end of the night, Sylvia was relieved it was over. She had been anxious before the evening began, but once Sylvia started speaking, she discovered she was actually enjoying the experience—the laughter, the tears, and the applause from the audience. And the congratulations on a job well done from Uncle Will.

In the years that followed, Sylvia found other opportunities to speak. She volunteered as a spokesperson for her city's Historical Society, she gave tribute speeches at a number of retirement dinners, and she even delivered the keynote address at a women's business

> *There are no gifted or ungifted. There are only those who give and those who withhold.*
> —MARTIN BUBER

retreat. Sylvia also taught in her church's adult education program and often served as the master of ceremonies for her company's special occasion dinners.

Sylvia chose to be a speaker for a lifetime.

Your public speaking experience and your role as a speaker doesn't have to end with this course. You can choose to continue your journey, perhaps for a lifetime.

10.2 Impromptu Speaking

During your lifetime, the vast majority of your public speaking will be impromptu—speaking without prior preparation and practice. You will not always be given an opportunity to research, outline, practice, and deliver a formal speech. Much of your speaking in public will be informal, less than 1–2 minutes in length, and delivered without preparation or practice. Every day you will be asked to present your ideas, opinions, and feelings during informal speaking situations. In this final chapter, we will look at two different types of impromptu speeches—the One-Point Impromptu Speech and the Standard Impromptu Speech.

The One-Point Impromptu Speech (One Minute)

Whether you're presenting your opinion at a city council meeting, responding to a question at a business meeting, or giving a toast at a family gathering, your speaking will most likely be spur of the moment. These impromptu speeches will usually be about one minute in length, so your effort and focus must be extremely specific—no time to develop a full-blown introduction, body, and conclusion as we've been learning and practicing in this book. These brief, spur-of-the-moment responses to questions, inquiries, or requests can be referred to as One-Point Impromptu Speeches. The One-Point Impromptu Speech contains three parts—statement of the point, development of the point, restatement of the point.

1. State the Point.   The most challenging task in the One-Point Impromptu Speech is just that, to decide on the one point (not two or three) you want to make to your audience. Once you've decided upon the one point, state that point clearly and concisely. Avoid using well-developed attention getters to open your impromptu speech. If you do, the audience might expect you to deliver a more developed body and conclusion, which is not the goal of the One-Point Impromptu Speech. Brevity is the goal. "I believe tax breaks will help the economy," "I disagree with the city council's proposal," and "Class attendance is a positive incentive to student success" are examples of one-point statements.

2. Develop the Point.   Once you've stated your point, you need to develop that point. Most likely, you will not have documented information, statistics, or expert testimony on the tip of your tongue, but you can give an example, illustration, or anecdote from your personal life to develop your point.

Your personal experience is the richest source of developmental material for your One-Point Impromptu Speech. "I'd like to develop this point with a brief story about how my tax break allowed me to purchase . . ." "I once lived in a community that did exactly what our city council is suggesting in its proposal, and I'd like to share the dreadful ramifications of such an unfortunate decision . . ." and "When I went to college, I had an experience that convinced me that class attendance is a positive incentive to class success . . ." are the beginnings to anecdotes or illustrations that support the point the speaker is attempting to make. You can also use examples or illustrations you've read about, heard from others, or seen in a movie. This section of your speech should constitute 90 percent of your One-Point Impromptu Speech.

3. Restate your Point.   Conclude your speech with a simple restatement of your original point. No need for a review of your developmental material or some impassioned emotional appeal. Simply remind your audience of your own point. "I believe tax breaks will help the economy," "I disagree with the city council's proposal," and "Class attendance is a positive incentive to student success." Keep it simple—the One-Point Impromptu Speech.

The Standard Impromptu Speech (Two or More Minutes)

Although most of your impromptu speaking requires that you present only one point in a brief fashion, opportunities may arise to deliver a more developed impromptu speech. If additional details are requested, a longer response is desired, or your public speaking instructor wants to develop your speaking skills, the Standard Impromptu Speech can be very helpful. The Standard Impromptu Speech is similar to the extemporaneous speech you've learned about in an earlier chapter with its introduction, body, and conclusion. The speech length is generally two or more minutes, and it provides a means to present two to three points in the body rather than just one. Here are the five steps that make for effective Standard Impromptu Speeches.

1. Select One Thought.   Your first step in the Standard Impromptu Speech is to select one thought, idea, or theme. We'll divide that thought into smaller parts later. But first, select just one thought you wish to communicate to your audience. It can be as simple as "Greg has been kind to us" or "Speech training is helpful." Many experienced impromptu speakers use a quotation or proverb as their main idea or thought, such as "Love your neighbor" or "A stitch in time saves nine." No matter what topic you're given, try to think of a one-sentence (a short one at that) idea or thought to work with. The shorter the better.

2. Organize Your Thought into a Pattern.   Once you've decided on a main thought or idea, the second step in the impromptu process is to organize it into a pattern. Here is a list of some ways you can organize your topic:

> **Chronological Order:** past/present/future, then/now
> **Topical Order:** three characteristics about . . . , two reasons we should . . .
> **Spatial Order:** near/far, up/down, kitchen/bedroom
> **Problem/Solution:** crime/education, inflation/reduce deficit

Let's try to organize the topic of "money" into the four organizational patterns just listed.

Chronological Order	**I.** Money I had in the past.
	II. Money I currently have.
	III. Money I will have in the future.
Topical Order	**I.** Money is difficult to earn.
	II. Money is easy to spend.
Spatial Order	**I.** Inflation rates in America.
	II. Inflation rates in Brazil.
Problem/Solution	**I.** Saving money is difficult.
	II. Enroll in a payroll-deduction program.

Notice how a single topic, such as "money," can be organized in a variety of patterns. With some practice, you can organize any topic into a number of patterns without much difficulty.

3. Support Your Points with Specifics.   Once you've selected your topic and have organized it into some pattern, you are ready to move to the third step of supporting the main points of your Standard Impromptu Speech. You can develop your main points with definitions, comparisons, specific examples, anecdotes, personal illustrations, statistics, facts, or quotations. One of the easiest methods of support is to reach back into your own life experience and share brief anecdotes or illustrations that relate to the point you are trying to make. This method helps the audience feel more involved with you, the speaker.

4. Construct an Introduction.   Now that you've selected an impromptu topic, organized the topic into a main-point pattern, and developed each point with supporting material, you're ready to construct a brief introduction for your talk. The introduction will consist of an attention getter and a preview of main points. Your entire introduction should take no more than 10–15 seconds for a two-minute Standard Impromptu Speech.

The attention getter can be an audience question, a personal statement of belief, or a brief anecdote. A preview of main points should follow your attention getter. This is simply a one-sentence statement of the two or three main points you want to present in your talk. For instance, "I'd like to tell you about two of Jane's wonderful traits—her dedication to her job and her dedication to her family."

5. Construct a Conclusion.   Your conclusion should contain a review of main points and a final thought or quotation. For a two-minute Standard Impromptu Speech, the conclusion should be about 10–15 seconds long. The review of main points should be a one-sentence review of the two points you presented in your talk. For example, "This evening I've told you about Jane's dedication to her job and her dedication to her family." After you've reviewed your points, you end your speech with a final thought or appeal.

> *There is enough time. I have exactly the right number of hours, minutes, and seconds to accomplish and do everything that I need to do in my lifetime.*
> —CLAIRE CLONINGER

One point to remember about your conclusion is to know when to end. Your conclusion should be short and to the point. Don't ramble. This is not the time to begin another point or share a second speech. Know when to put your impromptu speech to bed.

Standard Impromptu Speech Outline

Look at the outline of the impromptu speech that follows. Review each part of the outline to make sure you understand, and visualize the function of each component. This basic outline can be used in all speeches, regardless of length.

Introduction (10–15 seconds)	Attention getter
	Preview of main points
Body	**I.** Main point (45 seconds)
	Example, anecdote, or evidence
	II. Main point (45 seconds)
	Example, anecdote, or evidence
Conclusion (10–15 seconds)	Summary of main points
	Final thought

Some Helpful Suggestions When Giving Impromptu Speeches

Keep Your Speech Short.   If you are ever asked to give an impromptu speech, keep your speech short. If television advertisers are willing to spend hundreds of thousands of dollars for a 30- or 60-second advertising spot because they believe the message will reach their target audience, you should be able to get a thought or two across to your audience in one or two minutes.

Keep to Your Point.   Untrained speakers seem to wander and ramble in their speeches. When you give an impromptu talk, stick to your points. This is not a time for digressions or tangents. The old saying, "The more you say, the less you say. The less you say, the more you say," applies here. Stay focused.

Keep It Organized.   Follow the simple outline presented here. It will save you a great deal of decision making as you walk up to the podium. You won't have to think too much. Just fit your thoughts into the outline format, and you'll do fine. Simplicity is the basis of all beauty.

Keep It Colorful.   When you support your two or three main points with developmental material, remember to use colorful, descriptive language. Pretend that your audience is blind and that your responsibility is to paint mental pictures in their minds as you speak. This technique will help you utilize colorful language.

Keep It Conversational.   Use your regular conversational voice, but enlarge it a little so you will project to the people in the back of the audience. Don't try to sound like anyone else. Be yourself. Just enlarge it a bit. No one in the entire world has a voice pattern identical to yours, so enjoy your uniqueness.

Keep Your Cool. The natural tendency is to rush your impromptu speech, so remember to slow down. Walk to the podium slowly—there's no hurry. It will also give you time to organize your thoughts and locate supporting material from your life experience. Use pauses between the introduction, main points, and conclusion. Use pauses before and after important words or phrases. The use of pauses is one of the most powerful signs of speaker confidence.

> *Winston Churchill devoted the best years of his life to preparing his impromptu speeches.*
> —F. E. Smith

Keep It Natural. Your delivery—your voice, body movement, gestures, and facial expression—should be natural and relaxed. You should talk to the audience as if you are talking with friends. Remember, the audience wants you to succeed. Relax and enjoy the experience. Be yourself.

Keep It in Perspective. This speech is only 2 minutes out of your entire life. If you live to age 72, you will have experienced 37,324,800 minutes. Okay, so 12,614,400 of them are probably spent sleeping, but that still leaves you with at least 24,710,400 minutes of waking time. In round numbers, that's 25 million minutes! Your impromptu speech is only 2 minutes in length. That's only 0.000000001 percent of your life. With all that time left, maybe you should give two impromptu speeches before you leave the planet. Anyway, in light of eternity, it's not a big deal. Keep it in perspective.

10.3 Impromptu Word List

The following list of topics can be used for impromptu speaking practice. Select a number and decide on one of the two topics that follow it. Give yourself a few moments to prepare your speech using the five steps suggested. Then give your impromptu speech. You'll do well!

1. summer, friend	15. crisis, travel	29. secret, bill
2. police, season	16. star, computer	30. church, power
3. tool, universe	17. happiness, salt	31. plant, vacation
4. love, boy	18. boundary, heart	32. weep, picture
5. mistake, home	19. watch, store	33. miracle, toy
6. talk, fun	20. passion, boat	34. marriage, ball
7. ship, film	21. shock, passage	35. weather, hair
8. monster, foreign	22. furniture, car	36. gun, earth
9. holy, nation	23. doctor, regret	37. body, college
10. lamp, truth	24. nature, divorce	38. single, door
11. illness, shoe	25. energy, book	39. moral, soap
12. plastic, wonder	26. money, food	40. water, country
13. telephone, sin	27. habit, philosophy	41. gift, school
14. spirit, family	28. people, newspaper	42. temper, color

43. hate, furniture	51. logic, magazine	59. father, hope
44. music, path	52. freedom, girl	60. parade, recess
45. army, fear	53. history, mood	61. personality, bat
46. animal, bed	54. city, sensitive	62. joy, sister
47. wish, floor	55. teacher, clothes	63. paper, sex
48. ground, fish	56. dog, society	64. crime, carpet
49. ocean, art	57. farm, tax	65. change, plane
50. brother, map	58. insect, jewelry	66. worry, lamp

10.4 Special Occasion Speeches

In the course of your life, you may be called upon to speak at a special occasion, such as a wedding reception, anniversary party, retirement gathering, award ceremony, banquet, or funeral. During these special occasions, your speaking assignment could be to introduce a speaker, give a toast, present an award, accept an award, or pay tribute to an individual or group. Speakers at special events are not normally famous personalities or celebrities, but more often are friends, family members, and coworkers. The speeches are less formal than sales presentations, academic lectures, or training seminars. The goal of a special occasion speech is not to give enormous amounts of information or instruction, like an informative speech, nor to attempt to change the way an audience thinks about a controversial issue, like a persuasive speech. Rather, the goal of a special occasion speech is to unite the audience, reaffirm their beliefs, and honor specific individuals or a group. These occasions are more emotional than intellectual, more heart than head. In many respects, special occasion speeches can be the most significant, moving, and memorable of all the speeches you will ever give.

Guidelines for Special Occasion Speeches

Before we discuss specific special occasion speeches and how to deliver them effectively, let's take a moment and talk about three general guidelines to follow for all special occasion speaking.

Be Brief. More than anything else, the most important advice you can receive about special event speaking is to be brief. Please be brief. That's spelled S-H-O-R-T. You are not the reason for the special occasion. You are only a speaker, perhaps one of many, who has been asked to comment on the occasion. And often there are a number of speakers slated to share the podium, and the nightmare of all nightmares is to have each speaker deliver a full-length, keynote speech. Be kind to your audience and to yourself by being brief. We'll look at specific time limits for each kind of speech later, but for now, remember that no speech is entirely bad if it's short. Short is best. Less is more.

Be Prepared. No matter how brief, your speech should be delivered with skill, confidence, and enthusiasm. The easiest way to ensure a successful special occasion speech is to be prepared. That means to prepare and practice well in advance of the occasion. The last thing your audience wants is for you to be mumbling your words, fumbling through your note cards, and stumbling over names. Plan your speech in advance, organize it clearly, and practice it until it becomes part of you. It's best if you don't use a manuscript or note cards. Since your speech will be brief, maybe 1–3 minutes, try to memorize it. Your audience doesn't want to see the top of your head as you read a manuscript, nor are they dying to see you flip through note cards for your 30-second toast. They want to see your smiling face, speaking words that you know deep in your heart, and with enthusiasm that will make the occasion truly special. Anyone can read a manuscript or note card. Be different. Be practiced. Be prepared. Be a speaker who can walk away from the podium and walk into the hearts of the audience.

Be Heartfelt.   Special occasions are just that, special. These events are held for purposes out of the ordinary, not your everyday happening. Many are once in a lifetime. Whether it's a wedding reception, retirement party, baby dedication, or memorial service, these events are experienced in the heart, not the head. They're emotional, not intellectual. They pull us into the territory of the heart. They lead us into the realm of spirit, where laughter and tears, appreciation and gratitude, and wonder and love reign. And for a moment or two, the everyday is replaced by the eternal.

To touch the heart, you must speak from the heart. Avoid exaggeration, questionable humor, obscene language, and slapstick comedy. Most likely your special occasion speech will be taped, played, and replayed in the years to come, and the last thing you want is to be immortalized as the speaker who upset, slighted, insulted, or bored the audience. Instead, be heartfelt. No matter what kind of special occasion speech you give, be genuine and sincere. Slow down your speaking rate, smile, and look into the eyes of your audience. Be friendly. Touch the hearts of your audience by using a brief story or anecdote to illustrate a positive attribute about the individual, the group, or the occasion you are celebrating. A well-told story can move the hearts of your audience more than statistics or expert testimony and can be remembered years after the event. Stories have the power to capture the attention of the audience, to transport them to places they've never been, and make them feel emotions they rarely experience. Stories have the power to move the heart.

Types of Special Occasion Speeches

In the course of your life, you might be asked to introduce a speaker, give a toast, present an award, receive an award, deliver a tribute, give an after dinner speech, or present a eulogy. Let's look at each of these special occasion speeches.

Introducing a Speaker.   You may be asked to introduce a speaker at some special occasion. The first step in preparation for any introduction is to research the occasion, the background of the speaker, the title and brief summary of the speaker's talk, and any specific items the speaker might want you to mention in your introduction. Most important, make certain you know how to correctly pronounce the speaker's name. The worst thing you can do is stumble over the name of the individual you're introducing. Keep your introduction brief. You're there to introduce the speaker, not give the speech. A good rule is to spend no more than one-tenth of the speaker's speaking time with your introduction. So if the speaker's talk is 20 minutes in length, your introduction should be 1–2 minutes at most. Be brief.

Giving a Toast.   A toast is a very brief commemorative speech that lasts less than 30 seconds. Your remarks should be focused on the individual or individuals you are honoring. Usually everyone in the audience has his or her glass raised as you deliver your toast, so keep your comments short. Limit your remarks to one or two sentences that respect and honor the individual or individuals you're toasting, while inspiring the audience. Avoid trite clichés and worn-out phrases. Whatever brief remarks you choose, memorize your toast. This is not the time to read from a note card. Practice your toast with a champagne glass, a smile, and a strong voice. Remember to look at the individual or individuals you're honoring when you give your toast. Smile. You'll do well.

> *Life becomes harder for us when we live for others, but it also becomes much richer and happier.*
> —ALBERT SCHWEITZER

Presenting an Award.   One very common special occasion speech is the presentation of an award, which usually lasts about 2–3 minutes. Your main purpose is to explain the significance of the award and emphasize the accomplishments or worthiness of the person receiving it. Begin your speech by giving the name of the award, the reason or reasons it is being given, and any brief historical information about the award, including notable past recipients. You might also tell the audience what a privilege and honor it is for you to present the award. After this has been accomplished, announce the name of the recipient and the specific reasons he or she was selected. If possible, include a brief story that illustrates one of the reasons. Invite the recipient up to the podium to receive the award and to share some remarks with the audience. As always, practice your presentation speech to ensure that your delivery is smooth, natural, and enthusiastic. With this longer form of special occasion speech, a note card could prove helpful in keeping your remarks organized and your delivery confident. Use key words on your note card and keep your eyes on the audience and not on your note card.

Accepting an Award.   When you are accepting an award or honor, your remarks should be very brief, especially if there are other award recipients following you. However, you need to say more than "thank you," since your words should express your gratitude and recognize the significance of the award and the occasion. Your acceptance speech should be no more than 1–2 minutes long. If you know you are receiving the award before the event, prepare your speech ahead of time. Your speech should thank the donor and the presenter, express gratitude to those who have contributed to your success, and finally, tell them how pleased and honored you are to receive the award. Don't diminish the award or the occasion by saying, "I don't deserve this award," because this can insult the donors and audience. Also avoid exaggeration by saying, "This is the greatest day of my entire life," because that can sound disingenuous. Instead, demonstrate humility and grace by simply expressing your gratitude for the award and how you will try to live up to its high standards.

Paying Tribute.   Of all the special occasion speeches, the tribute speech is the one you will most likely give many times in your life. Paying tribute to an individual or a group is appropriate at many events, including an anniversary party, a retirement gathering, an awards banquet, an annual club dinner, and even a birthday celebration. Any occasion that honors or celebrates a person or group provides a wonderful opportunity to use a tribute speech. The primary purpose of a tribute speech is to recall and highlight past accomplishments and achievements. In the case of an individual, you can speak about his or her professional, community, family, and religious contributions and accomplishments. As you describe his or her achievements, use stories to demonstrate and illustrate the accomplishments that have been realized. You might also share brief testimonies from individuals who have benefited from the individual's life. Similar topics can be shared if you're paying tribute to a group of people, an organization, or a club. In organizing a tribute speech, you can use the introduction, body, and conclusion pattern, since this speech is more involved than all of the previous special occasion speeches we've discussed. A tribute speech can have a body of three to five points, depending on how comprehensive you want your talk to be. In terms of main-point order, one pattern to consider is "begin with laughter, end with tears." This arrangement begins with light-hearted and humorous points and ends with more serious, deep, and even inspirational ones. Whether you're paying tribute to an individual or a group, your purpose is to discuss the achievements that the individual or group has accomplished and how these accomplishments can encourage, unify, and even inspire the audience.

After-Dinner Speech.   One of the most difficult special occasion speeches is the after-dinner speech. Its primary purpose is entertainment. The audience is not expecting or desiring a speech that is serious or challenging, but instead they want something light and humorous. Consider that the audience has already sat through a day of workshops or put in a full day at work. Now they've just finished a big meal, maybe had a few drinks, and really want to finish off their dessert and go home. It is this situation that confronts the after-dinner speaker. What do you do?

First, your message must relate to the occasion and/or group you are addressing. Limit your message to a single, memorable theme or idea. Second, keep your speech brief, with a 10- to 12-minute limit. Anything longer places more strain on you and your audience than is necessary. Third, a humorous story or two to illustrate your message is really helpful in accomplishing your goal. Stories are easy to remember for the speaker and more engaging and entertaining for the audience. The audience doesn't want to hear a lecture or an impassioned persuasive oration. On the other hand, avoid stand-up comedy or reciting a string of jokes. Comedy requires a great deal of skill and experience, and rattling off a series of jokes can place you at the mercy of some of your more intoxicated audience members. Instead, your audience will pay more attention to a story than anything else you can share. Fourth, conclude your speech with a final thought that emphasizes a core value or goal that is shared by the audience. Even though you have presented entertaining material during your speech, you can leave your audience with a unifying thought or challenge that recognizes and commemorates the occasion.

Eulogy.   A eulogy is a speech that pays tribute to someone who has died. The primary purpose of a eulogy is to celebrate the positive aspects of an individual's life while consoling the family and friends. The funeral service is for the benefit of the deceased's family and friends, so your eulogy should show respect for the family. Mention all immediate family members by name and emphasize the many ways the deceased showed love and concern for them during his or her life. Talk to the immediate family and closest friends before you speak to discover what important memories they want you to share. Remember to emphasize the positive aspects of the individual's life and how his or her life benefited the lives of others. Avoid reciting long inventories of accomplishments. Instead, focus on positive character traits, accomplishments, and acts of love and sacrifice that the individual demonstrated in life. Keep your eulogy short. Don't read long quotations, lengthy letters, or drawn-out poems. The goal of your eulogy is to show how the individual made a positive difference in the lives of others and how he or she lives on in the memories of those left behind.

10.5 Developing the Heart of a Speaker

We began this book by discussing the significance of communication in your life and how your attitude is more important than your aptitude—your heart is more important than your head. And that's how we're going to end this book—by talking about your heart and the role it plays in your becoming a speaker for a lifetime.

You can acquire the knowledge and technical skills necessary to organize and deliver a speech, but if your attitude or heart is wrong, the speech will lack a certain vitality, wholeness, and impact. If your heart is one of insincerity, indifference, animosity, or arrogance, the audience will intuitively sense this and regard you with caution, defensiveness, and in some cases, even hostility.

But if your heart is sincere, positive, and helpful, the audience will receive you in a more open, receptive, and friendly manner. Your audience is much more aware of and sensitive to your attitude than you might suspect.

Carl Jung, a famous psychiatrist, believed that it was the integrated personality or soul of the therapist that ultimately brought healing to the injured or disintegrated soul of the patient. He felt that beneath the words in therapy, it was the healthy heart of the therapist that somehow reached out, touched, and brought wholeness to the unhealthy heart of the patient. All the talking, analyzing, theorizing, and interpreting in therapy were secondary to the mysterious, powerful, and silent music of the heart. Perhaps this offers some insight into why certain individuals are draining to be around, while others are a joy to be near. Could it be that our hearts communicate to one another in ways we are not yet aware of?

It's not enough to know how to research and organize a speech and deliver it without passing out from fright; you must possess an attitude or heart that communicates a positive message to the minds and hearts of your listeners. How does a speaker do this? Are some people born with the right attitude and others are not? What are the ingredients that make for this kind of heart?

As you may have guessed, there are no easy answers to these questions. Maybe this topic doesn't readily lend itself to simple definition or logical explanation. Perhaps what we can't define, measure, and dissect should be left alone. But we all know that unmistakable feeling when our hearts have been touched by the words or actions of another. Maybe you experienced this sensation during one of the speeches you listened to this semester in your public speaking course. That moment when the communication between speaker and listener transcended even language itself.

Although there is no clear-cut map into this territory of the heart, there are three ingredients or dispositions of the speaker that seem to bring the speaker closer to the hearts of the listeners. The speaker needs to love the topic he is speaking about. The speaker needs to love the audience. And the speaker needs to love himself or herself. Ideally, a speaker should possess each of these three ingredients, but at the very least, one of these three is necessary to touch the hearts of the listeners.

The Speaker Needs to Love the Topic

A romantic affection for the topic is not what we're talking about here. It's more of a passion for or commitment to the subject. The topic of any speech you give in the future must be important to you—something you feel strongly about, committed to. Anything less will not motivate you to speak well or compel your audience to listen deeply. If you don't feel strongly about something, don't waste the audience's time. You and your audience have other things to do, and life is short.

It's easy to say the speaker needs to love the topic, but maybe it's easier said than done. If you were given a blank piece of paper, a pencil, and three minutes, how many topics could you list that would fit this requirement? A recent study of college freshmen and sophomores found the average respondent could list only five topics that fit this description. Of all the thousands of things to list, most students could list only five. How many could you list?

As children, we loved just about everything we came in contact with: a butterfly, a creek, the smell of rain on asphalt, color crayons, and puppies. But as we grew older, this list grew smaller with each ensuing year. So why is it that years later we can list only five topics we love? What happened to our love affair with life?

In the future, you will be given many opportunities to speak in front of others. Don't speak unless you really care about the topic. But you also might want to examine the things and people you really love. Have your interests and passions of the heart diminished over the years? Is there anything you get excited about anymore? Don't let your heart become hard as you get older. Discover ways to remain open to life and to get excited and thrilled about the countless events and miracles that happen to you daily.

Whether it's giving a toast at a wedding reception or delivering a formal presentation to a scientific conference, your heart should reflect a love or passion for the topic at hand. If it doesn't, don't speak. If your heart's not really involved, then don't speak. Wait until the opportunity to toast a couple you care about arises, or wait until you discover a scientific topic that you feel deeply about before you walk up to the podium. Your love for the topic, regardless of what it is, will be communicated to your audience beyond your words.

Much of what passes for public speaking in this culture is really mediocre, unimpressive, and boring. Many of our professors, preachers, and politicians have lost their passion, and their lectures, sermons, and speeches reflect their weary hearts. Don't add to this debris. Remember to speak about topics you feel a passion for, or remain silent.

The Speaker Needs to Love the Audience

The audience is not the enemy. If that's all you learn from this book, you will have gotten your money's worth. And more. You see, the audience is like a Rorschach test—you know, the famous inkblot test. A person looks at an inkblot on a piece of paper and is asked to describe what he or she "sees." Some people see a monster. Others describe a train. And still others see a beautiful butterfly.

Of course, there is no correct answer because there is no "picture." Just a blot of ink squished between two halves of a cardboard screen. What the individual "sees" is really "who" that individual is. The paranoid man "sees" a dark, ominous monster. The divorced woman "sees" a train leaving a station. And the young bride "sees" a beautiful butterfly. It's been said that "We don't see the world the way the world is. We see the world the way we are." How true this is.

> *The supreme happiness of life is the conviction that we are loved.*
> —VICTOR HUGO

And "how" we are when we are novice speakers is inexperienced. The audience is more than just a collection of people who have assembled to listen to our speech. They can be seen as the ENEMY. Not the kind of enemy who will hurt us physically, but the enemy who will laugh at our mistakes, judge our inadequacies, and reject our opinions. The audience represents many of our deepest fears—fears of evaluation, rejection, and, ultimately, abandonment. The audience is the Rorschach test upon which we project all the fears we don't have names for—only that terrifying, empty feeling in the pit of our stomach.

But as you gain experience in speaking, you slowly realize that the audience is not the enemy. The laughter occurs only when you say something funny. The judgment is usually expressed in their applause. And the rejection doesn't occur. Instead, our speeches are usually met with compliments and congratulations. If you were fortunate during this semester in public speaking, the responses from your audience were positive and supportive. And your perception of audience-as-enemy shifted to audience-as-friend or, at least, audience-as-nonthreatening-acquaintance.

If you choose to become a speaker for your lifetime—to give speeches after the end of your public speaking course—your impact on your audience will be greatly enhanced if you can learn to love your audience.

The Speaker Needs to Love Himself or Herself

You will touch the hearts of the audience if they sense you love yourself. Not with a self-absorbed, narcissistic kind of love. Nor an arrogant, boastful kind of love either. But rather, an attitude of gentleness or softness toward yourself. An attitude of spaciousness. An attitude that says you don't have to be perfect when you speak. An attitude that says you can make mistakes as a speaker. You can be human. It's an attitude that says you don't have to be the best speaker, an impressive speaker, or even a good speaker. But more important, you can be a speaker with a message to share with an audience you are concerned about.

Loving yourself requires a softening toward yourself—an attitude of gentleness that isn't concerned so much with performance, action, or results as it is with supporting and nurturing your willingness to speak.

This love is also a softening of the fear or anxiety you may be feeling about speaking. Rather than tensing, hardening, and defending yourself against those butterflies in the stomach, it involves a process of welcoming, relaxing, and letting go. Softening allows your butterflies to fly wherever they want. Like watching children in a playground, you simply welcome the scene and do not attempt to control it. The paradoxical thing about accepting your fears is that they will have less control over you when you simply let them be. Don't try to get rid of them, redirect them, or control them. Give yourself permission to let them in for a while and notice what follows.

Finally, this love involves some level of acceptance of who you are. Your strengths and your weaknesses. Those things you do well and those things you don't do well. This acceptance of self requires a recognition of the fact that not everything you do has to be done well, or even done at all. And it requires a deeper appreciation for those so-called weaknesses. For it just might be that our weaknesses, whatever they may be, are the very aspects of ourselves that make us understanding, humble, caring, and connected to others—in the end, human.

When you speak in front of an audience, let them sense your love for the topic, your love for the audience, and your love for yourself. This may be your most important message in your journey to become a speaker for a lifetime.

COMMUNICATION ACTIVITIES

PERSONAL ACTIVITIES

1. **Your future speaking opportunities.**
   Think about your future for a few minutes—your professional life, your personal life, your family life, your community involvement, your recreational pursuits, and your spiritual development. Brainstorm two or three ways you might use your public speaking skills to communicate important ideas to others in each of these areas of your future life. Remember to be creative in your brainstorming. You'd be surprised at how your speaking skills might serve others in the future.

2. **What do you love?**
   In this chapter, you were introduced to the idea that to develop the heart of a speaker, you need to love your audience, your topic, and yourself. It's rare that you are ever asked to look at yourself and list those personal attributes, achievements, character traits, beliefs, convictions, and activities that you love about yourself. Well, this is the time. Take out a piece of paper and grab a pen or pencil, and list 10 things you love about yourself. Look at every aspect of your life and write your love list with gratitude and thanksgiving. After completing the list, look it over for a few minutes. How do you feel? How many of these things that you love about yourself can be used to serve and help others?

3. **Your 100-word eulogy.**
   The eulogy is one of the most important special occasion speeches you will ever deliver in your lifetime. Let's take a closer look at you for a moment. This exercise is simple, but not easy. In fact, most people will never do what you're about to do. Take the next 15 minutes and write your own eulogy. That's right—*your* eulogy. Imagine that you've died (at age 75), and you are now a different

person, who has lived a different life from the one you're actually living now. You've been asked to write *your* eulogy. In 100 words or fewer, write a brief summary of the highlights of your life (that is, the way you'd like your life to be). What were the important things you want to accomplish in your life? What was this exercise like for you?

Class Activities

1. **Your most significant lesson from public speaking.**
   Divide the class into groups of five students. Introduce yourselves, and then, as a group, take the next 10 to 15 minutes to have the group members share their responses to the question, "What was the most significant lesson I learned from this public speaking class?" Remember to listen to the responses of others without judgment or advice. What did you learn about the other students' lessons? Were there any common themes? What did you think about listening to others speak about what they learned?

2. **How will you change the world for the better?**
   Divide the class into groups of five students. Introduce yourselves, and then, as a group, take the next 10 to 15 minutes to have the group members share their responses to the question, "In the future, how will I use my public speaking skills to change the world for the better?" Have fun with this question. Think of creative, far-out, and even outlandish ways your future speaking can improve the world in some small (or big) way. How did this group exercise feel to you?

3. **Seeing beauty in everyone.**
   Divide the class into groups of five students. Introduce yourselves, and then, as a group, take the next 10 to 15 minutes to have the group members share their responses to the question, "What do I remember and appreciate about you?" This is a challenging group activity that can be both moving and memorable. Each student is to go around the circle and share one very brief memory of each of the other four members of the group (a particular speech, an interaction, a comment, an after-class conversation, etc.). After each of the five students has completed this sharing, the group is to repeat the process by having each member share one thing he or she appreciated about each of the other four members. What was this group experience like? What did you learn about the perceptions of others? What did you learn about yourself?

Index